THE COMMENTATORS' DESPAIR

KENNIKAT PRESS

NATIONAL UNIVERSITY PUBLICATIONS

SERIES ON LITERARY CRITICISM

General Editor

EUGENE GOODHEART

Professor of Literature, Massachusetts Institute of Technology

Stanley Corngold

THE COMMENTATORS' DESPAIR

The Interpretation of Kafka's *Metamorphosis*

National University Publications
KENNIKAT PRESS • 1973
Port Washington, N.Y. • London

Library of Congress Catalog Card No: 72-189558
ISBN: 0-8046-9051-0

Manufactured in the United States of America

Published by
Kennikat Press, Inc.
Port Washington, N.Y./London

PREFACE

The intention of this work is to stabilize to some degree the state of Kafka interpretation and to help create a point of departure for a self-conscious criticism of Kafka's fiction. For too long critics have disregarded the perspective they could gain from standing on the shoulders of their predecessors: they have either not known or not wanted to know that such help exists. According to Benno von Wiese, Kafka's interpreters ignore each other "although or perhaps precisely because they contradict each other in the crassest way."[1] But the lines of even contradictory arguments have since grown long, and positions have become entrenched; no one now writing about Kafka can suppose that he does so without entering a tradition.

My own reading of *The Metamorphosis* takes its starting point from a formal dimension of the work–the metamorphosis of a metaphor from conventional speech. This approach belongs to a tradition of critical analysis focusing on the intentions which originate the language and style of Kafka's fiction. These intentions can be deduced from the history of Kafka's profound commitment to the act of writing, a commitment inscribed in his fiction as well as in his confessional works.

The fact that no single reading of Kafka escapes blindness does not mean that Kafka is indecipherable or that all plausible interpretations are equally valid. "An interpretation is privileged," writes Heinrich Rombach, "if it can enlarge the foundation of other interpretations–hence, interpret them."[2] There is only a finite number of types of Kafka interpretation to which this criterion applies. These types can be identified and their validity measured by a scrutiny of the work, which unfolds as the adventurous combat of principles authorizing interpretations. These principles of symbolic and allegorical action organize the empirical history of interpretations of *The Metamorphosis*, and in many cases determine their correctness.

My work aims to provide an overview of this history. To this end I have paraphrased the work of American, English, German, French, Spanish and Italian critics of *The Metamorphosis*, consciously omitting none. The few Russian, Czech, Dutch, Scandinavian and Japanese commentaries which have come to my attention are not included, nor are unpublished dissertations, various transient reviews, and brief synopses of *The Metamorphosis* included in surveys of wider subjects.

Many of the abstracts printed here include a commentary; some do not, either for reasons of space or because my remarks would follow evidently from the introductory essay. The fact that I have not glossed an abstract should by no means be held to imply either that I think a particular interpretation uninteresting or that I necessarily agree with it.

Each abstract is intended to be fully representative of the work cited. Since this is the first truly thorough, although restricted bibliography of secondary literature on Kafka, a study of the reception of at least one of Kafka's texts is now possible. My own comments on these critiques aim to determine their correctness; another reader may wish to chart this criticism on the axes of historical sequence or schools or countries.

The bibliography should make available to any student of *The Metamorphosis* a knowledge of what critical approaches to this work have been tried, and with what success, as well as many specific insights of indubitable value. Insight into *The Metamorphosis* will open up other works of Kafka, especially those written before and soon after the breakthrough of 1912.

I should like to thank the editors of *Mosaic* for permission to reprint portions of my article, "Kafka's *Die Verwandlung*: Metamorphosis of the Metaphor," which appeared in the summer, 1970, issue. I am grateful to Eugene Goodheart for reading the manuscript, and to the reference staff of the Princeton University Library for helping me to locate many of the items in the bibliography.

CONTENTS

KEY TO ABBREVIATIONS

These abbreviations are used throughout the text, bibliography, and notes, followed by the appropriate page reference. A name in **bold type** refers to an entry under that author's name in the bibliography. If more than one work by an author appears, the appropriate bibliographic number follows the name.

A *Amerika*, trans. by Edwin and Willa Muir. London, 1938.

B *Beschreibung eines Kampfes*, ed. by Max Brod. Frankfurt am Main, 1954. See also DS.

BM *Briefe an Milena*, ed. by Willy Haas. New York, 1952. See also LM.

Br *Briefe, 1902-1924*, ed. by Max Brod. Frankfurt am Main, 1958.

DI *The Diaries of Franz Kafka, 1910-1913*, trans. by Joseph Kresh. New York, 1948. See also T.

DII *The Diaries of Franz Kafka, 1914-1923*, trans. by Martin Greenberg. New York, 1949. See also T.

DF *Dearest Father*, trans. by Ernst Kaiser and Eithne Wilkins. New York, 1954.

DS *Description of a Struggle*, trans. by Tania and James Stern. New York, 1958.

E *Erzählungen*, ed. by Max Brod. Frankfurt am Main, 1946.

F *Briefe an Felice*, ed. by Erich Heller and Jürgen Born. Frankfurt am Main, 1967.

GW *The Great Wall of China*, trans. by Willa and Edwin Muir. New York, 1960.

H *Hochzeitsvorbereitungen auf dem Lande und andere Prosa aus dem Nachlass*, ed. by Max Brod. Frankfurt am Main, 1953.

J Gustav Janouch, *Conversations with Kafka*, trans. by Goronwy Rees. New York, 1953.

LM *Letters to Milena*, trans. by Tania and James Stern. New York, 1953. See also BM.

P *The Penal Colony: Stories and Short Pieces*, trans. by Willa and Edwin Muir. New York, 1948.

T *Tagebücher*, ed. by Max Brod. Frankfurt am Main, 1951. See also DI, DII.

THE COMMENTATORS' DESPAIR

THE STRUCTURE OF KAFKA'S *Metamorphosis*

Metamorphosis of the Metaphor

To judge from its critical reception, Franz Kafka's *The Metamorphosis (Die Verwandlung)* is the most haunting and universal of all his stories; and yet Kafka never claimed for it any particular distinction. He never, for example, accorded it the importance he reserved for "The Judgment," a work it profoundly resembles but which it surpasses in intensity and scope. On the morning of September 23, 1912, after the night he spent composing "The Judgment," Kafka, with a fine elation, wrote in his diary, "Only *in this way* can writing be done, only with such coherence, with such a complete opening out of the body and the soul" (DI 276; T 294).[1] But throughout the period of the composition of *The Metamorphosis*—from November 17 to December 7, 1912, and until the beginning of the new year—his diary does not show an entry of any kind; and when it resumes on February 11, 1913, it is with an interpretation, not of *The Metamorphosis*, but of "The Judgment." The diary does finally acknowledge the new story, almost a year after its composition, with this remark: "I am now reading *The Metamorphosis* at home and find it bad" (DI 303; T 351).

Kafka was especially disappointed with the conclusion of the story. On January 19, 1914, he writes, "Great antipathy to 'Metamorphosis.' Unreadable ending" (DII 12; T 351), and he traces the botched conclusion to a business trip he was obliged to take just as he was well advanced into the piece. His annoyance and remorse at having to interrupt his work is vivid in the letters written at the time to his fiancée, Felice Bauer. These letters reveal Kafka's moods all during the composition of the story—moods almost entirely negative. The story originates "during my misery in bed [; it] oppresses me with inmost intensity *[innerlichst]*" (F 102). The tonality of the piece is again expressed as "hopelessness" (F 105) and "despair" (F 142). On November 23 the story is said to be "a bit horrible" (F 116); a day later, "exceptionally disgusting" (F 117). A trace of liking and concern for *The Metamorphosis* appears in a later letter: "A pity that in many passages in the story my states of exhaustion and other interruptions and worries about other things are clearly inscribed. It could certainly have been more cleanly done; you see that from the sweet pages" (F 160). But by this time Kafka has begun to consider *The Metamorphosis* more and more of an interruption to the writing of the novel that was to become *Amerika*. Finally, on the night of December 7, he states the complaint which will recur: "[M]y little story is finished, but today's conclusion doesn't make me happy at all; the conclusion should have been better, no doubt about it" (F 163).

Kafka's own sense of *The Metamorphosis* compels us to consider the work essentially unfinished. The interruptions which set in so frequently past the midpoint of the story tend to shift the weight of its significance toward its beginning. This view draws support from other evidence establishing what might be termed the general and fundamental priority of the beginning in Kafka's works. One thinks of the innumerable openings to stories scattered throughout the diaries and notebooks, suddenly appearing and as swiftly vanishing, leaving undeveloped the endless dialectical structures they contain. On October 16, 1921, Kafka explicitly invoked "The misery of a perpetual beginning, the lack of the illusion that anything is more than a beginning or even as much as a beginning" (DII 193; T 542). For Dieter Hasselblatt, "[Kafka's prose] is in flight from the beginning, it does not strive toward the end: *initiofugal*, not final. And since it takes the impulse of its progression from what is set forth or what is just present at the outset, it cannot be completed. The end, the conclusion, is unimportant compared to the opening situation."[2]

One is, it would seem, directed by these empirical and theoretical considerations to formulate the overwhelming question of

The Metamorphosis as the question of the meaning of its beginning. What is the fundamental intention that inspires the opening sentence of *The Metamorphosis*: "When Gregor Samsa woke up one morning from unsettling dreams, he found himself changed in his bed into a monstrous vermin [*ungeheueres Ungeziefer*]" (E 71)?[3] We shall do well to keep in mind, in the words of a recent critic, "the identity [of the beginning] as *radical* starting point; the intransitive and conceptual aspect, that which has no object but its own constant clarification."[4] Much of the action of *The Metamorphosis* consists of Kafka's attempt to come to terms with its beginning.

The opening of *The Metamorphosis* recounts the transformation of a man into a monstrous, verminous bug; in the process, it appears to accomplish still another change: it metamorphoses a common figure of speech. This second transformation emerges in the light of the hypothesis proposed in 1947 by Günther Anders: "Kafka's sole point of departure is . . . *ordinary language*. . . . More precisely: *he draws from the resources on hand, the figurative nature [Bildcharakter], of language*. He takes metaphors at their word [*beim Wort*]. For *example*: Because Gregor Samsa wants to live as an artist (i.e. as a *'Luftmensch'*—one who lives on air, lofty and free-floating), in the eyes of the highly respectable, hard-working world he is a 'nasty bug' [*'dreckiger Käfer'*]: and so in *The Metamorphosis* he wakes up as a beetle whose ideal of happiness is to be sticking to the ceiling." For Anders, *The Metamorphosis* originates in the transformation of a familiar metaphor into a fictional being literally existing as this metaphor. The story develops as aspects of the metaphor are enacted in minute detail.

Anders' evidence for this view is furnished partly by his total comprehension of Kafka: "What Kafka describes are . . . existing things, the world, as it appears to the stranger (namely strange)." Anders further adduces examples of everyday figures of speech which, taken literally, inspire stories and scenes in Kafka. "Language says, 'To feel it with your own body' [*'Am eignen Leibe etwas erfahren'*] when it wants to express the reality of experience. This is the basis of Kafka's *In the Penal Colony*, in which the criminal's punishment is not communicated to him by word of mouth, but is instead scratched into his body with a needle."[5]

Anders' hypothesis has been taken up in Walter Sokel's writings on *The Metamorphosis*. The notion of the "extended metaphor," which Sokel considers in an early essay to be "significant" and "interesting" though "insufficient as a total explanation of *Metamorphosis*,"[6] reemerges in *The Writer in Extremis* (105-B, p. 47) as a crucial determinant of Expressionism. "The character Gregor Samsa has been transformed into a metaphor that states his essential self, and this metaphor in turn is treated like an actual fact. Samsa does not call himself a cockroach; instead he wakes up to find himself one." Expressionist prose, for Sokel, is defined precisely by such "extended metaphors, metaphoric visualizations of emotional situations, uprooted from any explanatory context" (p. 46). In *Franz Kafka: Tragik und Ironie* (105-C, p. 99) the factual character of the Kafkan metaphor is reasserted: "In Kafka's work, as in the dream, symbol is fact. . . . A world of pure significance, of naked expression, is represented deceptively as a sequence of empirical facts." Not until his *Franz Kafka* (105-D, p. 5), however, does Sokel state the "pure significance" of Kafka's literalization of the metaphor:

> German usage applies the term *Ungeziefer* (vermin) to persons considered low and contemptible, even as our usage of "cockroach" describes a person deemed a spineless and miserable character. The traveling salesman Gregor Samsa, in Kafka's *The Metamorphosis*, is "like a cockroach" because of his spineless and abject behavior and parasitic wishes. However, Kafka drops the word "like" and has the metaphor become reality when Gregor Samsa wakes up finding himself turned into a giant vermin. With this metamorphosis, Kafka reverses the original act of metamorphosis carried out by thought when it forms metaphor; for metaphor is always "metamorphosis." Kafka transforms metaphor back into his fictional reality, and this counter-metamorphosis becomes the starting point of his tale.

The sequence of Sokel's reflections on Anders' hypothesis contains an important shift of emphasis. Initially the force of *The Metamorphosis* is felt to lie in the choice and "extension" (dramatization) of the powerful metaphor. To support his view, Sokel cites Johannes Urzidil's recollection of a conversation with Kafka: "Once Kafka said to me: 'To be a poet means to be strong in metaphors. The greatest poets were always the most metaphorical ones. They were those who recognized the deep mutual concern, yes, even the identity of things between which nobody noticed the slightest connection before. It is the range and the scope of the metaphor which makes one a poet.' "[7] But in his later work Sokel locates the origin of Kafka's "poetry," not in the metamorphosis of reality accomplished by the metaphor, but in the "counter-metamorphosis" accomplished by the transformation of the metaphor. Kafka's "taking over" images from ordinary speech enacts a second metaphorization *(metaphero=* "to carry over")—one that concludes in the literalization and hence the metamorphosis of the metaphor.[8] This point once made, the genuine importance of Kafka's remarks to Urzidil stands revealed through irony. In describing the poet as one "strong in metaphors," Kafka is describing writers other than himself; for he is the writer par excellence who came to detect in metaphorical language a crucial obstacle to his own enterprise.

Kafka's critique of the metaphor begins early, in the phantasmagoric story "Description of a Struggle" (1904-05). The first-person narrator addresses the supplicant—another persona of the author—with exaggerated severity:

"Now I realize, by God, that I guessed from the very beginning the state you are in. Isn't it something like a fever, a seasickness on land, a kind of leprosy? Don't you feel it's this very feverishness which is preventing you from being properly satisfied with the genuine *[wahrhaftigen]* names of things, and that now, in your frantic haste, you're just pelting them with any old *[zufällige]* names? You can't do it fast enough. But hardly have you run away from them when you've forgotten the names you gave them. The poplar in the fields, which you've called the 'Tower of Babel' because you didn't want to know it was a poplar, sways again without a name, so you have to call it 'Noah in his cups' " (DS 60; B 43).

Because "language is fundamentally metaphorical," designating the "significations to which words accrue" as the significations within words *(Sprachinhalte),*[9] this critique of naming amounts to a critique of the metaphor. But what is remarkable about this passage is its dissatisfaction with both ordinary and figurative names. With the irony of exaggerated emphasis, it calls the conventional link of name and thing "genuine" and the act of renaming things—an act which generates metaphors—arbitrary. The new metaphor leaves no permanent trace; it is the contingent product of a fever; or worse, it arises from deliberate bad faith, the refusal to accept the conventional bond of word and thing. The exact status of ordinary names remains unclear; what is important is that Kafka sees no advance in replacing them with the figures of poetic language.

In a diary entry for December 27, 1911, Kafka stated his despair of a particular attempt at metaphor. "An incoherent assumption is thrust like a board between the actual feeling and the metaphor of the description" (DI 201; T 217). Kafka had begun this diary entry confidently, claiming to have found an image analogous to a moral sentiment: "This feeling of falsity that I have while writing might be represented in the following image." A man stands before two holes in the ground, one to the right and one to the left; he is waiting for something that can rise up only out of the hole to the right. Instead, apparitions rise, one after the other, from the left; they try to attract his attention and finally even succeed in covering up the right-hand hole. At this stage of the construction, the materiality of the image predominates; as it is developed, however, so is the role of the spectator, who scatters these apparitions upward and in all directions in the hope "that after the false apparitions have been exhausted, the true will finally appear." But precisely at the point of conjuring up "truthful apparitions," the metaphorist feels most critically the inadequacy of this figurative language: "How weak this image is." And he concludes with the complaint that between his sentiment and figurative language there is no true coherence (though he cannot, ironically, say this without having recourse to a figure of speech). Now what is crucial here is that an image which is mainly material has failed to represent the sentiment of writing; and though it has been replaced by one which introduces the consciousness of an observer, between the moral sentiment of writing and an act of perception there is also no true connection. If the writer finds it difficult to construct metaphors for "a feeling of falsity," how much greater must be his difficulty in constructing figures for genuine feelings, figures for satisfying the desire "to write all my anxiety entirely out of me, write it into the depths of the paper just as it comes out of the depths of me, or write it in such a way that I can draw what I have written into me completely" (DI 173; T 185).

Kafka's awareness of the limitations of figurative language continues to grow. The desire to represent a state of mind directly in language, in a form consubstantial with that consciousness, and hence to create symbols, cannot be gratified by figurative language. "For everything outside the phenomenal world, language can only be used in the manner of an allusion *[andeutungsweise]* but never even approximately in the manner of the simile *[vergleichsweise]*, since corresponding as it does to the phenomenal world, it is concerned only with property and its relations" (DF 40; H 92). But try as language will to reduce itself to its allusive function, it continues to be dependent on the metaphor, on developing states of mind by means of material analogues. On December 6, 1921, Kafka wrote: "Metaphors are one among many things which make me despair of writing. Writing's lack of independence of the world, its dependence on the maid who tends the fire, on the cat warming itself by the stove; it is even dependent on the poor human being warming himself by the stove. All these are independent activities ruled by their own laws; only writing is helpless, cannot live in itself, is a joke and a despair" (DII 200-201; T 550-51). Indeed, the question arises of what truth even a language determinedly nonfigurative—in Kafka's word, "allusive"—could possess. The parable employs language allusively, but in the powerful fable "On Parables" Kafka writes: "All these parables really set out to say merely that the incomprehensible is incomprehensible, and we know that already" (GW 258; B 95). At this point, it is clear, the literary enterprise is seen in its radically problematical character. The growing desperation of Kafka's critique of metaphorical language leads to the result—in the words of Maurice Blanchot—that, at this time of Kafka's life, "the exigency of the truth of this other world [of sheer inwardness desiring salvation] henceforth surpasses in his eyes the exigency of the work of art."[10] This situation does not suggest the renunciation of writing, but only the clearest possible perception of its limitations, a perception which emerges through Kafka's perplexity before the metaphor in the work of art and his despair of escaping it.

Kafka's "counter-metamorphosis" of the metaphor in *The Metamorphosis* is inspired by his fundamental objection to the metaphor. His purpose is accomplished—so Anders and Sokel propose—through the literalization of the metaphor. But is this true? What does it mean, exactly, to literalize a metaphor?

The metaphor designates something (A) *as* something (B)—something in the quality of something not itself. To say that someone is a verminous bug is to designate a moral sensibility as something unlike itself, as a material sensation—complicated, of course, by the atmosphere of horror which this sensation evokes. With I. A. Richards, we shall call the *tenor* of the metaphor, (A), the thing designated, occulted, replaced, but otherwise established by the context of the figure; and the *vehicle*, the metaphor proper, (B), that thing *as* which the tenor is designated.[11] If the metaphor is taken out of its context, however, if it is taken literally, it no longer functions as a vehicle but as a name, directing us to (B) as an abstraction or an object in the world. Moreover, it directs us to (B) in the totality of its qualities, and not, as the vehicle, only to those qualities of (B) which can be assigned to (A).

This analysis will suggest the paradoxical consequence of "taking the metaphor literally," supposing now that such a thing is possible. Reading the figure literally, we go to (B), an object in the world in its totality; yet, reading it metaphorically, we go to (B) only in its quality as a predicate of (A). The object (B) is quite plainly unstable, and hence so is (A); as literalization proceeds, as we attempt to experience in (B) more and more qualities that can be accommodated by (A), we *metamorphose* (A); but if the metaphor is to be preserved and (A) is to remain unlike (B), we must stop before the metamorphosis is complete. If, now, the tenor—as in *The Metamorphosis*—is a human consciousness, the increasing literalization of the vehicle transforms the tenor into a monster.

This genesis of monsters occurs independently of the nature of the vehicle. The intent toward literalization of a metaphor linking a human consciousness and a material sensation produces a monster in every instance, no matter whether the vehicle is odious or not, whether we begin with the metaphor of a "louse" or of a man who is a jewel or a rock. But it now appears that Anders is not correct in suggesting that in *The Metamorphosis* literalization of the metaphor is actually accomplished; for then we should have, not an indefinite monster, but simply a bug. Indeed, the progressive deterioration of Gregor's body suggests ongoing metamorphosis, the *process* of literalization and not its end state. Nor would Sokel's earlier formulation appear to be tenable: the metaphor is not treated "like an actual fact." Only the alien cleaning woman gives Gregor Samsa the factual, entomological identity of a "dung beetle"; but precisely "to forms of address like these Gregor would not respond" (E 125). The cleaning woman does not know that a metamorphosis has occurred, that within this insect shape there is a human consciousness—one superior at times to the ordinary consciousness of Gregor Samsa. Analysis shows that the metamorphosis in the Samsa household of a man into a vermin is unsettling, not only because vermin are disturbing or because the vivid representation of a human "louse" is disturbing, but because the indeterminate, fluid crossing of a human tenor and a material vehicle is in itself unsettling. Gregor is at one moment pure rapture and at another very nearly pure dung beetle, at times grossly human, at times airily buglike. In shifting incessantly the relation of Gregor's mind and body, Kafka shatters the supposititious unity of ideal tenor and bodily vehicle within the metaphor. This destruction must distress common sense, which defines itself by such "genuine" relations, such natural assertions of analogues between consciousness and matter, and in this way masks the knowledge of its own strangeness. The ontological legitimation for asserting analogues is missing in Kafka, who maintains the most ruthless division between the fire of the spirit and the principle of the world: "What we call the world of the senses is the Evil in the spiritual world" (DF 39; H 44).

The distortion of the metaphor in *The Metamorphosis* is inspired by a radical aesthetic intention, which proceeds by destruction and results in creation—of a monster, virtually nameless, existing as an opaque sign.[12] "The name alone, revealed through a natural death, not the living soul, vouches for that in man which is immortal."[13] But what is remarkable in *The Metamorphosis* is that "the immortal part" of the writer accomplishes itself odiously, in the quality of an indeterminancy sheerly negative. The exact sense of his intention is captured in the "*Ungeziefer*," a word which cannot be expressed by the English words "bug" or "vermin." "*Ungeziefer*" derives (as Kafka probably knew) from the late Middle High German word originally meaning "the unclean animal not suited for sacrifice."[14] If for Kafka "writing is a form of prayer" (DF 312; H 348), this act of writing reflects its own hopelessness. As a distortion of the "genuine" names of things, without significance as a metaphor or as literal fact, the monster of *The Metamorphosis* is, like writing itself, a "fever" and a "despair."

Kafka's metamorphosis–through incomplete literalization–of the metaphor "this man is a vermin" appears to be an intricate and comprehensive act, in which it is possible to discern three orders of significance, all of which inform *The Metamorphosis*. These meanings emerge separately as we focus critically on three facts: that the metaphor distorted is a familiar element of ordinary language; that, the distortion being incomplete, the body of the original metaphor maintains a shadow existence within the metamorphosis, and the body of *this* metaphor–a verminous bug–is negative and repulsive; and finally, that the source of the metamorphosis is, properly speaking, not the familiar metaphor but a radical aesthetic intention. Together these meanings interpenetrate in a dialectical way. For example: the aesthetic intention reflects itself in a monster but does so by distorting an initially monstrous metaphor; the outcome of its destroying a negative is itself a negative. These relations illuminate both Kafka's saying, "In addition it is imposed on us to do the negative" (DF 36-37; H 42) and his remark to Milena Jesenská-Pollak, "But even the truth of longing is not so much its truth, rather it is an expression of the lie of everything else" (LM 200; BM 225). For the sake of analysis, each of the three intents must be separated and discussed independently.

Kafka metamorphoses a figure of speech embedded in ordinary language. The intent is to transform the familiar, not to invent the new; Kafka's diaries for the period around 1912 show that his invented metaphors are more complex than "this man is a vermin." To stress the estrangement of the monster from his familiar form in the metaphor—the dirty bug—is to stress Gregor Samsa's estrangement from his identity in the family. Gregor harks back to, yet defiantly resists, integration into the "ordinary language" of the family. The condition of the distorted metaphor estranged from familiar speech shapes the family drama of *The Metamorphosis*; the *Ungeziefer* is in the fullest sense of the word *ungeheuer* [monstrous]—a being that cannot be accommodated in a family.[15]

Is it too odd an idea to see this family drama as the conflict between ordinary language and a being having the character of an indecipherable word? It will seem less odd, at any rate, to grasp the family life of the Samsas as a characteristic language. The family defines itself by the ease with which it enters into collusion on the question of Gregor. Divisions of opinion do arise—touching, say, on the severity of the treatment due Gregor; but such differences issue at once into new decisions. The family's projects develop within the universe of their concerns, through transparent words and gestures that communicate without effort. At the end, images of family unity survive the story: the mother and father in complete union; mother, father, and daughter emerging arm in arm from the parents' bedroom to confront the boarders; mother and father "growing quieter and communicating almost unconsciously through glances" at the sight of their good-looking, shapely daughter.

Family language in *The Metamorphosis* has a precise symbolic correlative, Kimberly Sparks suggests, in the newspaper. The person in power at any moment reads or manipulates the newspaper.[16] Gregor has clipped the love object that hangs on his wall from an illustrated newspaper; his evening custom as head of the family had been to sit at the table and read the newspaper. It is a sorry comment on his loss of power and identity within the family that it is on newspaper that his first meal of garbage is served; the father meanwhile, downcast for a while, fails to read the newspaper aloud to the family. When the boarders come to dominate the family, it is they who ostentatiously read the newspaper at the dinner table. The newspaper represents an order of efficient language from which Gregor is excluded.

The task of interpreting the monstrous noun which Gregor has become is more difficult; his transformation is essentially obscure and can be understood only through approximations. One such approximation is the *intelligible* transformation that also results in Gregor's becoming an opaque sign.

If Gregor had lost the ability to make himself understood by the others but had preserved his human shape, the family would be inclined to interpret the change as temporary: it would encourage Gregor to speak; the mere loss of language would not result in isolation and insignificance. But if Kafka wished to suggest the solitude resulting from the absolute loss of all significance, he would have to present this condition as a consequence of the loss of the human form. The sense of Gregor's opaque body is thus to maintain him in a solitude without speech or intelligible gesture, in the solitude of an indecipherable sign. To put it another way: his body is the speech in which the impossibility of ordinary language expresses its own despair.

The conception of Gregor as a mutilated metaphor, uprooted from familiar language, brings another element of this family drama to light. The transformed metaphor preserves a trace of its original state. The consciousness of Gregor, like the uprooted metaphor, is defined by its reference to its former state: though Gregor cannot communicate, he continues to remember. This point underscores a feature of Kafka's metamorphosis which distinguishes it from the classical metamorphosis in Ovid, where a human consciousness is converted into a natural object. *The Metamorphosis* converts a word having a quasi-natural identity, the rooted and familiar identity of ordinary speech, into a word having the character of a unique consciousness. The distorted word, without presence or future, suggests a mind dominated by nostalgia for its former life–a life of obscure habit and occupation rewarded by secure family ties.

Gregor's future is mainly obstructed by a particular form of the tyranny of nostalgia, by the "consideration" (E 96, E 129) he shows his family. Kafka's word *Rücksicht*, with its connotations of hindsight, of looking backward, is exactly right for Gregor: his consideration arises from his clinging to a mythic past–one that is, in fact, hopelessly lost. The play of Gregor's "consideration" reveals his family feeling as necessarily ambivalent, moving between extremes of solicitude and indifference. The key passage has been pointed out by William Empson, though his interpretation of the passage is actually misleading. According to Empson, Kafka can only have been nodding when he wrote in the scene of the sister's violin playing: "It hardly surprised [Gregor] that lately he was showing so little consideration for the others; once such consideration had been his greatest pride. . . . [N]ow . . . his indifference to everything was much too deep for him to have gotten on his back and scrubbed himself clean against the carpet, as once he had done several times a day" (E 129). "After the apple incident," Empson points out, "there could surely be no question of . . . this,"[17] for the apple fired at Gregor by his father has lodged in his back and caused a festering wound. But Kafka's chiding Gregor for his indifference precisely at this point is not an "inconsistency." The moment teaches us to regard Gregor's consideration for the others as an aberration, an impulse opposite to his own most genuine concern, such as it is. It is in forgetting a useless consideration and pursuing the sound of the music that Gregor is able to discover his own condition, to perceive his irreducible strangeness. The abandonment of a *Rücksicht* that is bent on reintegration into ordinary life enables him for one moment (he did not formerly "understand" music) to imagine the music of the world in a finer tone. In our perspective this moment emerges as a restitution of language to Gregor, yet of a language fundamentally unlike the language he has lost. The character of the lost language is approximated by the abrupt fantasy of violence and incest following the violin music, into which Gregor's experience of music collapses. The language of music is degraded when it is made the means for the restitution of a family relationship.

Gregor's ambivalent relation to his family, inspired partly by the relationship between literary and conventional figurative language, suggests Kafka's own ambivalent feeling about intimacy. His ambivalence, centering as it does on an idea of renunciation, is spelled out in an early account of his love for the Yiddish actress Mrs. Tschissik. "A young man . . . declares to this woman his love to which he has completely fallen victim and . . . immediately renounces the woman. . . . Should I be grateful or should I curse the fact that despite all misfortune I can still feel love, an unearthly love but still for earthly objects?" (DI 139; T 148). We know that Kafka at times thought the utmost a man might achieve was to found a family; he liked to quote the words attributed to Flaubert describing a family full of children: *"Ils sont dans le vrai,"* "they are living the truthful life."[18] But he also wrote in a letter to Felice Bauer, "Rather put on blinkers and go my way to the limit than have the familiar pack *[das heimatliche Rudel]* mill around me and distract my gaze" (DII 167; T 551). The precarious existence which Kafka maintained outside "the house of life" required vigilant curbing of his nostalgia.

The separateness and nostalgia which inform Gregor's relation to his family (and which reflect Kafka's ambivalent feelings about intimate relations) dramatize still more sharply Kafka's relation to the familiar language on which he drew. In "Description of a Struggle," Kafka alluded to that fevered soul who could not be contented with the genuine names of things but had to scatter arbitrary names over familiar things. But later in the same text the same fictional persona declares, " 'When as a child I opened my eyes after a brief afternoon nap, still not quite sure I was alive, I heard my mother up on the balcony asking in a natural tone of voice: "What are you doing, my dear? Goodness, isn't it hot?" From the garden a woman answered: "Me, I'm having my tea on the lawn *[Ich jause so im Grünen]*." They spoke without thinking and not very distinctly, as though this woman had expected the question, my mother the answer' " (DS 62; B 44). In the model of a dialogue in ordinary language Kafka communicates his early, intense longing for and insistence on wholeness and clarity—in Klaus Wagenbach's phrase, Kafka's "direct marvelling at the magic of the simple." This is the simplicity of common speech in which names and things fit effortlessly together. Kafka's "idolatrous admiration of the truth, which grows more and more marked," Wagenbach continues, "is at the root of his decision to confine himself to the linguistic material offered him by his environment."[19] But another writer, Hermann Pongs, foresees in this decision a dangerous end—the result of Kafka's confining himself to the juiceless, stilted language of Prague is Gregor Samsa's ongoing metamorphosis. "The fate of the animal voice, into which human sound is changed, becomes a terrible symptom of Kafka's being cut off from the substrata of the inner form of language. Kafka scholarship has brought to light the fact that the Prague German available to Kafka, homeless between Germans, Jews and Czechs in the region of Prague, was an already etiolated literary German, obliged to do without any forces of rejuvenation through dialect."[20] There is some truth in this statement, to which Kafka's frequent animadversions on the German of Prague testify (but then, of course, the fate of the animal voice is not a "symptom" but a conscious reflection of Kafka's alienation). "Yesterday," writes Kafka, "it occurred to me that I did not always love my mother as she deserved and as I could, only because the German language prevented it. The Jewish mother is no 'Mutter' " (DI 111; T 115). In a letter to Max Brod composed in June, 1921, Kafka discusses the predicament of the Jewish writer writing in German. The literary language of such a Jew Kafka calls "*mauscheln*," which ordinarily means "to speak German with a Yiddish accent": "I'm not saying anything against this language; in itself it is even beautiful, it is an organic combination of wooden literary German *[Papierdeutsch]* and mimicry . . . and a product of a delicate flair for language, which has come to know that in German only the dialects and aside from them only the most personal standard German truly lives, while what remains, the middle-class of language, is nothing but ashes, which can only be brought to a semblance of life by ultralively Jewish hands rooting about in them" (Br 336-7). The "middle-class" of German which Kafka heard around him was frequently not the object of his nostalgia but mere "noise" (DI 220; T 240) or inanity (DI 258; 273)—"in the next room . . . they are talking about vermin."

Now it is precisely through this act of "rooting about" that Kafka names, elliptically and ironically, the kind of creative distortion to which he submitted the figures of the conventional idiom. That the metamorphic character of Kafka's relation to ordinary language is frequently misunderstood, however, is particularly clear from critics' speculations about the *source* of this act. Wagenbach suggests that Kafka's distortions are in fact the work of Prague German which "of its own accord" provoked the counter-metamorphosis of metaphors. Kafka's native German, Wagenbach writes, "always possessed a vestige of unfamiliarity; distance, too, vis-à-vis the individual word set in of its own accord. Removed from the leveling effect of everyday usage, words, metaphors, and verbal constructions recovered their original variety of meaning, became richer in images, richer in associative possibilities. As a result, in Kafka's work too on almost every page such chains of association are found arising from taking words with strict literalness."[21]

But it is as questionable to maintain that *of its own accord* Prague German proferred its metaphors literally as it is to maintain, as Martin Greenberg does, that Kafka's sociological situation determined his use of metaphor, that "thanks to his distance as a Prague Jew from the German language, he is able to see it in an 'analytic' way."[22] In the seven hundred closely printed pages of Kafka's letters to his fiancée Felice Bauer–letters written, of course, in Prague German–Kafka is not tempted to "root about" in the metaphors of the conventional idiom, to take them literally, or to see them in an analytic way. In these letters Kafka achieves the most palpable intimacy, the native coldness of Prague German notwithstanding; indeed, so intimate is this world he conjures up and creates through language that it becomes for him as much of the married state as he can bear. It is not Prague German that imposes on Kafka his sense of the untruthfulness of the metaphor and hence the fundamental form of his writing; the source lies prior to his reflections on a particular kind and state of language.

Kafka, writes Martin Walser, "accomplished the metamorphosis of reality prior to the work, by reducing–indeed, destroying–his bourgeois-biographical personality for the sake of a development which has for its goal the personality of the poet; this poetic personality, the *poetica personalità*, establishes the form."[23] It is Kafka's literary consciousness, reflecting itself in the destruction of all intimacy even with itself, which from the beginning puts distance between Kafka and the world of Prague German. Tzvetan Todorov, too, stresses "the difference in the hierarchy of the two ideas [of figurative language and poetic language]: figurative language is a sort of potential stock inside language, while poetic language is already a construction, a utilization of this raw material. . . . Figurative language opposes transparent language in order to impose the presence of words; literary language opposes ordinary language in order to impose the presence of things"[24]—things unheard before, new realities, reflections of the poetic self.

Kafka's attachment to the everyday language of Prague is only one impetus in the thrust of his poetic consciousness toward its own truth. His language probes the depths of the imaginary—a depth which lies concealed within ordinary language but which can be brought to light through the willful distortion of the figurative underlayer of ordinary language. The primitivity of the vermin reflects Kafka's radical thrust toward origins. Kafka's destruction of his native personality for the sake of a poetic development destroys the privilege of inherited language.

Conceiving, then, the opening of *The Metamorphosis* as the metamorphosis of a familiar metaphor, we can identify minor and major movements of Kafka's spirit: the retrospective attachment to the familiar, and the movement of the spirit toward its own reality. As opposite movements, they cannot be accommodated within the metaphor that asserts an analogy between the spirit and the common life it negates. Only the metamorphosis destroying the metaphor establishes their distinction.

Our second approach to *The Metamorphosis* stresses the presence in the fiction of Gregor Samsa of the residue of a real meaning—the real vermin in the conventional metaphor, "the man is a vermin." This method opens a path to that whole range of criticism aiming to relate *The Metamorphosis* to empirical experiences and, by extension, to Kafka's personal life. Kafka, the approach stresses, has distorted but preserved through distortion the sense of a man debased in the way that a vermin is debased. As Kafka incorporates in the story the empirical sense of a biting and sucking vermin—so this argument proceeds—he incorporates as well his sense of his empirical self.[25] An essentially realistic tale of humiliation and neurosis reflects Kafka's tortured personality.

Innumerable attempts have been made to explain Gregor's

debasement in terms of the ways in which a man can be humiliated. The Marxist critic Helmut Richter, for example, alludes to the deformed products of a mechanical work process, to Gregor the alienated salesman; Sokel, as a psychologist, stresses Gregor's intent to punish through his repulsiveness the family that had enslaved him. Kaiser views the metamorphosis as retribution for an Oedipal rebellion; the pathologist Wilfredo Dalmau Castañón sees it as the symptomatology of tuberculosis.[26] In most of these readings the evidence of Kafka's empirical personality is brought directly into court: the *ne plus ultra* of this sort of criticism is an essay by Giuliano Baioni, which sees the metamorphosis as repeating Kafka's feeling of guilt and absolving him of it. Kafka is guilty and must be punished simply for being himself, for being his father's son, for hating his father, for getting engaged, for not loving enough, for being incapable of loving, for being a writer who is thinking about his father, for being a factory manager and not writing, and finally, for being an imperfect creature whose body is a foreign body and who stands condemned by a Hasidic ideal of unity.[27] The critical bibliography of *The Metamorphosis* describes more than one hundred published critiques of an empirical or programmatic kind. Though all are plausible, they are privative; Kafka, this most highly conscious of artists, implacable skeptic of psychoanalysis, never conceived of writing as enactment of, or compensation for, his troubled personality.

For Kafka, personal happiness is not the goal but a stake and as such alienable—a means, functioning essentially through its renunciation, to an altogether different elation (and anxiety), which is at the heart of literature, his "real life" (DI 211; T 229). Karl Rossman, in a passage in *Amerika* written shortly before the composition of *The Metamorphosis,* feels, as he plays the piano, "rising within him a sorrow which reached past the end of the song, seeking another end which it could not find."[28] "Art for the artist," said Kafka, "is only suffering, through which he releases himself for further suffering."[29] In a letter to Max Brod of July 5, 1922, Kafka links his writing to the amelioration of his life in a merely concessive way: "Of course [I] don't mean that my life is better when I'm not writing. Rather, it is much worse then and completely insufferable and must end in madness" (Br 384). But this relation between not writing and madness obtains only because he is fundamentally a writer, and a writer who does not write is an absurdity *(Unding)* that would call down madness. The only madness that writing cures is the madness of not writing.

The attempt to interpret *The Metamorphosis* through Kafka's empirical personality suffers, by implication, from the difficulty of interpreting the vermin through the residual empirical sense of the metaphor of the vermin. The author of a recent monograph on *The Metamorphosis,* Jürg Schubiger, notes a concrete disparity between the form of the vermin and any bug which can be visualized:

> [The head] . . . ends in "nostrils" and in strong jaws, which take the place of human jaws. Compared with what we are accustomed to in bugs, the head is unusually mobile. Not only can the creature lower and raise it, draw it in and stretch it out, he can even turn it so far to the side that he sees just what is going on behind him. . . . Statements about the weight of the creature . . . "two able-bodied persons" would have been necessary to lift him out of bed (E 78) . . . are incompatible with Gregor's later ability to wander over the walls and ceiling; even with glue, a bug weighing at least seventy pounds cannot hang on to the ceiling.

"And so," Schubiger concludes, "the bodily 'data' must not be understood as facts . . . ; they are bodily imaged questions and answers in the bug's dialogue with the world."[30] Kafka himself confirmed this conclusion when he specifically forbade his publisher to illustrate the first edition of *The Metamorphosis* with a drawing of the creature: "The insect itself cannot be drawn" (Br 136).

The importance within *The Metamorphosis* of the original metaphor, "this man is a vermin," is not for Kafka the empirical identity of a bug. What is paramount is the form of the metaphor as such, which is then deformed; hence, any metaphor would do, with this provision (as formulated by Jacques Lacan): "Any conjunction of two signifiers would be equally sufficient to constitute a metaphor, except for the additional requirement of the greatest possible disparity of the images signified, needed for the production of the poetic spark, or in other words for there to be metaphoric creation."[31] In the most powerful metaphor, vehicle and tenor are poles apart; this power is appropriated by the act of aesthetic distortion. Kafka's metaphor is only impoverished when the tenor, a traveling salesman, is equated with Kafka's empirical personality as factory manager.

Lacan's insight helps, moreover, to clarify another crux. Anders originally saw the metaphor underlying *The Metamorphosis* as "This man, who wants to live as an artist, is a nasty bug." Dieter Hasselblatt has argued against this formulation, asserting, "Nowhere in the text is there any mention of the problem of the artist and society."[32] Of course it is true that Gregor Samsa is not an artist manqué. But as the occasion for a metamorphosis, he becomes an aesthetic object—the unique correlative of a poetic intention. Indeed, Hasselblatt's own view of *The Metamorphosis* as the response of the everyday world to the inconceivable gives the work an essential bearing on the theme of poetic language. The empirical identity of the tenor, be it artist or any other man, is inconsequential because *The Metamorphosis* is dominated by an aesthetic intent. The intent to literalize a metaphor produces a being wholly divorced from empirical reality.

The third approach focuses upon this aesthetic intent which aims, through metamorphosis of the metaphor, to assert its own autonomy. We can no longer take our bearings from the empirical sense of the vermin. Yet neither are we obliged to abandon every attempt at interpreting the signifier. For Kafka has already established a link between the bug and the activity of writing itself. In the story "Wedding Preparations in the Country" (1907), of which only a fragment survives, Kafka conjures a hero, Eduard Raban, reluctant to take action in the world (he is supposed to go to the country to arrange his wedding); Raban dreams instead of autonomy, self-sufficiency, and omnipotence. For this transparent reflection of his early literary consciousness Kafka finds the emblem of a beetle, about which there hovers an odd indeterminacy:

"And besides, can't I do it the way I always used to as a child in matters that were dangerous? I don't even need to go to the country myself, it isn't necessary. I'll send my clothed body. If it staggers out of the door of my room, the staggering will indicate not fear but its nothingness. Nor is it a sign of excitement if it stumbles on the stairs, if it travels into the country, sobbing as it goes, and there eats its supper in tears. For I myself am meanwhile lying on my bed, smoothly covered over with the yellow-brown blanket, exposed to the breeze that is wafted through that seldom aired room. The carriages and people in the street move and walk hesitantly on shining ground, for I am still dreaming. Coachmen and pedestrians are shy, and every step they want to advance they ask as a favor from me, by looking at me. I encourage them and they encounter no obstacle.

"As I lie in bed I assume the shape of a big beetle, a stag beetle or a cockchafer, I think.

. . .

"The form of a large beetle, yes. Then I would pretend it was a matter of hibernating, and I would press my little legs to my bulging belly. And I would whisper a few words, instructions to my sad body, which stands close beside me, bent. Soon I shall have done—it bows, it goes swiftly, and it will manage everything efficiently while I rest" (DF 6-7; H 11-12).

The figure of the omnipotent bug is positive throughout this passage and suggests the inwardness of the act of writing rendered in its power and freedom, in its mystic exaltation, evidence of which abounds in Kafka's early diary entries:

The special nature of my inspiration . . . is such that I can do everything, and not only what is directed to a definite piece of work. When I arbitrarily write a single sentence, for instance, "He looked out of the window," it already has perfection (DI 45; T 41-42).

My happiness, my abilities, and every possibility of being useful in any way have always been in the literary field. And here I have, to be sure, experienced states . . . in which I completely dwelt in every idea, but also filled every idea, and in which I not only felt myself at my boundary, but at the boundary of the human in general (DI 58; T 57).

How everything can be said, how for everything, for the strangest fancies, there waits a great fire in which they perish and rise up again (DI 276; T 293).

But this is only one side of Kafka's poetic consciousness. The other is expressed through the narrator's hesitation in defining his trance by means of an objective correlative ("a stag beetle . . . , I think"), which suggests beyond his particular distress, the general impossibility of the metaphor's naming, by means of a material image, the being of an inward state and hence a doubt that will go to the root of writing itself. After 1912 there are few such positive emblems for the inwardness and solitude of the act of writing; this "beautiful" bug[33] is projected in ignorance; the truer emblem of the alien poetic consciousness which "has no basis, no stability" (Br 385), which must suffer "the eternal torments of dying" (DII 77; T 420), becomes the vermin Gregor. The movement from the beautiful bug Raban to the monstrous bug Gregor marks an accession of self-knowledge–an increasing awareness of the poverty and shortcomings of writing.

The direction of Kafka's reflection on literature is fundamentally defined, however, by "The Judgment," the story written immediately before *The Mètamorphosis*. "The Judgment" struck Kafka as a breakthrough into his own style and produced an ecstatic notation in his diary. But in his later interpretation of the story, Kafka described it in a somewhat more sinister tonality, as having "come out of me like a regular birth, covered with filth and mucus" (DI 278: T 296). The image has the violence and inevitability of a natural process, but its filth and mucus cannot fail to remind the reader of the strange birth which is the subject of Kafka's next story–the incubus trailing filth and mucus through the household of its family.

Two major aspects of "The Judgment," I think, inspire in Kafka a sense of the authenticity of the story important enough for it to be commemorated in the figure of the vermin. First, the figure of the friend in Russia represents with the greatest clarity to date the negativity of the "business" of writing (the friend is said by the father to be "yellow enough to be thrown away": P 62; E 67); secondly, "The Judgment," like *The Metamorphosis,* develops as the implications of a distorted metaphor are enacted: "The Judgment" metamorphoses the father's "judgment" or "estimate" into a fatal "verdict," a death "sentence."[34]

Kafka's awareness that "The Judgment" originates from the distortion of the metaphor dictates the conclusion of his "interpretation." The highly formal tonality of this structural analysis surprises the reader, following as it does on the organic simile of the sudden birth: "The friend is the link between father and son, he is their strongest common bond. Sitting alone at his window, Georg rummages voluptuously in this consciousness of what they have in common, believes he has his father within him, and would be at peace with everything if it were not for a fleeting, sad thoughtfulness. In the course of the story the father . . . uses the common bond of the friend to set himself up as Georg's antagonist" (DI 278; T 296). This analysis employs the structural model of the metamorphosed metaphor. At first Georg considers the father as the friend; his friend, as the metaphor of the father. But Georg's doom is to take the metaphor literally, to suppose that, by sharing the quality of the friend, he possesses the father in fact. Now in a violent countermovement the father distorts the initial metaphor, drawing the friend's existence into himself; and Georg, who now feels "what they have in common . . . only as something foreign, something that has become independent, that he has never given enough protection . . . " (DI 279; T 296), accepts his sentence.

It is this new art, generated from the distortion of relations modeled on the metaphor, which came to Kafka as an elation, a gross new birth, and a sentence; the aesthetic intention comes to light negatively when it must express itself through so tormented and elliptical a strategem as the metamorphosis of the metaphor. The restriction and misery of this art is the explicit subject of *The Metamorphosis;* the invention which henceforth shapes Kafka's existence as a writer is original, arbitrary, and fundamentally strange. In a later autobiographical note he writes: "Everything he does seems to him extraordinarily new, it is true, but also, consistent with this incredible abundance of new things, extraordinarily amateurish, indeed scarcely tolerable, incapable of becoming history, breaking the chain of the generations, cutting off for the first time at its most profound source the music of the world, which before him could at least be divined. Sometimes in his arrogance he is more afraid for the world than for himself" (B 279; GW 263-64). Kafka's pride in his separateness equals his nostalgia for "the music of the world." His tension defines the violently distorted metaphor Gregor Samsa who, in responding to his sister's violin playing, causes this music to be broken off. That being who lives as a distortion of nature–and without a history and without a future still maintains a certain sovereignty–

conjures up through the extremity of his separation the clearest possible idea of the music he cannot possess.

In the light of the beautiful beetle of "Wedding Preparations" and the trail of filth and mucus which "The Judgment" leaves behind, the vermin in *The Metamorphosis* is revealed as expressing a hermeneutical relation, as reflecting Kafka's sense of his literary destiny. But the negative character of this vermin, this judgment, still has to be clarified.[35]

It is a seductive hypothesis to suppose that *The Metamorphosis* describes the fate of the writer who does not write, whose "business," like that of the Russian friend in "The Judgment," is not flourishing. For this assumption there is a good deal of evidence in Kafka's letters. On November 1, 1912, two weeks before conceiving *The Metamorphosis,* Kafka wrote to Felice, with uncanny relevance to the story: "My life consists and always consisted basically of attempts to write, mostly of abortive ones. But not to write was already to be lying on the floor, deserving to be swept out" (F 65).[36] It is as a wholly literary being, albeit one who is foundering, that Kafka identifies himself with the corpse that will be swept out of the bedroom. On November 18, *The Metamorphosis* becomes a "cautionary tale" for the writer at a standstill: "I just sat down to yesterday's story with a boundless yearning to pour myself into it, clearly goaded on by all my despair. Oppressed by so much, at loose ends about you, completely unable to cope with the office, with a wild desire, in view of this novel *[Amerika]* at a standstill for a day, to continue the new, equally cautionary tale" (F 105). Several days after completing *The Metamorphosis,* Kafka wrote to Felice, "And do not talk of the greatness which is in me, or do you perhaps consider it something great that on account of the two-day interruption in my writing, I pass these two days with the unrelenting fear of not being able to write anymore, a fear, by the way, which, as this evening has shown, was not so entirely groundless" (F 171). This matter is given definite formulation in 1922, when Kafka finds an image for the danger of not writing that is powerfully reminiscent of the vermin's attempt to cling to his human past: "For the existence of the writer is really dependent on his writing desk. If he intends to escape madness, he really must never leave his writing desk; he must hang on with his teeth" (Br 386). Here, then, as Erich Heller writes (in his edition of the letters to Felice), is "Kafka's curse: he is in Nothingness when he doesn't write." But he is also "in a Nothingness of another sort, when, rarely enough, writing does 'seize hold' of him" (F 24).

What is this "Nothingness of another sort" to which a vermin image for the act of writing bears witness? Can it be grasped, as many critics believe, through Kafka's impulse to view the writer in the perspective of the nonwriter, the normal *Bürger*? In Kafka's earliest works–in the story, for example, developed but unfinished in the *Diaries* of 1910 and 1911, beginning, " 'You,' I said . . . "–the writer appears in the eyes of others as the dim figure of the bachelor, the nonentity who must drag out his days in feeble solitude, without children or possessions (DI 22-24, 40). "The Judgment," too, presents the writer in an alien and insulting perspective; the essential character of this relation is stressed through the alliance said to exist between the vindictive father and the friend, a transparent persona of the writer. The clearest formulation of this theme occurs in 1919, in Kafka's "Letter to His Father": "My writing was all about you," Kafka declared to his father; "all I did there, after all, was to bemoan what I could not bemoan upon your breast. It was an intentionally long-drawn-out leave-taking from you, only although it was brought about by force on your part, it did not take its course in the direction determined by me" (DF 177; H 222). In these passages, the origin and destiny of the writer appears to be fundamentally shaped by the perspective of the father; Gregor Samsa, too, needs to have his metamorphosis confirmed by the judgment of his family.

But in fact this idea is neither predominant nor even highly significant in *The Metamorphosis*. For the work frequently stresses the son's defiance of the father; Gregor comes out in the open to hear the language of music despite his father's prohibition. What is more, the truth and pathos of the story stem from the reader's occupying throughout–with the exception of the "unsatisfactory" conclusion–a consciousness very nearly identical with Gregor's own. The center of gravity of the work is Gregor's sense of the world: he sees himself as a vermin, we do not see him as a vermin through the eyes of the others. Significantly, the omniscient narrator of the close of the story confirms Gregor's body to be actually verminous.

The negativity of the vermin has to be seen as rooted, in an absolute sense, in the literary enterprise itself, as coming to light in the perspective which the act of writing offers of itself. Here the activity of writing appears only autonomous enough to demand the loss of happiness and the renunciation of life. But of its own accord it has no power to restitute these sacrifices in a finer key. Over Kafka's writing stands a constant sign of negativity and incompleteness:

When it became clear in my organism that writing was the most productive direction for my being to take, everything rushed in that direction and left empty all those abilities which were directed toward the joys of sex, eating, drinking, philosophical reflection, and above all music. I atrophied in all these directions. . . . My development is now complete and, so far as I can see, there is nothing left to sacrifice; I need only to throw my work in the office out of this complex in order to begin my real life (DI 211; T 229).

The path to Kafka's "real life" is strewn with sacrifices; and the fact that he was never able to throw off his professional work until he had become fatally ill reflects the inherent inaccessibility of this ideal.

In a letter of July 5, 1922, to Max Brod, Kafka envisions the writer as inhabiting a place outside the house of life—as a dead man, one of those "departed," of the "Reflections," who long to be flooded back to us (DF 34; H 39). It cannot be otherwise; the writer has no genuine existence ("*[ist] etwas nicht Bestehendes*"); what he produces is devilish, "the reward for devil's duty—this descent to the dark forces, this unbinding of spirits by nature bound, dubious embraces and whatever else may go on below, of which one no longer knows anything above ground when in the sunlight one writes stories. Perhaps there is also another kind of writing. I only know this kind" (Br 385). "Yet," as Erich Heller remarks, "it remains dubious who this 'one' is who 'writes stories in the sunlight.' Kafka himself? 'The Judgment'—and sunlight? 'The Metamorphosis' . . . and sunlight . . . ? How must it have been 'below ground' if 'above ground' blossoms like these were put forth?" (F 22).

Kafka's art, which Kafka elsewhere calls a conjuration of spirits, brings into the light of language the experience of descent and doubt. And even this experience has to be repeated perpetually. "Thus I waver, continually fly to the summit of the mountain, but then fall back in a moment. . . . [I] t is not death, alas, but the eternal torments of dying" (DII 77; T 420). There is no true duration in this desperate flight; conjuring up his own death, Kafka writes: "The writer in me will, of course, die at once, for such a figure has no basis, has no substance, isn't even of dust; is only a construction of the craving for enjoyment. This is the writer" (Br 385). The self-indulgence which defines the writer is that of the being who perpetually reflects on himself and others. The word "figure" in the passage above can be taken *literally*: the writer is defined by his verbal figures, conceived at a distance from life, inspired by a devilish aesthetic detachment with a craving to indulge itself; but he suffers as well the meaninglessness of the figure uprooted from the language of life—the dead figure. Kafka's spirit, then, does spend itself *"zur Illuminierung meines Leichnams"* (Br 385), in lighting up—but also in furnishing figural decorations for—his corpse.

It is this dwelling outside the house of life, *"Schriftsteller-sein,"* the negative condition of writing as such, which is named in *The Metamorphosis*; but it cannot name itself directly, in a language that designates things that exist, or in the figures that suggest the relations between things constituting the common imagination of life. Instead, in *The Metamorphosis* Kafka utters a word for a being unacceptable to man (*ungeheuer*) and unacceptable to God (*Ungeziefer*), a word unsuited either to intimate speech or to prayer. This word evokes a distortion without visual identity of self-awareness—engenders, for a hero, a pure sign. The creature of *The Metamorphosis* is not a self speaking or keeping silent but language itself (*parole*)—a word broken loose from the context of language (*langage*), fallen into a void the meaning of which it cannot signify, near others who cannot understand it.

As the story of a metamorphosed metaphor, *The Metamorphosis* is not just one among Kafka's stories but an exemplary Kafkan story; the title reflects the generative principle of Kafka's fiction—a metamorphosis of the function of language. In organizing itself around a distortion of ordinary language, *The Meta-*

morphosis projects into its center a sign which absorbs its own significance (as Gregor's opaque body occludes his awareness of self) and thus aims in a direction opposite to the art of the symbol; for there, in the words of Merleau-Ponty, the sign is "devoured" by its signification.[37] The outcome of this tendency of *The Metamorphosis* is its ugliness. Symbolic art, modeled on the metaphor which occults the signifier to the level of signification, strikes us as beautiful: our notion of the beautiful harmony of sign and significance is one dominated by the human signification, by the form of the person which in Schiller's classical conception of art "extirpates the material reference." [38] These expectations are disappointed by the opaque and impoverished sign in Kafka. His art devours the human meaning of itself and, indeed, must soon raise the question of a suitable nourishment. It is thus internally coherent that the vermin–the word without significance–should divine fresh nourishment and affinity in music, the language of signs without significance.[39]

But the song which Gregor hears does not transform his suffering; the music breaks off; the monster finds nourishment in a cruder fantasy of anger and possession. This scene communicates the total discrepancy between the vermin's body and the cravings appropriate to it and the other sort of nourishment for which he yearns; the moment produces, not symbolic harmony, but the intolerable tension of irreconcilables. In Kafka's unfathomable sentence, "Was he an animal, that music could move him so?" (E 130), paradox echoes jarringly without end.

At the close of *The Metamorphosis* Gregor is issued a death sentence by his family which he promptly adopts as his own; he then passes into a vacant trance.

> He had pains, of course, throughout his whole body, but it seemed to him that they were gradually getting fainter and fainter and would finally go away altogether. The rotten apple in his back and the inflamed area around it, which were completely covered with fluffy dust, already hardly bothered him. He thought back on his family with deep emotion and love. His conviction that he would have to disappear was, if possible, even firmer than his sister's. He remained in this state of empty and peaceful reflection until the tower clock struck three in the morning (E 136).

He is empty of all practical concerns; his body has dwindled to a mere dry husk, substantial enough to have become sonorous, too substantial not to have been betrayed by the promise of harmony in music. He suggests the Christ of John (19:30)—but not the Christ of Matthew (27:50) or Mark (15:37)—for Gregor's last moment is silent and painless. "He still saw that outside the window everything was beginning to grow light. Then, without his consent, his head sank down to the floor, and from his nostrils streamed his last weak breath" (E 136-37). For a moment the dim desert of Gregor's world grows luminous; his opaque body, progressively impoverished, achieves a faint translucency. Through the destruction of the specious harmony of the metaphor and the aesthetic claims of the symbol, Kafka engenders another sort of beauty and, with this, closes a circle of reflection on his own work. For, in 1910, just before his mature art originates as the distortion of the metaphor, Kafka wrote in the story fragment, " 'You,' I said . . . ": "Already, what protected me seemed to dissolve here in the city. I was beautiful in the early days, for this dissolution takes place as an apotheosis, in which everything that holds us to life flies away, but even in flying away illumines us for the last time with its human light" (DI 28; T 23).

At the close of *The Metamorphosis*, the ongoing metamorphosis of the metaphor accomplishes itself through a consciousness empty of all practical attention and a body that preserves its opacity, but in so dwindled a form that it achieves the condition of a painless translucency, a kind of beauty. In creating in the vermin a figure for the distortion of the metaphor, the generative principle of his art, Kafka underscores the negativity of writing but at the same time enters the music of the historical world at a crucial juncture; his art reveals at its root a powerful Romantic aesthetic tradition associated with the names of Rousseau, Hölderlin, Wordsworth, and Schlegel, which criticizes symbolic form and metaphorical diction in the name of a kind of allegorical language.[40] The figures of this secular allegory do not refer doctrinally to Scripture; rather, they relate to the source of the decision to constitute them. They replace the dogmatic unity of sign and significance with the temporal relation of the sign to its luminous source. This relation comes to light through the temporal difference between the allegorical sign and the sign prefiguring it; the exact meaning of the signs is less important than the temporal character of their relation. The vermin that alludes to vermin-figures in Kafka's early work, and whose death amid increasing luminosity alludes casually to Christ's, is just such a figure. But to stress the temporal character of the metamorphosed metaphor of *The Metamorphosis* is to distinguish it fundamentally from the "extended metaphor" of Sokel's discussion; for in this organistic conception of the figure, sign and significance coincide as forms of extension. And if Expressionism is to be defined by its further extension of metaphor, then *The Metamorphosis* cannot be accommodated in an Expressionist tradition.

Though *The Metamorphosis* joins an allegorical tradition within Romanticism, it does so only for a moment, before departing radically from it. The light in which Gregor dies is said explicitly to emanate from outside the window and not from a source within the subject. The creature turned away from life, facing death, and as such a pure sign of the poetic consciousness, keeps for Kafka its opaque and tellurian character. It is as a distorted body that Gregor is struck by the light; and it is in this light, principally unlike the source of poetic creation, that the work of art barely comes to recognize its own truth. For, wrote Kafka, "our art is a way of being dazzled by truth; the light on the flinching, grimacing face *[zurückweichenden Fratzengesicht]* is true, and nothing else" (H 46). Because the language of Kafka's fiction originates so knowingly from a reflection on ordinary speech, it cannot show the truth except as a solid body reflecting the light, a blank fragment of "what we call the world of the senses, [which] is the Evil in the spiritual world (DF 41; H 44).

And so the figure of the nameless vermin remains principally opaque. More fundamental than the moment of translucency, reflected in the fact that this moment is obtained only at death and without a witness, is the horror that writing can never amount to anything more than the twisted grimace on which glances a light not its own. Here Kafka's essentially linguistic imagination joins him to a disruptive modern tradition, described by Michel Foucault:

> The literature in our day, fascinated by the being of language, . . . gives prominence, in all their empirical vivacity, to the fundamental forms of finitude. From within language experienced and traversed as language, in the play of its possibilities extended to their furthest point, what emerges is that man has "come to an end," and that, by reaching the summit of all possible speech, he arrives not at the very heart of himself but at the brink of that which limits him; in that region where death prowls, where thought is extinguished, where the promise of the origin interminably recedes. . . . And as if this experiencing of the forms of finitude in language were insupportable. . . . it is within madness that it manifested itself—the figure of finitude thus positing itself in language (as that which unveils itself within it), but also before it, preceding it, as that formless, mute, unsignifying region where language can find its freedom. And it is indeed in this space thus revealed that literature, . . . more and more purely, with Kafka, Bataille, and Blanchot, posited itself . . . as experience of finitude.[41]

Symbolic and Allegorical Interpretation

In recent years it has become the practice of many of Kafka's most intelligent critics to prove Kafka indecipherable.[1] The intention is admirable: to call a halt to Kafka interpretations which read an abundant and univocal meaning into Kafka and in this way depart further and further from the writer as he read himself and as he is read by his work. This new critical project demythologizes the figure of Kafka as *homo religiosus*, of Kafka the social philosopher—indeed, of Kafka the truth teller.[2] Instead, it presents us with Kafka the author of fictions, stressing the extreme degree to which Kafka considered himself an event in the history of *literature*—indeed, literature as such. But demythologizing is

A shorter version of this essay was read at a symposium on *The Metamorphosis* held on December 15, 1971, at the Graduate Center of the City University of New York.

that labor of the negative which always falls short of literature, for it ignores the intention of literature to speak the truth–albeit figuratively, in the mode of fiction. In the end the demythologizing criticism of Kafka replaces one myth about his work with another.

Such is the result of the insistence by the new criticism on the irreducible multivalence of Kafka's meaning, on the intention of Kafka's work to contain a variety of codes which cannot be integrated. It ends by offering us Kafka's *mystery*, by declaring Kafka's fiction constitutively obscure. It takes out of Kafka's work the consoling certainty of a *plenum* of meaning–however gruesome that message of the misery of cities, the insanity of bureaucracy, the bloodthirstiness of family, the neurasthenia of self-consciousness. But in its place it puts an abundance still more odd–a "magic" we can never dispel. How little this restful revelation would have contented Kafka, that fabulous crow who fully intended to storm the heavens![3]

In fact, nothing in the past twenty years of literary analysis of *The Metamorphosis* exacts the obscurantist view. Essays by **Beissner**, **Walser**, **Henel**, and **Binion** have clarified a key structural dimension of this story: its original point of view, which is not identical but congruent with the consciousness of the hero while it maintains a playful distance. It changes with the hero's death into omniscience, but not in order to declare the hero mystified. Other analyses reveal the profit of a more and more exact description of Kafka's rhetoric. For example, **Brod**, **Pongs**, and **Weinberg** have shown the importance of the phrase "*ungeheueres Ungeziefer*," the monstrous vermin designating the metamorphosis. These words do not name an insect or a bug or ultimately any natural being: Kafka–reader of etymologies–knew what depth of unbeing underlies this phrase. Again, the patient description by **Luke** and **Schubiger** of Gregor's tergiversating rhetoric gives interpretation a starting point in form, and hence a valid origin.

But the greatest value of the successive application of critical thought to *The Metamorphosis* has been, I think, in defining the levels of possible interpretations. It is no longer useful to note that *The Metamorphosis* invites a wide variety of apparently faithful interpretations; or that the indifferent coexistence of interpretations is a structural item in the constitution of this work. Criticism has begun to identify the kinds of interpretations which *The Metamorphosis* has attracted; it has begun to measure the validity of these separate kinds and to realize the extent to which Kafka's stories themselves thematize the principles on which Kafka interpretations are based. These stories exist as the adventurous combat of types of interpretation of their own action, types which will determine the nature and direction of Kafka's future work. Kafka's stories dramatize the principles authorizing kinds of interpretation and hence kinds of consciousness which the literary act has of itself. Martin **Greenberg**'s readings of "The Judgment" and *The Metamorphosis* have given a powerful impetus to this critical project.

It appears that interpretations of *The Metamorphosis* can be provisionally divided into the symbolic and the allegorical. Such a distinction is of some importance.

The nuclear fable of all symbolic readings goes somewhat as follows. Despite his transformation, Gregor Samsa remains an intact moral personality. He is fundamentally the homeless man, the outcast social man; his life is empty of meaningful work, friendship, sexual love, family loyalty. He does not become a riddle as a result of his transformation. The reader can correlate that transformation with naturalistic intentions and empirical effects—with intentions such as resentment and laceration, familiar from the popular philosophy of our time (Freudianism); and with effects such as dependency and sickness, which we recognize from our own bodily experience. We therefore say that Gregor's outcast state is symbolic of the estrangement which the empirical person sooner or later comes to feel—the humiliated self-consciousness which perpetuates its estrangement in an ignorant and guilty way.

Symbolic readings agree in viewing Gregor's sorrow as the sorrow of a defeat in experience. At this level of interpretation it is an indifferent matter whether his defeat is seen essentially as a failure in his work life (**Richter**, **Sokel**); as a failure in intrafamilial integration (the psychologists **Kaiser** and **Webster**); or as the failure of personal sufficiency according to the standards of a *Bildungs*-philosophy exacting full self-realization through experience. What is important in the symbolic reading is that Gregor's predicament is in principle remediable. Thus, while *The Metamorphosis* describes a man whose experience has been deficient, it is not finally a descriptive work, its thrust is prescriptive. Read symbolically, the work asks us to complete it by supplying Gregor's deficient experience with a compensatory fullness; and indeed, it gives us hints of this fullness. For example, Gregor's metamorphosis, which condemns him to fawn and to scuttle, to play the slave and the robot, is merely an extended metaphor of his deformed work life; his proletarianization and his political impotence within a pseudopatriarchal structure depict a work life as it must not be. The sense of the story is then its implicit prophecy of an economic alternative (**Richter**). And indeed, a hint of this reformation is given in the more or less happy renewal of the family's work life. Another reading at this symbolic level is the psychological. When Gregor becomes a cockroach, he simply realizes in a vivid way the intentions which define him within a schizophrenic family situation. He punishes the family with his odium and punishes himself by assuming a cripple's or pariah's existence. He is punished by his sick body and by his dependency but achieves the covert, doubly aggressive expressiveness of the tyrant invalid and the family idiot. Yet bodily and psychological restoration is forecast in the moment of painlessness and translucency which Gregor achieves at his death . . . and so on.

The gist of all symbolical readings is most clearly present in the psychoanalytical reading, which fills in the literary text as psychoanalysis fills in an oral report of a dream, as if both texts were essentially nonliteral communications, full of gaps and ellipses. This is the procedure of the critics **Kaiser** and **Webster**.

In sum the symbolic reading asserts: 1. the continuity of the empirical personality of Gregor Samsa with the monstrous vermin; 2. the meaningfulness of the metamorphosis in terms of intentions and effects taken from ordinary experience; 3. the deficiency and remediableness of the experience with which *The Metamorphosis* is correlated; 4. the prescriptive and prophetic bearing of the work, hinted at in Gregor's and the family's end: at his death Gregor is a *schöne Seele*; the family is restored to health and hope.

The allegorical reading opposes the symbolic reading in every detail. It takes literally the metamorphosis, the radical disjunction separating Gregor Samsa from the vermin. It considers the work as literally constituting an uncanny, unsettled existence. Hence, it reads Gregor's consciousness of his sister's violin playing, through which he senses the way to an unknown nourishment, not as compensation for his existence but rather as an integral condition of it. Finally, his situation is not seen as a defective or any other kind of empirical situation: it cannot be grasped through familiar experience.

Mainly because this reading stresses the absolute interval between Gregor Samsa and his new situation—his unbeing—it can be called *allegorical* according to Walter Benjamin's definition of allegory as the nonpresence—that is to say the nonexperienceable character—of what is signified.[4]

What, then, is allegorized in *The Metamorphosis*? What intention finds its correlative in the metamorphosis of a man into an *Ungeziefer*, an unbeing? It is, first of all, Kafka's intention to exist as literature, to write fiction; for this intention to write—to paraphrase Collingwood—is realized only insofar as it both lives in the historical process and knows itself as so living. In this story writing reflects itself, in the mode of allegory, as metamorphosis, literality, death, play, and reduction—the whole in a negative and embattled form.

The degree of Kafka's commitment to writing, to what he called *Schriftstellersein*, cannot be exaggerated, and his work necessarily reflects the conscious intensity of this commitment. But writing held different meanings for him at different times of his life; on no account should one overlook the historicity of Kafka's work as a reflection of the project of writing. This history nevertheless has a basic direction. Kafka came to realize more and more sharply the impoverishment, reduction, and shortcoming which writing entails.

The decisive turn away from a eudemonic conception of writing occurs with the composition, in 1912, of "The Judgment." This work stands beside *The Metamorphosis* in a special intimacy of act and interpretation. "The Judgment" simply happens to Kafka; it is a kind of breakthrough which he describes in his diaries in a very confused way—in language that is alternatively violently metaphorical and impenetrably abstruse. The story cries out for clearer interpretation; this is what it receives in *The Metamorphosis.*

The hero of *The Metamorphosis* is "The Judgment," the insight liberated in that story: that Kafka must not betray his writing either by marrying or by supposing that his father is the source and goal of his art. This judgment metamorphoses Kafka's existence into *Schriftstellersein* in the mode of allegory: the mode that definitively detaches the particular entity from the *plenum* of which it dreams, whether this plenitude be conceived as an expansive state of mind, interpersonal recognition, or metaphysical truth. After "The Judgment," when Kafka writes, when he "descends to the dark forces," he takes up a position irretrievably outside the house of life.

Kafka's radically figurative way of expressing the separation of literature from life is to declare literary existence to be outside of death. In his diaries Kafka wrote about the death scenes in his work: "But for me, who believe that I shall be able to lie contentedly on my deathbed, such scenes are secretly a game" (DII 102; T 448). This playfulness is present in *The Metamorphosis* in the profusion of its imagery of art and play and in the distance between the ghostly, smiling narrator and his monster. This distance reveals Kafka as always a little ahead of his subject; fundamentally, he is the narrator of the story who survives the death of his hero; he can be this narrator because he has already had the experience of death, existing now in the most radical estrangement from life. This is the point at which the play begins, and it is a play necessarily full of sorrow.

The sorrow belongs to the being who is literature, who is engaged in an exemplary way in the passage from particularity to generality and as a consequence must suffer death after death without hope of a goal. The emblem of literature in its desire for generality and its condemnation to particularity is its literality, the literal being the allegory of the literary. Literality is the main bearing of Kafka's point of view throughout his fiction: in *The Metamorphosis* we are so thoroughly immersed in the perspective of the vermin that we understand him only word by word, and always for the first time; we are bound to the text.

Kafka's crucial insight is the root separateness of literature and life—indeed, the antithetical character of literature and life conceived as *Bildung*, as an extensive totality of experience. This vision is given in the vermin's gradual reduction and impoverishment, his loss of eyesight and loss of locomotion. Kafka's art of constituting realities stripped bare bespeaks a movement of the mind that proceeds by reduction to radical immanence. Examples abound: in *Amerika*, the subject Karl Rossman is reduced to verminous existence in Brunelda's bedroom; in *The Castle* the object of experience, the village world, is blanketed by snow, reduced to the bare *factum brutum* of a material world.

Kafka's fiction now can be viewed as a contest between essentially symbolic and essentially allegorical interpretations of its own action. At every point the symbolic interpretation bespeaks the contrary of the allegorical: it invests the self with continuity, meaningfulness, expansiveness, and the prospect of reconciliation.

The constitution of tragic, allegorical consciousness in *The Metamorphosis* includes the representation of symbolic consciousness. This occurs whenever the vermin erroneously asserts his identity with Gregor Samsa and tries to restore his old situation within the family and again whenever his reflections appear to justify the metamorphosis as punishment. That the symbolic mode is a seduction and an error emerges through the vermin's attempts to speak in metaphorical language. Kafka's aversion to the metaphor is constant, but in the few places in *The Metamorphosis* where this language occurs, the reader patently finds himself inside an inauthentic consciousness. The vermin's attempt to come to terms with his experience through metaphor inspires derision, as when he likens his rivals to harem women or sees the office manager turn on the stairs, seeking transcendental deliverance.

It cannot be this creature's fate to know a symbolic unity with his world. The prospect of redemption at the end of *The Metamorphosis* is a grotesque delusion: Gregor—we read—"thought back on his family with deep emotion and love." To Kafka, immersion in the will of the family invariably means extinction in the state of greatest error: this is the case of Georg Bendemann at the close of "The Judgment."

The vermin is most an opaque bug, least the lucid beetle of the story "Wedding Preparations," whenever he uses his position in order to gain an expansive unity with the world. The music that summons him would provide him, he thinks, with an "unknown *nourishment*" (italics added), even though it cannot mean anything to him in terms of his former experience. To turn that experience to account, to go after the playing as if it were the player, would be to use literature as Kafka describes it in his most deluded work, the "Letter to His Father"—it would be to bemoan in writing what he wished to bemoan on his father's breast. The vermin is the blood-sucking louse to which Kafka compares himself in his struggle with his father only when he attempts to deny his separateness, to deny his character as an allegorical figure.

In Kafka's letters to Felice Bauer written during the composition of *The Metamorphosis*, he noted that the story was bearable on account of its "sweet pages." When he read the story aloud to friends, they all laughed. These remarks can only refer to the narrator's playful relation to his protagonist, a distance which means, not detachment, but being ahead of the hero in the sense of knowing his errors. All Gregor's errors come under the head of action in the symbolic mode—the mode which asserts the continuity of consciousness and being.

The priority of literalness and play over meaning in the story is the statement of the priority for Kafka of literature as allegory over literature as symbol, but this priority is one that has to be perpetually reasserted. It requires a corresponding priority of interpretative modes. Yet to find Kafka's stories essentially constituted by the combat of interpretative modes—one of which, the allegorical, has priority—is not to declare Kafka ambivalent or indecipherable. The allegorical stands to the symbolic in Kafka, not in ambivalent relation, but in the relation of priority.

A CRITICAL BIBLIOGRAPHY OF *The Metamorphosis*

This bibliography has been assisted by the following bibliographical works:

1. **Beebe, Maurice** and **Christensen, Naomi.** "Criticism of Franz Kafka: A Selected Checklist. *Metamorphosis.*" *Modern Fiction Studies,* VIII (Spring 1962), 96-97.
2. **Flores, Angel,** ed. *The Kafka Problem*. New York: New Directions, 1946. Pp. 455-77.
3. **Flores, Angel** and **Swander, Homer,** eds. *Franz Kafka Today*. Madison: University of Wisconsin Press, 1958. Pp. 259-85.
4. *Germanistik.*
5. **Hemmerle, Rudolf.** *Franz Kafka: Eine Bibliographie*. Munich: Robert Lerche, 1958.
6. **Järv, Harry.** *Die Kafka-Literatur: Eine Bibliographie*. Malmo and Lund, Sweden: Bo Cavefors, 1961.
7. *Publications of the Modern Language Association of America: Annual Bibliographies.*

German Texts

1. The original manuscript, privately owned. It has not been possible to see this text. One page can be found in *Expressionismus, Literatur und Kunst 1910-1923:* Eine Ausstellung des dt. Literaturarchivs im Schiller-Nationalmuseum, Marbach a.N., 1961, p. 140.

2. "Die Verwandlung." *Die Weissen Blätter 1915*, Heft 10-12, 1177-1230. Kafka did not correct the proofs of this first printing. It contains many printer's errors.
3. *Die Verwandlung. Der jüngste Tag.* Leipzig: Kurt Wolff Verlag, 1916. [On p. 2: Gedruckt bei Poeschel & Trepte in Leipzig, November 1915, als Band 22/23 (Doppelband) der Bücherei "Der jüngste Tag" mit einem Titelbild von Ottomar Starke. Copyright 1915 by Kurt Wolff Verlag, Leipzig.] This text is the most reliable.
4. *Die Verwandlung. Der jüngste Tag*. Leipzig: Kurt Wolff Verlag [1918]. [On p. 4: Bücherei "Der jüngste Tag," Band 22/23, Gedruckt bei Dietsch & Brückner, Weimar. Copyright Kurt Wolff Verlag, Leipzig, 1917.] It is difficult to decide whether Kafka had a hand in this edition. I count fifty-seven changes between item 3 and this edition, of which I judge eleven to be degradations, ten to be improvements, and the rest to be of minimal consequence. The very few variants that alter the sense of the text (the great majority of the changes are concerned with orthography and punctuation) are indicated in my translation.
5. "Die Verwandlung." *Erzählungen und Kleine Prosa*, ed. by Max Brod. New York: Schocken Books, 1946. Brod reproduces item 3 with a few changes in punctuation and some indefensible adjustments of the orthography of separable verbs.
6. "Die Verwandlung." *Die Erzählungen*, ed. by Klaus Wagenbach. Frankfurt am Main: S. Fischer Verlag, 1961. Wagenbach's edition appears to be based by chance on item 4, with all the glaring printer's errors of this text corrected. At other places, however, he incorporates item 5, sometimes introducing Brod's adjustments, sometimes not. See **Dietz**.
7. "Die Verwandlung." *Sämtliche Erzählungen*, ed. by Paul Raabe. Frankfurt am Main: S. Fischer Bücherei, 1970. Raabe declares that his texts are based on the first edition, "but of course follow Max Brod's readable text" (390). In fact, his version of *The Metamorphosis* is not based on the first edition, item 2; neither does it follow item 5. He reprints item 3, with two minor deviations.

English Translations

1. "The Metamorphosis," trans. by Eugene Jolas. *Transition* (Paris), No. 25 (Fall 1936), 27-38; No. 26 (Winter 1937), 53-72; No. 27 (April-May 1938), 79-103.
2. *The Metamorphosis*, trans. by A. L. Lloyd. London: The Parton Press, 1937. Again as *Metamorphosis*. New York: The Vanguard Press, 1946.
3. "The Metamorphosis." In *The Penal Colony: Stories and Short Pieces*, trans. by Willa and Edwin Muir. New York: Schocken Books, 1948. Again in *Selected Short Stories of Franz Kafka*. New York: Random House, The Modern Library, 1952.
4. *The Metamorphosis*, trans. and ed. by Stanley Corngold. New York: Bantam Books, 1972.

Critical Works

1. Adams, Robert M. *Strains of Discord: Studies in Literary Openness*. Ithaca, New York: Cornell University Press, 1958. Pp. 168-79.

Kafka's constitution of meaning can be traced to his numerological speculations. In *The Metamorphosis*, triads (one leader and two followers) have structural and symbolic significance. Gregor's metamorphosis and his later struggles are expressed in threes which either reject or potentially include him. He has been occupying the central one of three bedrooms, and he will be driven back into his room by a triad of authorities. Gregor's isolation from the masculine number three symbolizes his sexual failure—his fetishism, withdrawal, and isolation. The pattern to which he is hopelessly extraneous is formed by the father flanked by the mother and sister. This triad, which menaces Gregor, is afterward duplicated by the triad of lodgers. Their behavior always involves a reversal; what they first appear to do is just the opposite of their final intent. Perhaps this reversal mocks Gregor's undue deference to the triad which has so far communicated order, community, and strength. When the lodgers are faced firmly, they disappear; if Gregor had faced up to the triad of the family at the start, he might have triumphed. "The inhumanly rigid law which turns out to be no law at all–at least for the person who supposed it applied to him–is a frequent component of Kafka's writing" (175-76). When the sister hastily makes up the lodgers' beds, she acknowledges an authority which may be bogus, but her tribute only confirms Gregor's self-abasing belief in it. The triad thus undergoes a reversal in the course of the story from a good and healthy principle, from which Gregor has been cut off, to a vicious folly. As in "The Judgment," "the protagonist approves and relishes his own abolition, as if by this final humility to ingratiate himself with a superior power" (177). The ending supports the view that Gregor, more humble than is good for him, dies in deference to a bogus deity; but an equally plausible conclusion is that Gregor is indeed sick and that the triads which oppose him genuinely symbolize the health and community from which he is isolated. "These two interpretations are wholly incompatible; they are also equally cogent" (177).

Here is a good example of the New Critical approach to Kafka. Through close reading Adams traces the destiny of a key structural element within *The Metamorphosis*–the image of triads–and concludes, from its ambiguous and paradoxical character, Kafka's "equivocation and ambivalence," the "equally cogent and wholly incompatible" meanings of his work. This conclusion is premature: it does not take into explicit account the various points of view determining the story, and it does not connect the meanings of this story with Kafka's reflective consciousness as a whole. From Gregor's point of view, the triad of the family is never a bogus deity. The family makes up almost his whole world, and it is as indubitable and as truly a "superior power" as anyone's world must be. Gregor strives to be more deeply a part of it; it is real enough, too, to provoke his rage and aggression. From the narrator's point of view, however–a point of view congruent with Gregor's own but not identical with it (see **Henel**)–the family is pettily self-obsessed, mindless, and cruel. Gregor stands condemned for pursuing the world of the family as a satisfying world of health and community. His sickness is his immersion in his world. We move here within a modern, "post-theodicean" ontology in which the self is a derelict mode of being-in-the-world (see **Bense**). The other Samsas are healthy only in the sense that they do not make life with Gregor, who is no better than they, the goal of their strivings.

When the story is seen as opposing Gregor's dreams of domestic happiness to the family's blind complacency, it cannot make a statement about genuine health and community. The consciousness that is unfolded on the surface of such a story is only an impoverished version of Kafka's self-consciousness—a stoic and amused reflection on the part of the self or mask which Kafka calls "the bachelor." The decisively Kafkan element, something expressive of Kafka's intense concern for writing, is all but hidden in the world of the Samsas. Gregor merely reflects the bachelor's (neurotic) interest in imagining himself exclusively from the standpoint of the Other who is hostile to his concerns.

When Gregor leaves the world of the family to pursue his conception of music, however, the deep structure of the story emerges. In this instant Gregor is explicitly identified with the condition of writing itself. And from the standpoint of writing, the Other is of no importance (see pp. 25-27).

Aside from this moment, the *surface* of the story lacks explicit self-reflection. Thus there is, quite consistently, even less evidence than Adams gives for asserting the bogus character of the family triad. The triad of lodgers, whose insectlike movements suggest Gregor, does not puncture the authority of the family so much as it punctures the validity of Gregor's wish to restore the happiness of former times (see **Sparks**).

Gregor is very "sick"—but the family does not signify the "health and community" from which he is alienated. These two propositions, though equally cogent, are not incompatible.

2. **Adorno, Theodor W.** "Aufzeichnungen zu Kafka." *Neue Rundschau* (Frankfurt), LXIV (July-Sept. 1953), 325-53. Reprinted in *Prismen: Kulturkritik und Gesellschaft*. Frankfurt am Main: Suhrkamp, 1955. Pp. 302-42. "Notes on Kafka," trans. by Samuel and Shierry Weber. In *Prisms*. London: Spearman, 1967. Pp. 245-72.

Most criticism of Kafka is existentialist and does not deal with the core mystery, the scandal. It does not help to call Kafka a symbolist using realistic themes. His intention is not symbolic. Particular moments of his art do not, on the strength of their connections, point beyond themselves; the totality of these moments is not absorbed into a single meaning. An abyss gapes between the literal sense of Kafka's sentences and their meaning.

They are, finally, parabolic; they express themselves through their rupture with expression, but this rupture still does not make up the content of the work.

Every sentence both invites and resists interpretation, yet correct interpretation seems a matter of life and death. The force with which Kafka exacts interpretation collapses all aesthetic distance. The works aim for an aggressive physical closeness preventing the reader's identification yet compelling him to produce the interpretative word.

It is doubtful whether Kafka's aphorisms and theoretical writings constitute an interpretation of his fiction. The metaphysical content of the work is not the philosophy which the artist "pumps" into his forms. The correct interpretation of Kafka must take everything literally, it must not cloak the word in notions. True, many of Kafka's texts provide no basis for this principle of literalness; "at times words and particularly metaphors detach themselves and achieve a separate existence" (*Prismen*, 306). They fuse associations, frequently wittily, and are full of psychological insights, such as the connection between the instinctual and the compulsive personality. But without the principle of literalness, Kafka's polysemy would dissolve into indifferent meaning. One of the components of Kafka's shock effect is the fact that he takes dreams *literally*. Everything unlike the dream and its prelogical logic is excluded—including dreams themselves. What is shocking is not the monstrous, but its matter-of-factness. The reader's attitude toward Kafka should adopt Kafka's attitude toward the dream; he should dwell on "the blind spots, the incommensurate, opaque details" (*Prismen*, 307). The gesture, frequently in counterpoint with language, has an exact meaning; the gesture is the trace of an experience which has become muffled in meaning. The gesture, not the shattered configuration of language, reveals the way things are.

Kafka's note that everything he wrote could be psychoanalytically interpreted, but that this interpretation would require further interpretation *ad infinitum*, does not negate the real affinity between Kafka and Freud, specifically in their representation of taboo, of the *délire de toucher*, which in Kafka brings together higher and lower orders, and of the temptation of parricide. Freud and Kafka share a nonpsychological psychoanalytical verism: for Freud, archetypal scenes were real events.[1] "In Freud as in Kafka the validity of the soulful dimension of the mind is excluded" (in Freud the personality loses substance and becomes the mere organizing principle of somatic impulses) (*Prismen*, 311). Yet Kafka surpasses Freud in his skepticism toward the ego.

Kafka imbues the evidence of psychoanalysis not merely with mental and metaphoric, but also with concrete existence and then studies the consequences; the result is that civilization and bourgeois individuation are convicted of pretense. He sins against aesthetic tradition in creating art out of nothing but the trash of reality, in the way that psychoanalysis attended to the "dross of the phenomenal world." Furthermore, he projects the future of society through the waste products which modernity extracts from the decaying present. "Instead of curing neurosis, he seeks in neurosis the curative power, that of knowledge: the wounds with which society brands the individual are read by the individual as signs of social untruth, as the negative of truth" (*Prismen*, 312). Kafka's is a power of demolition—not only of the controlled gratifications of society, not only of the subject, but also of the merely material existence which comes to light at the subjective level of the compliant, nonassertive consciousness. Kafka's epic itinerary is the flight through man into the nonhuman. Kafka names the collapse of the spirit in a language of compelling authority. The slack consciousness, strained to the bursting point, experiences what once was metaphor and meaning as something immediate and nonintentional. Only in solitude, when the spirit is immersed in itself, is that common existence laid hold of which individuation transcends and conceals. Kafka's art makes accessible the *déjà vu* of all men—eternalizes the past and curses it; this experience is betrayed when his writings are made to yield generalities.

The frozen, immortalized gesture in Kafka fuses the ephemeral and the permanent. A perception of sameness in variety inspires his mechanically reproduced doubles. "In the end the social origin of the individual is revealed as the power of annihilating his individuality" (*Prismen*, 315). The hermetic principle in Kafka, the mind's knowledge of insanity, has a protective function: to keep at bay the madness assaulting it from without—that is, its own collectivization.[2] The work that unsettles individuation wants at no cost to be imitated; it is for this reason that Kafka wanted his work destroyed.

The force of many of Kafka's images tears open their insulation—the penal colony, the metamorphosis. In these extremes Kafka's work shows a kind of hope, the power to hold out against the worst by converting it into language. These works are very probably the key to Kafka. "In *The Metamorphosis* the path of the experience can be reconstructed, as an extension of the lines, from the literal sense of the figure of speech: 'These traveling salesmen are like bedbugs.'[3] . . . . What happens to a man who is a man-sized bedbug?" (*Prismen*, 317). The child has the experience of such gigantism: grown-ups, to his terrified gaze, are enormous, distorted beings with huge trampling legs and remote tiny heads. To keep the vision of such enormities, one has to transform oneself into a child. Then the father is seen anew as the ogre whom the child feared; the disgust at cheese parings reveals itself as a despicable prehuman craving for them; from the boarders—the roomers (*die Zimmerherren*)—emanates an atmosphere of horror which is present in their name.[4] The literary technique which battens on words through their associations produces something opposite from reflection on what is human—the trying out of a type of dehumanization.[5] The pressure of this technique compels its subjects to undergo a biological regression, so to speak. Everything in Kafka tends to the revelation that men are not selves but things. Though men are like copies of each other, they share a fundamental nonidentity. The individual and the social character of the same man gape wide apart.[6] Kafka's work contains the social genesis of schizophrenia.

"The whole of Kafka's imagery is sad and broken. . . . Most of his work is a reaction to unlimited power" (*Prismen*, 318). W. **Benjamin** called the power of the raging patriarchs parasitic: it lives off the life it oppresses. "But the parasitic moment is characteristically displaced; Gregor Samsa, and not his father, becomes a bug. Not the powers, but the powerless heroes seem superfluous; none does socially useful work . . . . They crawl around between stage properties which have long been amortized and which grant them their existence only as charity" (*Prismen*, 318-19). This shift is based on the ideological habit of glorifying the reproduction of life into an act of grace on the part of the employer. The element of shabbiness in Kafka is the cryptogram of capitalism's brilliant late phase.

"In Kafka's compulsive universe everything which occurs combines the expression of the pure necessity with that of the pure contingency that goes with shabbiness" (*Prismen*, 320). Kafka bares the totalitarian system that sustains itself by its persecution of the deviant, who fatally endangers its principle merely by slipping through its meshes. Kafka prophesies with the dregs of the system, as one contingent with respect to the system that must assimilate all contingencies. "Consummate untruth is its own contradiction, therefore it does not need to be expressly contradicted" (*Prismen,* 320). Kafka sees into the heart of monopoly capitalism through the waste products of the liberal era which the former is liquidating. His metaphysics is crystallized in this historical moment and not in a putative supertemporal being gleaming throughout history. His sense of eternity is that of the endlessly repeated present sacrifice. Today's sacrifice is always yesterday's: hence the exclusion in Kafka's work of almost every reference to actual history. "His work stands in a hermetic relation to history; this concept is taboo. To the eternity of the historical moment corresponds his view of the world's course as fallen by nature and invariant; the moment, the absolutely transitory, is the symbol of the eternity of lapsing *[Vergehen]*, of damnation" (*Prismen*, 321).

The content of Kafka's works alludes more cogently to the subsequent Nazi reality than to the hidden sway of God. Kafka cannot be confiscated by dialectical theology, for, as **Benjamin** has pointed out, his powers have a mythic character; more than this, ambiguity and obscurity are not due strictly to the operations of a divine Other, but also to men and to their living conditions. Kafka levels the infinite qualitative distinction between man and God. In Kafka's world "unbridled violence is exercised by various subaltern types like noncommissioned officers, regular soldiers, concierges. These are all *déclassés* caught up in the collapse of the organized collective and permitted to survive, like Gregor Samsa's father. As in the eras of defective capitalism, the burden of guilt is shunted off from the order of production onto agents for the circulation [of wealth] or onto those providing services—traveling salesmen, bank employees, waiters" (*Prismen,* 325). Kafka is well aware of economic trends that only later became completely evident. For Kafka the newest phase of social power manifests the earliest phase through the things that are eliminated because they are considered prehistoric. He perceives traces of the Stone Age in the gaps and deformations of modernity; the bourgeois ends as a translation into archetypes. "The surrender of his individual features, the disclosure of the terror swarming under the stone of culture, marks the downfall of individuality itself . . . . As in Kafka's perverse epics, the thing which perished in concentration camps was that from which experience takes its measure—life, lived out of itself to its end" (*Prismen*, 325-36).

Kafka's writings have an exact historical provenance. Precisely as hermetic works they played a role in the literary movement of the ten years around the First World War; one of its focal points was Kafka's own milieu in Prague. Kafka's authentic horizon is Expressionism. In liquidating the dream by making it omnipresent, Kafka alone pursued the Expressionistic impulse as far as did the radical lyric poets.

"Kafka's hermetic principle is that of completely alienated subjectivity . . . . He is Kierkegaard's disciple only through the category of 'objectless inwardness' " (*Prismen,* 327). The medium of Kafka's consciousness is more monotonous, and hence even more ghastly, than the social system outside. "In absolute subjective space and time there is no room for anything which might disturb its inherent principle—implacable alienation. . . . The absence of distinctions within autarchic subjectivity strengthens the feeling of uncertainty and the monotony of the repetition compulsion. This inwardness, revolving within itself without resistance, is denied whatever might put a stop to the 'bad infinity' of its movement, and which then becomes mysterious . . . . Shut up in itself, it holds its breath, as if it did not dare to touch anything unlike itself. Under this spell pure subjectivity turns into mythology" (*Prismen*, 327-28). At the same time it is itself without a subject. "The self exists only in becoming other than itself. As the stable residue of the subject that encapsulates itself in the face of alien things, it becomes the opaque residue of the world. The more the Expressionist self is thrown back upon itself, the more it becomes a likeness of the excluded world of things" (*Prismen*, 328). "Pure subjectivity, necessarily alienated from itself and changed into a thing, turns into an objective reality expressing itself through its own alienation. The line between the human world and the world of things grows blurred" (*Prismen*, 328-29).[7] Precisely the external determination of interior beings lends Kafka's prose the appearance of sober objectivity. "The zone of not being able to die is at the same time the no-man's-land between man and thing" (*Prismen*, 329).

Depersonalization runs through the sexuality of Kafka's work. As the archaic collective, the family triumphs over its later individualized form. Kafka penetrates beneath current conceptions of eroticism. The relations of white-collar workers in big cities, without choice or memory, become an image of a condition that vanished ages ago. Patriarchal society reveals its mainspring as directed, brutal oppression. Women are used as the means to an end–as sexual objects and as connections. But in the middle of this gloom Kafka seeks an image of happiness. "It is produced out of the astonishment of the hermetically sealed subject at the paradox that he can be loved all the same" (*Prismen*, 330). Kafka's difficulty is in finding a language for this ecstasy that will preserve the character of objectless inwardness. He awards this function to the gesture. The privileged moment of feeling can be told visually, at the same time that, having become an image, it is wholly alienated from itself. Kafka's writing is a kind of translation of Expressionist painting. "To the panic gaze which has withdrawn from objects all affective cathexis, objects freeze into a third thing, neither dream, which can only be falsified, nor the mimicry of reality, but its jigsaw puzzle, pieced together out of its scattered fragments" (*Prismen*, 331). Kafka's world of images is shored up by the strict exclusion of everything resembling music.

"An Expressionist epic is a paradox. It narrates the unnarratable, the subject wholly restricted to itself and so at the same time unfree, indeed not even truly existing. Dissociated into the compulsive components of its own restricted existence, robbed of identity with itself, its life has no duration; objectless inwardness is space in the precise sense that everything which it originates obeys the law of timeless repetition" (*Prismen*, 332).

In the modern detective novel, the world of things preponderates over the abstract subject; and Kafka employs this aspect to convert things into omnipresent emblems. "The longer works are, as it were, detective novels which fail to unmask the criminal" (*Prismen*, 333). There are links to Sade; like Sade's innocents, the Kafkan subject lands in one hopeless situation after another. The stations of epic adventure become like those of the Passion; the sense of the epic is a flight from jails. Reason is at work here, through the stylizations of madness bringing objective madness to light. Kafka shows the way things are, without any illusions as to the subject, which in the most acute consciousness of itself—of its nullity—flings itself onto the junkheap.

The parable is informed with the intent of Enlightenment thought, which Kafka shares. By embedding human meanings and morals in natural life, the mind recognizes itself in them. The eclipse of the parabolic intent is equally the consequence of the Enlightenment. "The more objective reality which it reduces to man, the more barren and impenetrable are the outlines of the merely existing things which he can never dissolve fully into subjectivity and which he has already sucked dry of everything familiar" (*Prismen*, 337).

Kafka's God is opposite to the God of Enlightenment freethinking *and* of dialectical theology—the *deus absconditus*. Kafka's God converges with the mythic powers, awakening anxiety and terror. "Absolute alienation, delivered over to the existence from which it has withdrawn, is explored as the hell [it is]" (*Prismen*, 338). The aesthetic means Kafka uses to make objective alienation visible takes its legitimation from the content of the work. "His work fabricates a standpoint from which the creation seems as scored and battered as it itself imagines hell must be" (*Prismen*, 339). Kafka does not present an absurd God, but an absurd world. The subject objectifies itself in renouncing the last of its understanding with the world. Kafka preached, not humility toward bizarre powers, but cunning. "He seeks salvation in incorporating the powers of the adversary" (*Prismen*, 340). The spell of reification is broken when the subject reifies itself.

"Kafka's figures are instructed to leave their soul at the door at a moment of the social struggle in which the one chance of the bourgeois individual lies in negating his own composition and that of the class situation which has condemned him to be what he is . . . . The salutary recollection of man's likeness to the animal, which nourishes a whole class of his stories, replaces the highest bourgeois idea, that of human dignity. Immersion in the inner space of individuation, which culminates in self-reflection of this kind, hits upon the principle of individuation, the positing of the self by the self. . . . The self seeks to make amends by giving this up" (*Prismen*, 340).

Kafka resists the world through nonviolence. The mythic god shall succumb to its mirror image, but not through the victim's insisting on his being right, as is the custom of the world. Hence the silly and naive quality of the clever speeches of his heroes. "Their sound reasoning strengthens the delusion against which it protests" (*Prismen*, 348). Through the reification of the subject, which the world demands anyway, Kafka wants to surpass it where he can. That is the reverse side of Kafka's doctrine of the death which fails: the battered creation which cannot die. Here is a promise of immortality. It connects to the salvation enjoyed by things which are useless and no longer part of the guilty network of exchange. The universe of Kafka's ideas is like a universe of white elephants; it can be grasped through the movie title, "Shopworn Angel." While disaster plagues the interiors inhabited by men, children's hide-outs, such abandoned spots as stairs, are places of hope. The innocence of useless things creates a counterpoint to parasitic things. According to the testimony of Kafka's works, all labor which reproduces life in this entangled world only furthers the entanglement. The one remedy for the half-uselessness of life is its complete uselessness. Thus Kafka links himself intimately with death. The created universe takes priority over the living. The self is shattered, a fraud of mere nature. There is only a name to survive death.

The argument which runs beneath the brilliant surface of this essay is profound and consistent; yet it is only true in part. When Adorno's principal ideas are applied to *The Metamorphosis*, the result is suggestive but also misleading.

If it is true that Gregor has been branded by a repressive social order, *he* does not consistently read his wounds as "signs of social untruth." His desires, for example, remain what they were. From the start and well into the second section he wants to return to work. And his family is always an object of desire. These facts could be rescued for Adorno's theory only if it is argued that society perpetuates repression by insinuating itself as an attractive or coercive object into the desires of its victim; only if it is argued, in Adorno's terms, that society imposes the relation between compulsion (or coercion) and drive. However, it is impossible to find evidence for this view in *The Metamorphosis*. Gregor's desire to work appears to have an origin separate from the coercions of his father and the office manager. Again and again Gregor is the author of his own repression. Society—indeed, a principle of masked exploitation—seems to originate for Gregor with his desire to turn it to his own account. Certain distinctions must therefore be made with greater clarity: what Kafka may be asserted to know must be distinguished from what Gregor surely does not know—the truth of his predicament; again, the distinction must be maintained between society as something not subjective and society as a mode of inauthentic being perpetuated by the self. *The Metamorphosis* shows Gregor so deeply sunk in bad faith that it is impossible to obtain evidence from him for the social causation of psychosis.

Adorno stresses the destruction of the individual self in Kafka's world by another, more comprehensive process. The self of the hero is a pure subjectivity wholly detached from the world. But, Adorno argues, the self can live only as part of a subject that engages with others and from this encounter constitutes a personal world of objects and intentions. The alienated and solipsistic self, Adorno continues, thus exists at a presubjective stratum of itself—as animal-like and as pure social determination; in effect, as pure products for social consumption. Kafka, who in his diaries and letters frequently represents himself as a thing and as an animal, does in part illustrate this "demolition" of the self while remaining, of course, wholly aware of it. One correction has to be made, however: the things to which he likens himself in his letters to Felice Bauer are not obsolete consumer's goods, but purely natural substances—"a stone," "a piece of wood"; or else things whose names have suggestive connotations: for example, "a tiny trolley" used in the office, the word for which also means "bier." Now Adorno's description of the end state of the process of self-demolition—the regression into an animal and into a kind of "gear"—is marvelously apt for Gregor. But his description of the process leading to this end state cannot be applied to *The Metamorphosis* without violating the sequence of its moments.[8]

Before his metamorphosis Gregor is not alienated from the world as a pure solipsistic subjectivity, as an "objectless inwardness." He is wholly immersed in the world; he is hardly a subjectivity at all. His regression into an animal, into a sort of living "stuff," results in–it is not itself the result of–his becoming a wholly alienated subjectivity. As the regression becomes more and more radical, so does his human consciousness, which, at the point of Gregor's deepest degradation, first achieves a moment of transparency to itself. Yet Gregor's discovery of a desire for another sort of nourishment is not a demystification; it moves in quite a different direction from an insight into the experience of having been "demolished." True, he notes that he has been reduced in some sense to an animal when he puts this very experience into question. "Was he an animal that music could move him so?" But he already had this insight on the occasion of his sister's wanting to clear out all the furniture from his room. Now his experience at the deepest level of his demolition is of something not his individuated self and yet not archaic nor reified nor of social provenance. At this moment, which is only a moment, he is at once free from the myth of absolute, self-posited subjectivity and of the social force that destroys this assertion. But Adorno's thesis is beautifully illustrated when Gregor immediately falls back into a regressive state constituted by archaic desire (he wants incest), social power (he would rob his parents of his sister), and reversion into a thing (he and his sister will freeze into the members of a tableau emblematizing desire).

Adorno's "Notes" offer various centers from which systematic interpretations of Kafka's works could proceed. One should like to see him develop the pregnant clue that it is through writing that Kafka absolutely resists the world, but his description of consciousness within Kafka's world as *essentially* shaped and stressed by the burden of social existence can be accepted only with many reservations.

3. **Albérès, R.-M.** (pseudonym of **Marill, René**) and **De Boisdeffre, Pierre**. *Franz Kafka.* Paris: Editions Universitaires, 1960. Pp. 62-63. *Kafka; the Torment of Man,* trans. by Wade Baskin. New York: The Philosophical Library, 1968. Pp. 49-50.

The myth of *The Metamorphosis* is crueler than the myths of *The Trial* and *The Castle*: it is pure horror. We should be close to the romantic horror story here if tone and style did not banish every suggestion of mere effect. Everything in *The Metamorphosis* remains sober, banal. The Samsa family is stirred up by the metamorphosis, but no worse than if they were dealing with a bad cold; and if Gregor suffers from his change, Kafka takes pains not to say so. "He averts our attention from that which should occasion scandal and rebellion. Gregor should start screaming, think that he's gone mad . . . . Nothing of the sort." The improbable is not emphasized but is submitted to in the natural way in which ordinary people accept disaster: this is what makes it atrocious. The sole meaning of this atrociousness is unfathomable sadness.

Although it is true that Kafka plays down the scandalous and revolting character of the metamorphosis, this does not justify reducing the experience of this scandal to helpless pathos.

4. Alvárez, Alberto Quintero. "La Fatalidad en Kafka." *Taller* (April 1939), 37-39.

There would appear to be two kinds of anguish: the anguish born of a fervent desire for a wider "space" and the anguish of "terrestrial dissatisfaction." Kafka's characters do not experience anguish; this experience is reserved for the reader.

Kafka's characters are unfree; everything is over before they come on the scene and begins after they have passed on. They encounter neither limit nor explanation; "they are accustomed to suffering and obedient to death." The characters accept resignation and apathy sooner than experience anguish.

The experience of waking up as a bug is the experience of discovering oneself as sheerly strange and problematical existence. "If during the night we lose the memory of our corporeal form and on awakening contemplate our strange limbs, do we not experience the same discomfort that Gregor Samsa experiences from his chitinous back?" Gregor awakes into this experience without feelings of protest where we would precisely expect him to experience the fatality of his own being as anguish. Kafka's figures are men doomed to suffer the fatality of their own being without question, anguish, or resentment. They let themselves be led through a slow and tortuous process of dissolution.

5. Anders, Günther. "Franz Kafka–pro und contra." *Die neue Rundschau*, LVIII (Spring 1947), 119-57. Incorporated in *Kafka, pro und contra*. Munich: Beck, 1951. English version (not a literal translation) in Anders, *Franz Kafka*, trans. by A. Steer and A. K. Thorlby. London: Bowes and Bowes, 1960.

It is impossible to paraphrase in summary the argument of this original, complex, and erudite study of Kafka–a work marred only by its blurring of the two domains of Kafka's bourgeois and poetic personality. Fortunately Anders' study is available in English, though in an inevitably flattened version. The notes which follow suggest only those of Anders' arguments which bear directly on *The Metamorphosis*. It should be kept in mind, however, that the whole of Anders' study is indispensable to an understanding of Kafka's fiction.

It is not clear with what degree of personal liability Kafka speaks to the reader through his work. The result is, in any case, unsettling. The fact that Kafka's fiction has been interpreted so variously is based on its real ambiguity.

Kafka distorts the apparently normal surface of our demented world in order to make its madness visible. Kafka "alienates" his subject–presents it under a different name without giving us the key to his permutations. Alienation is not a mere literary trick employed by Kafka; it is a real phenomenon of the modern world. But alienation is ordinarily concealed under the mask of habit.

In our alienated universe, nature is *nature morte*; worse, human beings are reduced to mere things. If modern man seems inhuman, this is not because he has a "bestial" nature, but because he has been forced to perform the functions of things.

More unsettling than Kafka's themes and events is the fact that he responds to them as if they were normal themes or events–in an unexceptional manner. "What makes the reading [of Kafka] so terrifying is the everyday banality of his grotesque: not the fact that Gregor Samsa wakes up in the morning as a beetle, but that he does not see this as something amazing. . . . This anti-sensationalism of tone, the refusal to advertise the unusual, gives the unusual and often even the horrible a very peculiar petty-bourgeois cosiness" (*Kafka*, 13-14). This desensationalizing effect is achieved through the technique of inversion mentioned earlier. If Kafka wants to say that the matter-of-fact character of our world is horrible, his formulation will run: the horrible is matter of fact. Kafka's images are highly aestheticized, at several removes from reality; yet they are drawn with an extreme degree of precision. The result is a *"discrepancy between extreme unreality and extreme accuracy; this discrepancy in turn produces a shock effect; and this shock effect [produces], once again, the feeling of the most acute reality"* (*Kafka*, 16).

Kafka had the sharpest possible sensation of not belonging to the world, of *not being* (see p.26). The self which Kafka reveals is an alien, a stranger, one that *is* not and belongs nowhere. Kafka describes nonbeing—"or, more precisely: things which have being—the world—as it appears to the alienated man (namely, as alien); and the desperate efforts of the man who has no being (namely, of the man who does not belong) to be accepted by the world. . . . The degree to which the hero of *The Castle* is in the world is just sufficient to make it clear to him that he is not in it" (*Kafka*, 20-21).

Bourgeois novels interpret man's growing up in the world as "education"; Kafka describes the world from the outside, and growing up in it is sheer foundering. The curious degree of existence or nonexistence which his figures have is represented temporally, as something that is no longer or not yet a being.

For the man who is homeless in the world, everything that happens to him is uncanny, unsettling. Since he can count on nothing, everything that does happen to him is terrifying, with the result that for him the terrible becomes the normal. In his passionate desire to belong to the world, Kafka's outsider conforms; but because he cannot simply acknowledge the moral rightness of what he is asked to do, he harbors a perpetual bad conscience. His relation to women is shaped by the particular role which women play in Kafka's world; they are a sort of gap in the wall which separates the outsider from the world. "She represents what is called a 'connection,' that is, unofficial access to those who count" (*Kafka*, 30). In Kafka, pity appears as sex.

The hero who perpetually desires to enter the world, but cannot, consumes his life in perpetual, futile repetitions. "Where there is only repetition, there is no progression in time. In fact, all of the situations in Kafka's novels are paralyzed images" (*Kafka,* 34).

Though there is apparent movement, there is no fundamental change. The driving force behind these fictions is not the actions of the hero but his discussion and interpretation of an initial shocking *fait accompli* coming from the outside. The hero's "act" is a meditation on the possibilities that radiate from each event.[9] The form of Kafka's fiction is circular; his stories are marked by the repetition of a trauma.[10] The man thus condemned to repeat his failures is a prisoner. "The *paralysis of time* is taken so far that Kafka . . . can reverse the sequence of cause and effect (*Kafka*, 36).[11] In Kafka, "the crime follows on the heels of the punishment" (*Kafka*, 37).

Kafka is neither an allegorist (substituting images for concepts) nor a symbolist (representing one object by another with which it is actually consubstantial). Kafka cannot create symbols because he cannot believe in the *sym*–the holding together of things. His starting point is the common language: *"he draws from the resources on hand, the figurative character, of language.* He takes metaphors at their word. *For example*: Because Gregor Samsa wants to live as an artist (i.e. as a *Luftmensch*–one who lives on air, lofty and free-floating), in the eyes of the highly respectable hard-working world he is a 'nasty bug' (*'dreckiger Käfer'*): and so in *The Metamorphosis* Samsa wakes up as a beetle whose notion of happiness is to be sticking to the ceiling" (*Kafka*, 40).[12] We shall see that, though the world terrifies him, Kafka also woos the world.

Kafka does not attempt to define man's authentic nature, because modern man's total identification with his job prevents the question from arising.[13] Kafka's agnosticism is one reason for his collapsing the authorial standpoint into that of his characters, who are full of ignorance and tribulation. As a result, he sometimes allows different positions to exist alongside each other, unable to say which one is really his.[14]

In Kafka's fiction there is scarcely any plot. "Where man starts out already condemned, and is driven to repeat himself again and again, one can expect neither a gradual crescendo ending in a climax nor a development leading to a catastrophe" (*Kafka*, 53).

Kafka concentrates active sentences into images; for example, the sentence "Men are bugs" becomes the image of Gregor Samsa, man-bug. "His objects are frozen truths" (*Kafka*, 55).

Though Kafka's language is no more ceremonious than everyday language, it is elevated in the sense that it is even prosier than everyday language. "With Kafka, probably for the first time in literature, the elevated character of a style is not the consequence of the distance between one class of men and a higher class within the same world but of the *distance from the world as a whole*" (*Kafka*, 66). Kafka's language is free of mood. "Many of his sentences have the frightening precision of official notices; others the accuracy, the laborious definitions and flexibility of laws which demand the most careful reading . . . ; others again sound like parts of a medical record; while some have the modest tone of petitions" (*Kafka*, 67; Steer-Thorlby trans., 69). "But his language always speaks for the record; and *protocol language* is probably the most appropriate expression for Kafka's idiom" (*Kafka*, 67).

Commenting on Anders' view of *The Metamorphosis* as the extension of a metaphor taken literally, **Sokel**, 105-A (204), writes: "To see nothing but an extended metaphor in Kafka's work is not enough. The tale is too long, too packed with statements, too rich in meaning to be defined simply as a metaphor, no matter how extended. As a first approach to a formal analysis of Kafka's opus Anders' concept is excellent . . . ; as the sole key to his long work it does not suffice. It ignores, for example, the numerous statements in the narrative dealing with the situation of Gregor and his family before the metamorphosis. These alone make for a textual and poetic complexity which overburdens the theory of the single metaphor."

For other critical comments on Anders' work, see Brod's hostile reply, "Ermordung einer Puppe namens Franz Kafka," *Neue Schweizer Rundschau* (Zurich), XIX, no. 10 (Feb. 1952), 613-25, and further contributions to this discussion by Anders and Brod, "Franz Kafka: pro und contra," *Neue Schweizer Rundschau*, XX (May 1952), 43-50. See, too, Michael Kowal, "Kafka and the Emigrés: A Chapter in the History of Kafka Criticism," *The Germanic Review*, XLI (Nov. 1966), 291-301.

6. **Angus, Douglas**. "Kafka's 'Metamorphosis' and 'The Beauty and the Beast' Tale." *Journal of English and Germanic Philology*, LII (Jan. 1954), 69-71.

Angus points out that *The Metamorphosis* reproduces certain traits found in folklore and thus supports "the theory that dream and myth are intimately related," but he does not explain how it is possible to regard *The Metamorphosis* as a dream. The metamorphosis, followed by "the thrice repeated appeal for pity," is characteristic of the "beauty and the beast" and "loathly lady" tales. In the folktale the appeal for love is usually granted and is followed by magic transformation and marriage—but not in Kafka. Here no tenderheartedness on Grete's part overcomes her revulsion; the bug is not redeemed.

The more opaque elements of the "beauty and the beast" tale are "the evil metamorphosis itself and the strangely exaggerated and repeated appeal of the beast for Beauty's love." These are the elements which *The Metamorphosis* takes up in order to express Kafka's sense of his own personality: the metamorphosis expresses "his lifelong sense of loneliness and exclusion, of physical inferiority, and of an ingrained hypochondria"; the appeal for love; and his craving for affection. The myth in Kafka's hands thus becomes a repetition of his "narcissistic neurosis." The myth in the hands of other writers is wiser, claims Angus; it seems to say that the feeling of repulsiveness is "in the mind" and that redemption lies in another's love.

Angus' conclusion is wholly regressive; by revealing the shortcomings of Kafka's tale, he turns us away from it and towards a "source" admittedly opposite to its sense. In Angus' interpretation, *The Metamorphosis* emerges not as what is claimed for it—"a symbolistic projection of this [narcissistic] psychic pattern" (71)—but as much less, a mere verbal imitation of neurosis blocking out (by an undescribed mechanism) the happier features of an archetype.

Spilka's comment (110-A, 305-06), meanwhile, at the close of his persuasive study of the literary sources of *The Metamorphosis*, refutes all simplistic biographical interpretations: "The thought seems inescapable here: Gregor Samsa is not simply the young Kafka, as critics often hold; he is also the young Dickens, the young Copperfield, even the balding Golyadkin, . . . all synthesized into one regressive hero. . . . Kafka was a projective, not a subjective stylist."

Two other critics take issue with the "inverted fairy tale hypothesis." **Sokel**, 105-A (204), writes: "It fails to take into account the background of Gregor's metamorphosis, his relation to his work and his employer. (Nor does it accord with the fact that Gregor consents to his rejection by the family and dies without bitterness toward them)." **Loeb** (58, n. 27) argues that, since Gregor's acquiescence at the close is not in itself proof of a hidden nobility of soul, the theme of beauty and the beast does not apply. For this theme does not center only on the redemptive power of love; the hidden nobility of soul must also show itself to be worthy of redemption.

7. **Anon**. "Franz Kafka: Die Verwandlung." *Schulfunk*, Bayerischer Rundfunk, CX (1957), 130-31.

Not seen.

8. **Asher, J. A.** "Turning-Points in Kafka's Stories." *Modern Language Review*, LVII (Jan. 1962), 47-52.

The Metamorphosis is typical of Kafka's stories in that the hero awakens from a state of distraction into a dreamlike world but untypical in that this moment occurs at the outset of the story, without being preceded by a more normal consciousness. In his diaries Kafka described a "twilight state" of creativity which, Asher suggests, Kafka entered while writing his stories and which causes a characteristic change in their atmosphere in the direction of unreality. Because "Kafka identifies himself with his heroes to a degree unique in German prose-writing" (51), the heroes of his stories also register the mental change in which distraction, sleepiness, and physical exhaustion play a role. Though this phenomenon is "in keeping with a schizophrenic personality," Kafka's stories nonetheless "defy psychoanalytic investigation." Asher therefore proposes another possibility: the hero's condition of distraction is a "conscious and deliberate warning . . . of an imminent step into the 'dream' " (52).

Asher sees this structure, if it indeed signifies "that Kafka's stories were written in a twilight state, [as] eliminat[ing] the possibility of sustained and reasoned allegory" (52). It would also eliminate the possibility of sustained and reasoned interpretation. Consistently, Asher disclaims the task of interpreting his description of typical and untypical structures.

9. **Baioni, Giuliano**. *Kafka, Romanzo e parabola*. Milan: Feltrinelli, 1962. Pp. 81-100.

The Metamorphosis is, in the language of Musil, an edifice constructed on invisible pillars, in rapport with us as a fourth dimension. Kafka eliminates naturalistic reality from his fiction in order to obey an ideal of musical rhythm in which every object, emotion, and gesture is invested with a moral valency. He also uses the instruments of naturalism to construct a perfectly equilibrated form by means of a precise language, though the reader seeks in vain the finite objective correlative for it.

Gregor's passive adherence to the body of the insect makes the rest of the narrative obvious and predictable.[15] The narrator does not intervene in the mechanism of his story except to introduce a certain remote humor. This radical objectivity represents an extreme degree of subjectivity. Kafka is dominated by a sort of *idée fixe*, a monomania of narration, which excludes all counterpoint. But in the case of *The Metamorphosis*, Kafka was troubled by the extreme rigidity of the piece which made the end, Gregor's death, inevitable from the start. Kafka's preference for "The Judgment" is a preference for a work admitting surprising developments.

At the stage of writing "The Judgment" and *The Metamorphosis*, Kafka was ready to link the condition of being a son with that of being a culprit.[16] (By 1916, at the stage of writing *The Trial*, he broke down this identification, and guilt became the very condition of being a man.) This link justifies a psychoanalytical reading of *The Metamorphosis* in the manner of **Kaiser**, even though it cannot be interpreted wholly within the limits of the biography of the author. The two biographical predicaments confronting Kafka at the time of *The Metamorphosis* were the problem of marriage and the problem of freeing time from his work in the factory in order to write.[17] Both entail his relation to his father. If *The Metamorphosis* is a reflection of Kafka's masochism, it also reflects his sadism, which seeks to involve in the metamorphosis the ideal reader—that is to say, his father.

Is the meaning of the metamorphosis the judgment pronounced by the father, as in "The Judgment," or a transcendence of the father by the wisdom of another tribunal? [18]

Gregor is punished for the fault of simply being himself—a reflection of Kafka's guilt produced within the very act of writing this story and thinking of his own father. [19]

What does the metamorphosis bring to light? Kafka repeatedly reports in his diaries the experience of the obtuseness of his consciousness, which prevents him from talking to others. More insistently he reports his struggle with his own body in the form of observations made on it as if it were a foreign body. His body was the principal obstacle to his spiritual development, not in the Christian but in the Hebrew, Hasidic sense; for in this view, body and spirit must constitute a unity, and Kafka's body was too weak. Kafka's poetic intent aims at the restitution of the unity between body and spirit.

Baioni opposes the view of **Emrich** on the grounds of its extreme unspecificity. What is the meaning of the image of the *insect*? Any other creature could equally well represent the abstract idea of the self.

Though it is true that Kafka's work is informed by a consciousness of the schism between mind and body, this schism should not be grasped as that between self and mask, as in Gogol (see **Erlich**, **Parry**, and **Spilka**, 110-A). Kafka aims to "represent the fracture of the Hasidic rapport between soul and body" (91). Gregor Samsa's sin is one of omission, of the failure of the self to perfect itself in accordance with a Hasidic and cabalistic doctrine of emanations. Gregor Samsa's fate is not to represent the adventure of the self which is divided from the body, but the progressive darkening of the self in the obtuseness of the body. Kafka values sensation. He desires to see, to experience the sensation of himself in front of himself. He expresses the alienation of the self from the world, from itself, and from others as a loss of sensation. Gregor Samsa is the negation of thought, the progressive deterioration of knowledge. His destiny illustrates the relation between the life of the body and the inner life which is basically Kafka's own.

Because the fundamental theme of *The Metamorphosis*, as **Landsberg** has pointed out, is moral responsibility, or the effort to exist as a moral unity, **Emrich**'s interpretation in social and economic terms is not the most relevant. At the center of all of Kafka's works is the theme of the culpable refusal of reality.

In *The Metamorphosis* this moral struggle can be expressed in Freudian terms: the work illustrates a conflict between the libido and the death wish, in which eros becomes overwhelmed and can no longer neutralize the process of self-destruction, the ultimate aim of which is a return to the inorganic. Yet surely in *The Metamorphosis* this drama is represented not so much by a son crushed by his father as by a man incapable of loving. *The Metamorphosis* is the one major work of Kafka in which the theme of (nonincestuous) love does not appear.

The Metamorphosis is the most passive and the coldest, and perhaps the poorest, of Kafka's stories because it marks his renunciation of love; thereafter Kafka does not wish to live. In his imagination he executes the will of the father who condemned his engagement, and he condemns himself to the state of a filthy vermin cut off from the human world.

The true rapport between son and father in Kafka's world is parasitic, and the father is the host. The figure of the father is invented by Kafka to justify his own discomfiture at loving. On the one hand, the betrothal induces him to challenge the paternal deity and infallibly exposes him to the judgment of the angry god. Hence, Georg Bendemann's ecstatic joy in submitting himself to his father's judgment and Gregor Samsa's pleasure in abandoning himself to his animality. On the other hand, the act of betrothal drains the son of all his vital energies.

The Metamorphosis is a translation of the Talmudic maxim: "A man without a woman is not a human being" (T 174; DI 162). It is no accident that the insect motif appears for the first time in "Wedding Preparations in the Country." The diary entry for October 22, 1913, describes love as a state of wanting both to die and not yet to yield. Kafka's definition of love is the key to *The Metamorphosis*. The work is horrible not only because it lacks moral justification for the metamorphosis but because, most important, it lacks any strident cry of grief.

In truth the tale makes only scant allusion to Kafka's biography, but at the same time Kafka guards against being seduced by the mythological possibilities of his tale. The character of Gregor Samsa is maintained as such. The myth is one of daily life. The significance of the tale lies not so much in the horrifying appearance of the beast as in his heartrending resignation. The crux of the story is in the impossibility of man in a hateful world—hateful not because of a moral dimension dialectically opposite to love, but because of its impotence and absence of love. The fundamental drama of Kafka's need to love a woman and inability to love becomes transformed into the family drama of his inability to be loved. From this arises Kafka's perception of his own worthlessness and the need to be loved for his own worthlessness; from this, too, the cold and malignant aspect of *The Metamorphosis*. Kafka wrote in his *Diaries* on December 5, 1914: "My relation to her [Felice's] family acquires a coherent meaning for me only when I consider myself its ruination. This is the only organic explanation" (T 445; DII 99).

His family responds to Gregor in characteristic ways: the mother in a half-preoccupied fashion, the father harshly, the sister with embarrassed sympathy. As Gregor disintegrates, these attitudes are more and more sharply profiled. It is his sister who helps him progressively to annul his humanity and confirms his bestial nature—bringing him garbage to eat, emptying his room of the objects he loved and which constitute his human past, and finally pronouncing his death-sentence. The mother in *The Metamorphosis* represents the Kafkan definition of the mother figure as an image of reason,[20] but in this world reason and love are discomfited. Her sympathy for Gregor is too weak to survive. A world empty of love, of redemptive force, is fascinated by the insect as its own mirror-image, but cannot understand and does not want to understand this image. Kafka's insistence that the insect was not to be drawn[21] confirms our view that the true meaning of *The Metamorphosis* is not in the insect who in himself signifies nothing but in the human beings incapable of giving significance to the metamorphosis. Their emptiness explains his passivity.

Kafka views from a distance associated with comedy the grotesque anguish of the insect. The tone is one of chilling humor. At the same time the world of malign human beings figures for Kafka incomprehensibly as a region of grace and happiness from which he has been inexplicably excluded.

One can only invoke **Freedman**'s dictum: "Kafka's obscurity is mirrored in the confusions of his critics." Baioni sees *The Metamorphosis* as alternately repeating Kafka's sentiment of culpability and absolving it. Guilt attaches to Gregor simply for being himself, for being his father's son, for hating his father, for becoming engaged, for not loving enough, for being incapable of loving, for being a writer who thinks of his father, for being a factory manager and not writing, and finally for being an imperfect creature whose body is a foreign body and who stands condemned by a Hasidic ethos of unity. On the other hand, Gregor is nothing; the guilt in the story belongs to the members of the family, incapable of interpreting the metamorphosis. This failure incriminates the father, who is in turn the real object of a sadistic impulse, an invention, a god.

This essay goes beyond asserting the guilt which attaches to a failure of interpretation; it exhibits this very guilt as irremediable, as the despair of ultimate interpretation. Yet through the debacle of its attempt made with unavailing delicacy and scrupulousness, the essay unwittingly gives criticism a starting point in the fact that Kafka's art, intending to accommodate a wide variety of interpretations and consequently not to be captured by any one, also intends to incorporate the truth of the insufficiency of interpretation. His is an art of aesthetic reflection; in approximating the condition of sheer interpretability, it attains to the Kantian canon of beauty.

But with one reservation: not all interpretations are equally legitimate. Within Kafka's art, one order of interpretation has priority over another; that interpretation is privileged which takes into account the disjunction of the narrator from his fiction (see pp. 36).

10. Barnes, Hazel. "Myth and Human Experience." *The Classical Journal*, LI (Dec. 1955), 121-27.

A study of *The Metamorphosis* throws light on the function of myth in general. Myth may be thought of as an emotional analogue to the Platonic Idea, as one of the universals within which human life moves and has its meaning. "The quality of imperishability in myth stems from the fact that one way or another it depicts all of the fundamental emotional situations possible for human beings" (122). But the language of myth conceals as it reveals. It challenges interpretation.

Ours is an age of reinterpretation: we employ myths not so much to allude to a complex of immediately intelligible experiences, but as occasions for fundamental reinterpretation. *The Metamorphosis* is a wholly new myth; yet as a tale of metamorphosis, it constitutes a reinterpretation of the fundamental meanings of Greek myths dealing with the same experience. Greek myths of metamorphosis probably reflect primitive societies which did not make a sharp distinction between animal and human worlds. Many of these myths are stories about origins; in many, the metamorphosis illustrates poetic justice. The theme of the inability to communicate recurs.

In Orphic theories of metempsychosis, animal metamorphosis figures as animal reincarnation. In non-Orphic myths such hybrids as centaurs and satyrs may represent the presence of bestial elements in the human soul. What is the underlying sense of these persistent myths of animal transformation?

There are three probable motives. 1) We are curious about animal experience and guilty about exploiting these creatures. 2) We are driven by our defaults and our sense of guilt to consider the animal within us. 3) We are curious to know what animals would say if they had language: we are frightened by the predicament they suggest "of being unable to communicate what one knows and wishes to express. Hence the animal may be used to express the extreme limit of one of man's most dreadful fears–total isolation from all human understanding and contact" (125).

The representation of Gregor's consciousness satisfies our curiosity, and he is treated by his family in such a way as to produce in them a feeling of repressed guilt. Second, "Gregor's metamorphosis into a cockroach comes as a kind of self-revelation of his inner state and of his fundamental guilt. The guilt is what I would call existential; i.e., it is not due to any actual evil which Gregor has committed" (125). His is the guilt which anyone experiences who seeks self-realization within the conflict of generations. It is the guilt of dependence on the body, of submission to and glorification in a shoddy everyday morality Gregor has always lived as an insect.

Finally, *The Metamorphosis* is a study of the difficulties of human communication. Before his metamorphosis, Gregor had made no genuine effort to communicate with his family; and he had not wished to communicate with anything higher than man. After the metamorphosis he is unable to express himself without being misunderstood. "The human in animal form is chosen as the ultimate in horror since here the need for communication is the greatest, and possibilities are non-existent" (126). In this image Kafka radicalizes and isolates the experience of frustration and meaninglessness. This is the horror of the fates of Tantalus, Sisyphus, and the daughters of Danaus. While the metamorphosis in Apuleius' *The Golden Ass* concludes with redemption and enlightenment, in *The Metamorphosis* there is no salvation from torment. This is Kafka's crucial variation on a similar theme.

11. **Baumer, Franz.** *Franz Kafka*. Berlin: Colloquium, 1960. Pp. 23, 78, and passim.

In *The Metamorphosis* the motif of making oneself small and ugly to the point of becoming a louse is present in partly autobiographical form.

This insect metamorphosis contains a dimension of social prognosis. The work documents the later manifestation of an age of automation and functionalism, which has been characterized as the "insectification" of modern life. The motif is not new (though Kafka's poetic mastery of the theme is exceptional). Other works documenting the same phenomenon are Ensor's self-portrait as an insect, in the picture "The Insect Family," and the beehive style of the architecture of Frank Lloyd Wright and Le Corbusier.

12. **Beck, Evelyn Torton.** "Kafkas 'Durchbruch': der Einfluss des jiddischen Theaters auf sein Schaffen." *Basis*, I (1970), 204-23.

Kafka's work beginning in the fall of 1912 is marked by a new dramatic style. The action of "The Judgment" is theatrical, visualizable, informed by intense feeling, marked by tension, and plotted in a language of great simplicity and immediacy. This breakthrough is intimately linked with Kafka's experience of the Jewish-East European theater company which performed Yiddish plays in Prague in 1912. Kafka's diaries for 1911 and 1912 are full of testimony to his frequent attendance at these performances and his enthusiasm for them. The Yiddish theater marks a change not only in Kafka's literary consciousness but also in his attitude toward all things Jewish. From 1911-12 on, Kafka's diaries and letters reveal for the first time an interest in Jewry and Judaism.

But the influence of the Jewish theater on Kafka's art is not only stylistic; in all his work after 1912 there are more or less explicit traces of the themes, symbols, and motifs of these Yiddish plays, even though they are typically transmuted.

These themes are predominantly tragic; but the melodramatic way they were dramatized in Prague, on a stage barely large enough to accommodate a table and a few chairs, as often as not transformed them into unwitting comedy. "Kafka's taste for confined spaces, theatrical gestures, exaggerated plots and piercing glances can therefore be seen as wholly bound up with the Yiddish drama and the spatial limitations of the Café Savoy. The same holds true for the underground humor of so many of his stories, which recalls the tragicomic effects characteristic of the Yiddish theater" (208).

These plays are informed by a quite specific Jewish humor, which mingles negative consciousness (irony, sadness, self-mockery) with hope. "Even in the most dangerous and tragic circumstances their 'heroes' maintain a sense of the fundamental absurdity of their situation, at which point a peculiar shift into irony occurs" (208). Those characters who are unable to grasp their true condition inspire laughter. Something of this humor persists in Kafka, whose stance toward the tragedy of his figures is often ironical–consider the predicament of Gregor Samsa. "By revealing so clearly his own consciousness of the absurdity of his hero, Kafka forces the reader to view his protagonist with an irony to which the character is wholly blind" (209).

The Metamorphosis was conceived under the influence of

Jakob Gordin's Yiddish play *Der vilde Mensh* (*The Wild Man*). Kafka devoted several pages of his diary to a summary and interpretation of the play. The five main characters of *The Metamorphosis* (father, mother, son, daughter, and maid) have direct parallels in Gordin's work. Moreover, the son Lemekh, who is "backward," resembles Gregor in many important ways. "Both are treated at once as 'persons' and as 'things'; both are outcasts, a painful disgrace to their families. Both are depicted as modest, simple, retiring beings; their bestial transformation comes to a climax in Gregor's death and in Lemekh's murder of his stepmother" (214). True, Gregor's metamorphosis has occurred before the work begins, and Lemekh's occurs by degrees throughout the play, but both works awaken the same sense of gradual decay.

The central metaphor of *The Metamorphosis* is the mutation of man into beast; this also holds true for Lemekh. "Like Gregor, who has been locked into his room, Lemekh is isolated from his family, lies day after day on his bed, and is finally compared to an 'animal,' waiting 'to be sacrificed' " (214). Like Gregor, Lemekh, who stares at others with the dumb gaze of an animal, oozes gratitude for permission to be able to share in the life of the family by looking at them through a crack in the door. The spiritual and physical abnormality of the two sons inspires in their parents sensations of fear and mistrust, and both families hope to cure these sicknesses with the help of a doctor. The straightjacket into which Lemekh is forced at the close is like Gregor's back, "as hard as armorplate." At the close of *The Wild Man* Lemekh crawls around on all fours. Both sons are incapable of human contact. Both are assumed incapable of understanding what is said about them because they cannot make themselves understood. There is a crucial parallel between the works in the way that the progressive disintegration of both characters is intensified and expressed by their refusal to eat. In all the Yiddish plays the theme of food is crucial; this theme appears in several of Kafka's stories in an inverted form, as the refusal to take in food. "The loss of appetite, which 'heroes' like Georg, Gregor, the hunger artist, and the dog [of *Investigations of a Dog*] suffer, signifies a conscious refusal–even, indeed, an inversion–of the Jewish ritual of eating" (215).

The function of music in *The Metamorphosis* has an affinity with the function of music in the Yiddish plays, which "symbolizes the divine or the absolute" (209). In several Yiddish plays, too, sublime music can substitute for earthly nourishment.

In short, "there is hardly anything in Kafka which cannot be understood as an abstraction or 'alienation' or elaboration of those cultural symbols current in the Jewish theater around 1900" (223).

13-A. Beissner, Friedrich. *Der Erzähler Franz Kafka.* Stuttgart: Kohlhammer, 1952.

Kafka's works must be examined for their poetic form. Kafka would have agreed; consider the diary entry for February 19, 1911: "I can do everything, not only with respect to a particular work. When I indiscriminately write down a sentence, for example, 'He looked out the window,' it is already perfect as it is" (DI45; T42). Kafka is talking about mastery in a poetic sense. Now a close reading of Kafka's works, moving from individual words and sentences to the meaning and structure of the whole, is as yet impossible, since a reliably edited text does not exist. Therefore, discussion must be restricted to Kafka's mode of narration.

"Kafka has achieved and is able to maintain a narrative stance which in a godforsaken century permits him to create epic works, each of which, even the smallest, presents a world structured as a unity" (9-10). He turns from the external world and focuses on the self as the fit object of epic art, a being no less extensive and full of possibilities than the external world. The unity and unified character of the inner world is indestructible, provided the narrator renounces the role of the psychologist who, equally curious about the inner life of all his characters, slips from one subjectivity into another. Until now it has not been noted that Kafka narrates from a unique standpoint, conferring a unity of meaning (*einsinnig*), whether he employs the first or the third person. Since as narrator he does not have to be bound to the steady temporal progression of the external world as it is constituted in the typical discursive plot, he regains an essential dimension of the epic—the independence of its parts.

"If, now, the inner world with all its experiences, insights, desires, dreams, thoughts, joys, and vexations is the object of Kafka's story telling, and if the narrator does not stand outside as the coldly observing psychologist, then there remains no other place for him than in the subjectivity of his main figure: he narrates himself, he transforms himself into Josef K. and into the land surveyor K." (29). A famous diary entry of Kafka's reads: "The sense for the representation of my dreamlike inner life has put everything else to one side" (T 420; DII 77). Here Kafka himself reduces the essentials of his art to a formula–the representation of his dreamlike inner life. Of course the word "dreamlike" must not be taken in the narrow sense only of things perceived below the threshold of consciousness. The crucial point is that his fiction is narrated from a place within the consciousness of its main character.

The story "The Couple" exhibits a typically Kafkan trait; this story, told in the first person, does not presuppose anything; the narrator does not seem to know anything that the reader does not know. "The narrator–that is the secret of its effect–is nowhere ahead of what is narrated, even when he employs the past absolute tense. The event narrates itself in the moment of its happening in paradoxically preteritive form; it narrates itself from a one-sided but thoroughly 'unitive' optic and does not correct . . . the error which is possible and almost unavoidable in such an optic" (32).

In Kafka's epic, "the narrator is at one not only with the main character . . . but with what is narrated as well. The distance between what is happening and the telling is abolished" (34). Kafka's fiction is narrated in the epic mode, "although the narrator has wholly transformed himself into the main character. Even there where the main character appears in the third person, Kafka represents his own dreamlike inner life. . . . in Gregor Samsa, the hero of *The Metamorphosis*" (35).

In Kafka's work, then, there is no gap between narrator and fictional character. No reflections on these characters intrude. "There is only the self-narrating (paradoxically preteritive) event" (35): hence the reader's sense of being inextricably, oppressively caught in the event. "Kafka . . . transforms not only himself but also the reader into the main character" (36). He never leaves the domain of the subjectivity of the main character and its expansion toward the world.

The narrative standpoint of *The Metamorphosis* is rigorously identical with the hero's subjectivity. "For the narrator, and consequently for the reader, Gregor *is* transformed into a monstrous bug." But the metamorphosis is in fact the delusion of the sick hero, though there is no intimation of this within the story. The intimation comes from close scrutiny of the cover drawing done by Ottomar Starke for the first edition in book form, "presumably not without the author's consent, very probably even with his cooperation or at his request" (37).

The cover depicts a man "in a dressing gown and slippers, who desperately throws up his hands in front of his face and moves with a long stride into the center of the room toward the spectator, away from the opened door, which is not open for him; for outside is–do you see the black?–outside is darkness, nothingness. The man can only be Gregor Samsa himself–not, say, his elderly father. This is proved by the dark hair and the youthful vigor of the movement of the striding figure. This, then, must be Gregor Samsa, the Gregor Samsa who in the first sentence of the story was already transformed into a monstrous bug" (37). Kafka reveals the sense of his story through the cover drawing.

Beissner's thesis of the total coincidence of Kafka's poetic consciousness, the consciousness of the main character, and the consciousness of the reader is developed and refined by Martin Walser, *Beschreibung einer Form: Versuch über Franz Kafka* (Reihe, *Literatur als Kunst,* Munich: Hanser, 1961), denied by **Starke**, and submitted to a thoroughgoing critique by **Dentan** and **Henel**. The main bearing on *The Metamorphosis* of this critique is that "from the outset a clearer grasp of the real situation is made available to the reader than to the victim" (**Luke**, 34). This distinction is the basis of the comic and tragic incongruity of *The Metamorphosis.*

13-B. Beissner, Friedrich. *Kafka der Dichter.* Stuttgart: Kohlhammer, 1958. Pp. 40-42. "Kafka the Artist," trans. by Ronald Gray, in *Kafka, A Collection of Critical Essays*, ed. by Ronald Gray. Englewood Cliffs, N.J.: Prentice-Hall, 1962. Pp. 15-31. [This translation does not include the pages summarized below.]

Ottomar **Starke** has denied acceding to any request on Kafka's part to interpret *The Metamorphosis* by means of a cover drawing for the first edition in book form. But this does not rule out the fact that Kafka did actually see and approve a draft of this illustration. The opposite hypothesis—that given the immense respect Kurt Wolff, Kafka's publisher, had for him, Wolff should have left the illustration of *The Metamorphosis* entirely to the discretion of Starke, who was then very young—would be unthinkable. In all likelihood, Wolff, in agreement with Kafka or entirely on his own, suggested this cover drawing to Starke.

Here, meanwhile, is Starke's account of his intention in executing this drawing. He did not mean to establish the metamorphosis as the delusion of the sick hero. His aim was, rather, "to condense the content of the book into a sort of slogan. The slogan for Kafka's *The Metamorphosis* was: Horror! Despair! . . . The figure fleeing in terror has black hair because the head is black on white, thus, for pictorial reasons, and if he wears dressing-gown and slippers, then that is to show the irruption of a very 'nonbourgeois' catastrophe into a very 'humdrum bourgeois' existence" (41).

But Starke must simply be suffering a memory lapse if he maintains that the male figure in the drawing never appears in the story. And, surely, the hair of the male figure is not black because the background is white, but the background is white because the hair is black. Other details of the picture corroborate this hypothesis.

Binion, who considers Beissner's interpretation fruitful, writes, "Even so the evidence would be equivocal at best; Gregor reminisces much, and the scene may be one prior to his illness. Furthermore, some of the details do not fit the tale however construed. On the other hand, the tale does afford full *internal* evidence that Kafka meant Gregor's illness as mental, and not physical" (214-15).

For a further contribution to this discussion, see **Henel** as well as Kafka's letter to Wolff (Br 135).

14. Benjamin, Walter. "Franz Kafka. Zur zehnten Wiederkehr seines Todestages." Sections in *Jüdische Rundschau*, XXXIX, no. 102/103 (1934), 8; no. 104 (1934), 6. Complete in *Schriften*, II, ed. by T. W. Adorno und Gretel Adorno. Frankfurt am Main: Suhrkamp, 1955. Pp. 196-228. Reprinted in *Über Literatur*. Frankfurt am Main: Suhrkamp, 1969. Pp. 154-193. "Franz Kafka. On the Tenth Anniversary of his Death," trans. by Harry Zohn. In *Illuminations*, ed. by Hannah Arendt. New York: Harcourt, Brace and World, 1968. Pp. 111-40.

In its richness and subtlety and fidelity to the text, Benjamin's essay will make one resent the intrusions and dislocations of symbolizing interpreters. With great originality (Benjamin's essay appeared in 1934) he describes and accumulates clusters of related images, gestures, and motifs; these clusters constitute Kafka's worlds–or the dimensions of Kafka's world.

The fate which governs this world is partly the unwritten justice of prehistory, partly a function of social organization. The gesture of the father in the second section of *The Metamorphosis*, his head slumped down on his chest, is typically that of Kafka's authorities, burdened with the weight of a huge forgetfulness. That these authorities are always fallen beings or beings about to fall means that they can suddenly crop up in all their power in those figures who are basest and who have sunk the lowest. They are never more terrifying than when they spring up from the deepest degeneracy–from the fathers.

In the Kafkan family the father nourishes his own life at the expense of his son's: he devours his power and his rights. The father, the punisher, is also the accuser. He accuses his son of a sort of original sin, which consists for Kafka in the complaint which men constantly make that an original sin was committed against them. Hope appears to exist only for those beings in Kafka who have escaped the spell of the family; it is crucial that Gregor Samsa awakens as an insect precisely in his father's house. To regenerate the relation of father and son, the father must make a gesture which bears an enormous weight.

The world of the officials and the world of the fathers appears to be the same. Both figures punish; both are attracted by guilt. The parallel is based on the filthiness, decrepitude, and decay which is the circumstance of their power. The uniform of Gregor's father is spotted through and through. Uncleanliness is so much the attribute of the officials that they seem almost gigantic parasites.

For Kafka, music and song could be "an expression or at least a security" for hope, for escape from everyday reality, but for him "the sirens were silent" (*Schriften*, 203). (See F 92.)

The life in exile led by K. in the castle village is the life of modern man in his body. "It can happen that a man wakes up one morning, and he is changed into a bug. Exile–his exile–has taken him over" (*Schriften*, 213). The precondition of the action of Kafka's novels is forgetfulness; his novels are set in the world of a swamp, among original beginnings. "That this stage of existence is forgotten does not mean that it does not extend into the present. More: it is present by virtue of this oblivion. . . . What has been forgotten . . . never has a merely individual identity. It mingles with other things that lie in the oblivion of the prehistoric world, enters with them into innumerable, uncertain, changing compounds to produce perpetual monstrous offshoots. Oblivion is the receptacle from which the inexhaustible in-between world in Kafka's stories pushes its way into the light. . . . And the world of Kafka's ancestors, like the totem poles of the primitives, led down to the animals" (*Schriften*, 219). Gregor's metamorphosis is the form his forgetfulness takes; animals, Benjamin shows, are the form which forgotten guilt assumes. Though these creatures think, there is something scatterbrained about their thought. It feeds on every source of anxiety "and has the flightiness of despair. . . . Among all Kafka's creatures it is his animals who get to reflect the most. What corruption is in the law, anxiety is in their thinking. It ruins the procedure and yet is the only hopeful thing in it." In oblivion all things become disfigured, like the bug which we nonetheless know is Gregor Samsa.

Benjamin offers a highly suggestive theory of Gregor's metamorphosis. The primitive insect form does not immediately represent a substratum of the mind having no connection with consciousness; it has the character of a privation of consciousness, being "present by virtue of this oblivion." At this point, however, Benjamin fails to distinguish sharply between the sense of the metamorphosis itself and Gregor's response to the metamorphosis. In Benjamin's discussion, event and response appear to have the same character. The event is present through Gregor's forgetfulness, and so is his response; the guilt, flightiness, and anxiety of his reflections repeat the essential character of forgetting.

The question then arises: is the forgetfulness of the insect form the same forgetfulness which enables Gregor to hear the music of his sister's violin? Presumably not, if music is indeed for Kafka, as Benjamin maintains, a "security" for hope, for escape from the tyranny of everyday obliviousness.

And yet, for Gregor, music is a hope that fails. It swiftly becomes another occasion for expressing his anxiety, now in the form of a wish-dream of eroticism and violence; in effect, it becomes an inducement to Gregor to forget himself; it, too, has the character of forgetting.

Must we conclude, then, that Gregor's failure to maintain the experience of music was inescapable, being implicit in the privative character of its origin? Or is not his failure, rather, a culpable, specific defect of moral imagination, forgetfulness in another mode, a sheer refusal of an authentic awareness of the self? If this is so, then Gregor's aggressive, erotic fantasy would illuminate as well the experience which precedes his experience of the music. This is his forgetting to show the family consideration, a forgetfulness which enables him, in a contingent sense, to have the experience of music. The self-forgetting into which music collapses reveals that in this story we are dealing most fundamentally with a sequence of different types of forgetfulness: an initial forgetfulness of a superficial escapist benevolence toward others; a deeper, constitutive forgetfulness which is the mode of being in which an experience of the origin occurs; finally, a forgetfulness of the sense of this authentic experience. Thus Benjamin does not sufficiently discriminate and explore the types of forgetfulness which are, as he rightly suggests, the basic experiences of Kafka's work. (See further the commentary to **Goodman**.)

It is in other respects clear that Benjamin's essay is at the bottom of the reflections of **Emrich** on the theme of self-forgetfulness and **Adorno** on the theme of "social organization." Michael Kowal writes, "Benjamin was the first to point out the Old Testament elements of myth and parable, the significance of gestures, and the burden of distortion in Kafka's work. . . . His critical conception of poetry as the interaction of myth and social reality seems to me to be the underlying principle of all [the interpretations of Kafka we are to consider here]"—namely, those of T. W. Adorno, Günther Anders, Hannah Arendt, Hermann Broch, and Erich Kahler. ("Kafka and the Emigrés: A Chapter in the History of Kafka Criticism." *The Germanic Review*, XLI [Nov. 1966], 291-301.)

15. **Bennett, E. K.** *A History of the German Novelle*. Revised and continued by H. M. Waidson. Cambridge University Press, 1961. Pp. 267-68.

The reader of *The Metamorphosis* is thrown "into a world of psychotic delusion which [Kafka's] narrative art preserves as a reality in its own right" (268). He must "contend with two layers of 'reality': the reactions of the family, and Gregor's consciousness that he is undeniably an insect."

Gregor might be interpreted as the victim of a sick delusion. In revolt against exasperating work, but guilty for neglecting his duty, he takes refuge in lunacy.[22] Yet everyone sees Gregor as an insect.

"The humiliation of his animal shape is perhaps the necessary rejection of materialistic values before the attainment of spiritual reality." But the revulsion he inspires in the others breaks his will: he soon dies.

If the world which Kafka constitutes in *The Metamorphosis* is "a reality in its own right," if in it all the principals are aware of Gregor's being a bug, then it is irrelevant to speak of "psychotic delusion." Moreover, it can hardly be maintained that a basic "layer of 'reality' " of the story is Gregor's consciousness of undeniably being an insect, since what is distinctive about him is the way he resists reflecting on or interpreting his animal carcass or his sleepy animal consciousness. Significantly, Gregor is called by an animal name on only five occasions in the story. Because of the poverty of Gregor's self-consciousness, it is impossible to assert that he has rejected materialistic values. The moment of his spiritual illumination is immediately followed by the grossest fantasy of possession. Gregor's spiritual illumination comes in the form of an experience of violin music that addresses him from outside. Similarly, the metamorphosis has taken shape independently of his consciousness. It is extremely important not to destroy Kafka's presentation of Gregor's degradation and uplift as objectifications of meaning which Gregor does not consciously possess. Gregor's experiences do not occur as modulations of a self-consciousness which is viewed in post-Romantic fashion as its own destroyer and its own redeemer. The story makes a new departure in its disenfranchisement of self-consciousness; it has no theory of progressive self-development, no Idealist notion of *Bildung*; it denies the Hegelian assumption that absolute spiritual reality can be present in a moment of self-consciousness.

Even Gregor's moment of ethical vision—"his conviction that he would have to disappear was, if possible, even firmer than his sister's"—merely duplicates another's moral consciousness; and in this case it is his sister's, an unreliable one.

16. **Bense, Max.** *Die Theorie Kafkas*. Cologne and Berlin: Kiepenheuer und Witsch, 1952. Pp. 51-54.

To understand the theme of being which runs through Kafka's works, one must distinguish between classical ontology and so-called fundamental ontology, to which Kafka's conception of being is related. In classical ontology God is the first cause, the ground to which all beings are related; in fundamental ontology man is the subject, in relation to whom everything becomes intelligible and interpretable (51). As a consequence of this starting point, fundamental ontology does not know the explicit problem of objective reality, of the *real* world. The kind of literature indebted to fundamental ontology is Surrealism, which does not have the notion of a distinctively real world. "And it is certain that essential parts of Kafka's writings also belong to surrealism and constitute surreality in the sense of a world in which the distinction between real and unreal constituents no longer has any ontological meaning" (52). It is not among Kafka's tasks to be realistic. "Surrealistic" literature is not in any explicit sense psychological or sociological or mythological, though it does not shun the devices which prompt such interpretations. Neither is it intrinsically nonrational, since "the rational structure is in fact as much at home in possible as in real worlds . . . . Accordingly, the observable, real accuracy of the unreal found in Kafka–his precision with the imaginary–is not peculiar: rational precision in the unreal is not itself anything unreal, as is confirmed by the impression aroused, for example, by the 'metamorphosis' of Gregor Samsa into a 'monstrous vermin' " (53). In this kind of literature all modes of being possess logical equivalence; the aesthetic being thus constituted is distinguished by the play of its modes–a play, in fact, favored by the neglect of reality.

17. **Bezzel, Christoph.** *Natur bei Kafka: Studien zur Aesthetik des Poetischen Zeichens*. Erlanger Beiträge zur Sprach- und Kunstwissenschaft, XV. Nuremberg: Hans Carl, 1964. Pp. 67-71.

Natural details in *The Metamorphosis* have the character of signs. The circumstance that Gregor's response to the overcast weather at the outset of the story is still entirely normal signifies that the author can "react realistically" (68) even well within the world of his fiction. The rain and the later morning fog constitute the basic mood of the story, and like the metamorphosis itself, they are "signs of an epic world." Specifically, the fog is a sign of Gregor's "new life"; Gregor awaits both its dissolution and the return of normal conditions.

Bezzel proposes other subtle effects, underscorings of meaning, produced by the limited number of natural signs within the "formally composed, semantically closed" epic world of the story (71). For example, the inclusion in Gregor's death of the natural world outside the room heightens the forlorn and abandoned condition of his subjectivity, which never struggles against "the objectivity of the world, the law of the world" (70).

18-A. Binder, Hartmut. *Motiv und Gestaltung bei Franz Kafka.* Abhandlungen zur Kunst-, Musik- und Literaturwissenschaft, XXXVII. Bonn: Bouvier & Co., 1966. Passim.

At the time of writing *The Metamorphosis,* Kafka had a keen awareness of psychoanalysis; the story constitutes a literary reply to Freud.

The Metamorphosis cannot be characterized as Expressionist by virtue of its alleged affinity with typical Expressionist treatments of the father-son conflict. The works of Sorge, Hasenclever, Bronnen, and the later Werfel, frequently instanced in this discussion, date at the earliest from 1913.

The mode of narration called *erlebte Rede* invariably appears at crucial moments in the story. It is possible to establish the rules governing its use, such as the way in which, an obstacle in the action, it is linked to other modes of narration. Among these other modes are passages of inner monologue which at the outset of the story function as signs of Gregor's flight from an admission of the metamorphosis.

If a story is to represent only the experienced reality of its characters, summative reports of the action must be avoided, since they shift the perceptual center of the story away from the situation itself. Kafka's construction of *The Metamorphosis* aims at being situational in this sense. An obstacle to this procedure is the representation of recurrent actions; but minute formal analysis can show the devices Kafka employed in *The Metamorphosis* to overcome this difficulty.

Throughout *The Metamorphosis* there is no narrator asserting values distinct from the values of the central figure. Despite this hermetic unity of perspective, it is nonetheless possible to reconstruct in detail the context of actions independent of Gregor's consciousness. Thus the so-called epilogue, revealing the life of the family after Gregor's death, is not felt as a real rupture. That is because Gregor's perceptual range has been stretched from the start so as to register the life of the family with the comprehensiveness of the narrator's vision. Their life makes up a second strand of the action present from beginning to end. This dimension of the narrative has implications for an interpretation of the story, which must be viewed as a family story. It is the nature of this family—in distinction to the cleaning woman and the three roomers, say—that it considers Gregor revolting and not comical. The central event of *The Metamorphosis* is a psychic reality for Gregor and the family.

Many earlier interpretations of *The Metamorphosis* (e.g. **Emrich**'s) are contradictory in seeing in Gregor the ineluctably verminous condition of life lived inhumanely but in interpreting his ecstasy at his sister's violin playing as a sign of spiritual grandeur. A second group of interpreters (see **Edel**) considers the metamorphosis as an act of liberation from negative conditions; the family, however, fails to read the sign of Gregor's spiritual distinctiveness and imprisons him within the circle of its practical concerns. This reading runs counter to the text. Gregor has wanted to quit his work, but it is not his family that forces him to remain. He chooses to remain for their sake. Even as a vermin he has no intention of abandoning the family.

The story is properly to be understood through its basic pattern. In the beginning the father is an independent businessman, the son, a petty clerk. After the failure of the father's business, the father is humiliated, but the son enjoys swift elevation and success. With the metamorphosis Gregor is monstrously degraded. The relation between father and son is reversed: the father is once again powerful; furthermore, the family is forced to support itself. If Gregor intended at the outset of *The Metamorphosis* to break with the family for the sake of still greater independence, he is thwarted by the metamorphosis. "But why is the son unable to liberate himself from parental authority? Because *inwardly* he is still dependent on the family!" (357). He has only a rudimentary connection to women. He squanders his leisure on adolescent diversions. Taking "The Judgment" and *The Metamorphosis* together, we can conclude the following rule: "as regards the family situation, every strengthening of the position of the father must result in a weakening of the son's and vice versa" (359). The life context out of which these stories arose is the relation of father and son; this fact is confirmed by the stories themselves. The interpretation (e.g. **Pfeiffer**'s) that sees Gregor's predicament as a parable of the loneliness and extremity of the man who does not belong to the world of practical concerns is unjustified. Precisely the opposite is true: "The disaster comes from the fact that the son is unsuccessful in gaining a secure footing in what the interpreters term with contempt the null everyday world. . . . The son has not fallen captive to the world but wants to conquer it—from which he is prevented by his unfortunate relation to his family" (359-60).

Kafka wrote in his diaries that at the time of composing "The Judgment" he was thinking of Freud. The same concern informs *The Metamorphosis*—the concern, not to confirm Freud, but to criticize him. *The Metamorphosis* cannot be interpreted in Freudian fashion primarily because of the unmotivated double shift in the family situation. Nor can the relation of father and son be explained by reference to their characters. These objections are countered if we say that "an anthropological law is demonstrated here which is independent of the personal presuppositions of the individual figures. This would be a step beyond Freud's personalism" (369) [see **Adorno**]. The son does not struggle with the real father and with his particular contingent characteristics; his struggle is with an inner image for which the real father is only the occasion. The story cannot be accounted for through the personalistic-causal bias of Freud. Gregor's death would be unintelligible, and so would the opposition of mother and son.

18-B. Binder, Hartmut. "Kafka und 'Die neue Rundschau.' Mit einem bisher unpublizierten Brief des Dichters zur Druckgeschichte der 'Verwandlung.' " *Jahrbuch der deutschen Schillergesellschaft,* XII. Stuttgart: Alfred Kröner, 1968. Pp. 94-111.

Kafka was an ardent reader of *Die neue Rundschau*, and it was to this important journal that he first submitted *The Metamorphosis*. The story was accepted, then allowed to lie in the publisher's office for several months before Kafka was asked to shorten it by one-third. Kafka proposed that either the story be printed in its entirety at some later date or that only the first section of it be printed immediately. In the end, he withdrew the story and let it be published, instead, in *Die Weissen Blätter* (see **Dietz**, 35-A).

Binder discusses in detail the fate of the manuscript of *The Metamorphosis* before publication.

> **18-C. Binder, Hartmut.** "Kafka und seine Schwester Ottla: Zur Biographie der Familiensituation des Dichters unter besonderer Berücksichtigung der Erzählung 'Die Verwandlung' und 'Der Bau.' " *Jahrbuch der deutschen Schillergesellschaft*, XII. Stuttgart: Alfred Kröner, 1968. Pp. 403-57.

The main tendency of Kafka criticism has been "intrinsic"; little has been accomplished in the way of research into the biographical and historical circumstances of Kafka's fiction. Yet it would be false to consider Kafka's life a mere imitative footnote to his fiction, to which, it is alleged, he sacrificed every other side of his personality. True, "Kafka's productions are not merely imitative; but they are nevertheless precise expressions of his life situation and thus have a real basis in experience, the knowledge of which rules out from the start certain interpretations and makes others possible for the first time" (404).

Binder describes in convincing detail the analogues and reciprocal prefigurations existing between Kafka's life and the events of *The Metamorphosis*. It is impossible within this narrow compass to reproduce this net of relations.

> **19. Binion, Rudolph.** "What *The Metamorphosis* Means." *Symposium*, XV (Fall 1961), 214-20.

By and large, critiques of *The Metamorphosis* have taken the following constructions: 1) as a supernatural magnification of natural anguish; 2) as a surrealistic intensification of self-consciousness in its absurdity or nonbeing; 3) as an allegorical figuration "of the reincarnation of Christ, the isolation of the artist, neurotic illness or alienation at large" (214).

However, another and fruitful line of interpretation has been proposed by **Beissner**, 13-A; Gregor is the victim of a sick delusion. "[*The Metamorphosis*] is the story of a man who thinks he has become a bug, told as if the content of his delusion were physical reality. The narrator's perspective is equivalent to that of the hero himself, who, like a typical victim of hallucinosis, sees the world accurately in all of its particulars save one" (215).

Gregor's delusion is triggered by the impossibility of his job, for which he has lost all incentive. Now that he is ill he can miss work yet avoid blame. His oversleeping is justified "by his having been in the throes of becoming a bug" (216). His aphasia enables him to avoid any further discussion about his sister's future.

His symptoms have the unconscious sense of a reversion to infancy, as if to reinforce his emotional regression. "In neurosis 'vile little animal' means 'infant,' and Gregor impersonates a baby no less than a bug. He is speechless and helpless; he crawls, feeds on pap, and knows no disgust; he resumes his infantile gazing, and he gradually loses his sense of time and his concern for the outside world" (217). His family, meanwhile, do not treat him as if he were in fact metamorphosed; their behavior is appropriate to a disgusting lunatic. When Gregor does not recover, as the family expects, his sister insists that he be removed, presumably to a madhouse.

The narrative maintains the very form of Gregor's delusion. "Following his peculiarly psychotic pattern of awareness, it tends to fix unnaturally on single elements of a whole physical complex, ones having special meaning for Gregor, which then become self-sustaining and quasi-absolute; the father's uniform, . . . the sound of the lodgers' teeth" (217). Nor does it permit evidence that would refute Gregor's delusion.

It is not necessary to de-hallucinate the entire narrative—that is, supply a physical description of all the events which Gregor interprets neurotically. This can be done when there is the dramatic urgency of another's response to Gregor—as when his mother catches sight of a great brown blotch on the wallpaper, in reality "Gregor on tiptoe or perhaps kneeling on a table, flat against the wall, naked, filthy, emaciated, glaring defiantly" (219). Once one grasps the logic of the composition, it can be reconstructed on the realistic premise of Gregor's neurosis.

Through the irony of a double perspective—both Gregor's and

the narrator's perspectives being false—truths about neurosis and about the behavior of families emerge. Gregor's situation is a desperate one, but his neurotic response is fatal—"as fatal to his personality as resignation would have been. It is, however, beneficent to his family—his decline revitalizes them—and so by way of his morbid choice, a free and deliberate one in the end, he acquires tragic dignity" (219-20). Gregor's predicament is part of a wider social and historical problem—of financial insecurity and stultifying work—and indicts mankind for "having generated social and domestic institutions destructive of its own humanity" (220).

See **Beissner**, 13-A, and **Henel**.

20. Blanchot, Maurice. "Kafka et l'exigence de l'oeuvre." In *L'Espace littéraire*. Paris: Gallimard, 1955. Pp. 52-81. "The Diaries: The Exigency of the Work of Art," trans. by Lyall H. Powers. In *Franz Kafka Today*, ed. by Angel Flores and Homer Swander. Madison: The University of Wisconsin Press, 1964. Pp. 195-220.

Kafka's struggle with his own solitude is comparable to Jewish speculations seeking to overcome exile by pushing it to its limits. As Gershom Scholem writes in *Major Trends in Jewish Mysticism*: "There was an ardent desire to overcome Exile by aggravating its torments, by savoring its bitterness in the extreme (including the night of Shekinah itself)." Blanchot continues: "That the theme of *The Metamorphosis* (as well as the obsessive fictions of animality) is a reminiscence, an allusion to the tradition of the cabalistic metempsychosis, can well be imagined, even though we are not sure whether 'Samsa' is a recollection of 'samsara' " (*L'Espace*, 67).

Boisdeffre, Pierre de. See **Albérès.**

21. **Booth, Wayne C.** *The Rhetoric of Fiction*. Chicago: The University of Chicago Press, 1961. Pp. 281-82.

Booth describes the effect of the impersonal narration in *The Metamorphosis* which **Beissner**, 13-A, has placed in a literary-historical context. The reader sees everything through the "isolated sufferer's vision"; for his own part, the author maintains a strict silence. The result of this narrative mode is that the reader's physical revulsion for the man-cockroach Gregor Samsa is overcome. "Because we are absolutely bound to his experience, our sympathy is entirely with him." The narrative perspective which confines itself to Gregor's isolated vision insures throughout a peculiar "combination of revulsion with . . . absolute forgiveness." Our reading is sympathetic, and even after his death, when "the technical point of view inevitably shifts, the full effect of the various metamorphoses we see in his family, based on Gregor's unwilling sacrifice, still depends on our maintaining his moral point of view as our own."

Adorno has argued, on the other hand, that the powerful demand for interpretation implicit in the work, and its "aggressive physical proximity," prevent the reader from identifying himself with any of its characters. Booth's observations have to be modified; at the conclusion of *The Metamorphosis* we are a considerable distance from Gregor's point of view even if we do not take the position of the family, and this is very naturally the result of the radical shift in point of view.

22. **Borges, Jorge Luis**. "Prefacio." In *La Metamorfosis*. Buenos Aires: Losada, 1938. Pp. 7-11.

Kafka has himself said that all his work proceeds from the conflict with his father and from his "tenacious meditations on the mysterious mercies and the limitless demands of paternal power" (7). Theological interpretations of Kafka are not arbitrary—we know that he was a devoté of Pascal and Kierkegaard—but they are not useful. Two ideas—or rather, two obsessions—dominate his work: the first is subordination; the second, the infinite. In almost all his works there are hierarchies, and these hierarchies are infinite. There is only one kind of man: *homo domesticus*–part Jewish, part German–looking for his place in some kind of order, whether in the universe or in a jail. Kafka's works are informed by the theme of infinite procrastination.

Kafka's surest skill is in the invention of intolerable situations. His art is one of economy, stronger in invention than in elaboration. "The plot and the ambience are the essential thing, not the development of the story or its psychological penetration. Hence the primacy of his stories over his novels" (11).

23. **Born, Jürgen**. "Vom 'Urteil' zum 'Prozess': Zu Kafkas Leben und Schaffen in den Jahren 1912-1914." *Zeitschrift für deutsche Philolgie*, 86, no. 2, 186ff.

The summer months, from June to August, were never a time of literary productivity for Kafka. Kafka began writing *The Metamorphosis* on the night of November 17, 1912. Passages from Kafka's letters to Felice Bauer describe the genesis of the novella.

24. **Brod, Max**. *Franz Kafka: Eine Biographie*. Frankfurt am Main and Hamburg: Fischer Bücherei, 1966. P. 164. *Franz Kafka. A Biography*, trans. by G. Humphreys Roberts and Richard Winston. New York: Schocken Books, 1960. P. 134.

In the midst of Kafka's stories a whole free world stands open: these stories are not "on principle" horrifying, they are the opposite–idyllic, perhaps, or heroic, upright, healthy, positive. Brod instances the "blooming body of the girl which at the close of *The Metamorphosis* suddenly shines over the carrion of the hero." But the text shows Gregor's sister only "stretching" her body; there is in this action no spiritual radiance but at most a lazy animal health. Brod continues: Kafka does not reject the goodness of life; he does not quarrel with God but with himself, for whom this life is not accessible. Hence, Kafka passes judgment with a terrible severity: in *The Metamorphosis* Kafka debases a man who is imperfect to an animal, an insect.

25. **Brück, Max von.** "Versuch über Kafka." In *Der Sphinx ist nicht tot: Figuren*. Cologne and Berlin: Kiepenheuer und Witsch, 1956. Pp. 117-35.

In Kafka's art, death is present but not as in Proust, not in the exhausted material of his fiction; Kafka is no psychological novelist. Death is felt as the metaphysical limit of existence. Kafka's art sets up existential patterns. In these patterns, interior and exterior flow into one another; thus it is not possible for psychological interiors to establish inner positions and dimensions. The movement of existence in Kafka's works seeks duration—the *Augenblick* or moment of vision. This is not a sociological or psychological permanence; Von Brück cites Kafka's aphorism: "The decisive moment is everlasting [*immerwährend*]" and concludes that it promises a fulfillment of being, time transcended in the everlastingness of the moment of vision. Kafka's world of fiction corresponds to the depth of our sensuous and intellectual existence; besides it has, as art, its own ontological order. Thus Kafka's heroes possess a genuine aesthetic generality: at bottom they are the same figure, expressive of a general predicament, no more or less Kafka's than our own; they are "models," "exemplary" figures. Kafka's images are not signs and symbols of existence; they are, rather, reality, which reveals itself in a veiled manner.

The Metamorphosis is a shockingly radical experiment within Kafka's art of exhibiting transitions: human nature is shattered, then cast into a final stage of unfree, inhuman isolation. Gregor, who cannot speak, is to some extent a caricature of the solitary hero of *The Castle*; he is cast out from human speech, this house of being. A mere mechanistic nothingness follows upon his destruction. But the course of *The Metamorphosis* is not full of the grave exigency of arriving at decisions, which is the way of the hero of *The Castle*.

Many passages of this essay derive from **Adorno**, but run counter to their source by substituting "existentialism" for criticism and by failing to dwell on the dense, concrete passages of Kafka's art. For example: Gregor's corpse is not carried on a shovel to the window and then tossed out. There is another troublesome point. Von Brück writes: "The metamorphosed creature is still half *animal rationale:* he hears and understands human language but cannot himself speak" (130). To this first point **Hasselblatt** replies that it is incorrect to interpret *The Metamorphosis* on the basis of Gregor's at least half-*animal* dimension. Gregor's animal nature is hardly or never mentioned in the text. If the cleaning woman calls Gregor an old dung beetle, Kafka's intent is only to express her contempt. If Gregor asks himself whether he is an animal, his animal nature is precisely not being asserted but being put into question. On Von Brück's second point **Hasselblatt** comments that it is not quite true that Gregor cannot speak; he can speak but cannot make himself understood by doing so (203).

26. **Busacca, Basil.** "A Country Doctor." In *Franz Kafka Today,* ed. by Angel Flores and Homer Swander. Madison: The University of Wisconsin Press, 1958. P. 49.

Gregor's transformation into an insect is not literal; it is symbolic realization of the insect nature of his life, of its distance from human life. "His instinctive wish to get on with his job and fill his role in the hive of commerce . . . demonstrates . . . how his former life was bounded by the terms of insect society." The new Gregor is less of a bug than the Gregor of before, for the metamorphosis enacts the realization of his having become a bug. The Samsa family, too, dimly realizes that the metamorphosis accuses them of their failure. The conclusion dramatizes the truth which Gregor, in fact, only partly grasps: "The serenity (and sub-humanity) of ignorance" is posed against "the anguish (and human achievement) of self-knowledge."

This analysis sets up a contradiction which it does not resolve. It asserts at one and the same time that the metamorphosis is a complete expression of Gregor's awareness of having been a bug; and that Gregor's interpretation of the metamorphosis is "dim"–in fact, evasive and incomplete.

27. **Camus, Albert**. "L'espoir et l'absurde dans l'oeuvre de Kafka." In *Le Mythe de Sisyphe.* Paris: Gallimard, 1942. Pp. 171-87. "Hope and Absurdity," trans. by William Barrett. In *The Kafka Problem,* ed. by Angel Flores. New York: New Directions, 1946. Pp. 251-61. Also, as "Hope and the Absurd in the Work of Franz Kafka," trans. by Justin O'Brien. In *The Myth of Sisyphus*. New York: Alfred A. Knopf, 1955. Pp. 124-38.

"By an odd but obvious paradox, the more extraordinary the adventures of the character, the more noticeable will be the naturalness of the story: this is proportional to the gap that can be felt between the strangeness of a man's life and the simplicity with which he accepts it. This, it seems, is the naturalness of Kafka" ("L'espoir," 172-73). Kafka's work is absurd in the sense that it speaks of a life condemned to death—one which, if it tries to cope with this fate, does so without surprise; one which "will never be sufficiently astonished at this lack of astonishment" ("L'espoir," 173).

The Metamorphosis is informed by a concern for ethics whose highest value is lucidity. Through Gregor's lack of astonishment another astonishment is communicated, that which a "man feels in perceiving the beast he is capable of becoming without effort" ("L'espoir," 174). Kafka's work is informed by the paradox and contradiction of "the natural and the extraordinary, the individual and the universal, the tragic and the everyday, the absurd and the logical" ("L'espoir," 174).

An essential feature of tragedy is the ordinary logic with which disaster ensues. The complicity between the everyday and the logical is accomplished through the figure of the traveling salesman Gregor Samsa. "The only thing which disturbs him in the strange adventure that reduces him to a vermin is that his boss will be angry at his absence . . . . The whole art of Kafka is in this nuance" ("L'espoir," 174).

28. **Carrouges, Michel.** *Kafka Contra Kafka*. Paris: Plon, 1962. Passim. *Kafka Versus Kafka,* trans. by Emmett Parker. University of Alabama Press, 1962. Passim.

The Metamorphosis is concerned with the family, with the father. "Is it not, from beginning to end, the story of a young man whose mysterious illness renders him incapable of a normal life and unrecognizable to his family?" (French, 31).

Gregor Samsa's metamorphosis foreshadows Kafka's tuberculosis. "*The Metamorphosis* evokes the most degrading torture, prolonged to the very death" (French, 89).

There is nothing fantastic or incredible about a man's being transformed into a vermin. This is the condition of death; Gregor is death in life. "Instead of being posterior and waiting for the grave, the metamorphosis begins with illness and, step by step, in complete evidence, accompanies the progress of the agony" (French, 101-02).

29. **Cermák, Josef.** "Franz Kafkas Ironie." *Philologica Pragensia,* VIII, no. 4, 391-400.

The mysterious event that stands at the beginning of *The Metamorphosis* can be deciphered only with the key of irony. The "absurd dialectic of irony" is Kafka's response to a world that has lost the rule of consistency and meaning. Kafka's irony is a mode of conceiving the world. "He keeps himself alive through the scathing contradictoriness of his inner struggle" (397). The erroneous view that Kafka's absurdity is only a half-conscious and merely poetically inspired reflection of chaos is found above all among Czech writers who were influenced by Kafka.

30. **Chaix-Ruy, J.** *Kafka: la peur de l'absurde.* Paris: Editions du Centurion, 1968. Passim.

Gregor Samsa, transformed into a vermin by the hate which simmers within the family, is the victim of the stranger's hostile or indifferent gaze. Fixed by the intolerable stares of the roomers, he crawls into a darkened corner of his room to die.

31. **Clive, Geoffrey**. "The Breakdown of Romantic Enlightenment: Kafka and Dehumanization." In *The Romantic Enlightenment: Ambiguity and Paradox in the Western Mind.* New York: Meridian Books, 1960. Pp. 170-84, passim.

Clive shows that *The Metamorphosis* exhibits in Gregor Samsa a life of solitude, soullessness, unfreedom, despair, matter-of-factness, and, because of his repulsive insect shape, "wholly other-ness" (Kierkegaard). These are the qualities of modern man's sense of himself—apostate from the Pelagian virtues of self-love, community, liberty, joy, which characterized the epoch of "Romantic Enlightenment." True, Kafka's heroes "in their rigid isolation succumb to the temptation of the ethical"; "each has a religious experience"; but in the end they "exemplify the inversion of self-reliance. They have the power to damn themselves" (181).

Clive's analysis is vitiated by simplifications: Gregor does not exhibit "unyielding kindliness" (172). It is very moot that Gregor's family "long ago crushed . . . his will to lead a life of his own" (173). The language of Gregor's privileged moment does not justify attributing to him "a stream of love and affection" for his sister (177). Does "Gregor's integrity" at the close "shine like a star" (178)? Clive's method of treating Kafka's fictions as vehicles of topiclike ideas is put into question by the opacity of the metamorphosis, by the radical disjunction within the story of reason and being.

31-A. **Corngold, Stanley**. "Kafka's *Die Verwandlung:* Metamorphosis of the Metaphor." *Mosaic*, III, no. 4 (1970), 91-106.

See pp. 1-31.

31-B. Corngold, Stanley. "Introduction." In *The Metamorphosis*, trans. by Stanley Corngold. New York: Bantam Books, 1972. Pp. xi-xxii.

This essay gives a short biographical account: "Kafka's real history is his life as literature" (xiii). " 'The Judgment' liberated in Kafka the insight essential to his life: he must not betray his writing, either by marrying or by supposing that his father is the source and goal of his art " (xvi). The argument of the essays introducing the present work is restated. Kafka's central experience was one of estrangement, taken to its limit in literature. "From this experience flows the power of Kafka's work to comprehend all forms of alienation, and to suggest a response to political estrangement different from political counterterror: the effort to illuminate this condition by grasping through literature that play is the reward for the courage of accepting death" (xxii).

32. **Dalmau Castañón, Wilfredo.** "El Caso clinico de Kafka en 'La Metamorfosis.' " *Cuadernos Hispanoamericanos* (Madrid), XXVII (March 1952), 385-88.

In the egoistic eyes of society, Gregor Samsa is transformed into a bug, but there is a prior metamorphosis: Kafka transforms himself into his protagonist, and the story springs from his tuberculosis.

There is an element of reality in *The Metamorphosis*—namely, the changes produced in Kafka by his tuberculosis. *The Metamorphosis* reflects an obsession with this disease and includes its symptomatology. The story is a kind of clinical report of Kafka's tuberculosis.

Kafka's physique is asthenic; his constitution is typical of the consumptive. Gregor's room—small, cold, high-ceilinged—is like those rooms one reads about in clinical histories of consumptives. (Kafka's work is informed with sheer physical misery.) The pain Gregor feels in his side is possibly of tubercular origin. Kafka himself probably suffered from the colds to which Gregor alludes. The liquid which streams from Gregor's mouth as he attempts to turn the key with his jaws stems from hemoptysic vomiting. Two clinical manifestations accompany this process of debilitation: breathlessness and weight loss. As a literary work, however, *The Metamorphosis* is selective and does not reproduce all the important symptoms.

The family reflects the structure of the society which gives rise to the consumptive. Under the burden of his work to maintain this group, Gregor suffers from debilitating fatigue. Fatigue lowers resistance against disease and particularly against tuberculosis. What is more, there is a family history increasing Gregor's susceptibility to tuberculosis: his mother suffers from bronchial asthma.

Gregor, as he himself says, has never had trustworthy lungs, but he hopes to recover without having to stay at home; he is under the pressure of having to support his family and of wanting to send Grete to the conservatory.

The violent recoil of the office manager, the horror of the maid, Grete's fear, are inspired by the danger of contagion; hence their desire to keep him confined. His outbreaks inspire horror in the others. Gregor's emotions–his tender feelings for his family and his outbursts of irritation at their neglect–reflect the neurovegetative disequilibrium of the consumptive.

The Metamorphosis is a reflection of Kafka's bitterness at his sickness. The work is penetrated by truth, the truth of Kafka's sickness–the truth which, as Kafka said, blinds and is our art.

"But being a literary work," says Dr. Dalmau Castañón, *"The Metamorphosis* is selective." It selects those details of the truth of Kafka's sickness which serve its truth. The truth which "is our art" cannot then be the truth of Kafka's sickness.

The Metamorphosis was composed between November 17 and December 7, 1912. According to Kafka's biographer Klaus **Wagenbach** (106-07), the beginning of Kafka's tuberculosis dates from the notation of August 1917 in his octavo notebook: "Coughed up blood." The existence of the disease was confirmed a month later. There is nothing in Kafka's diary and letters during the period of the composition of *The Metamorphosis* to establish Kafka's concern with the disease which first came to light five years later.

In **Politzer**'s words (91-A, 80-81), "The power which transformed Gregor Samsa is infinitely more than an image of bodily disease. Nowhere does Kafka encourage us to interpret Gregor's insect shape as an expression of his physical or even mental disorder."

33. **Dentan, Michel.** *Humour et création littéraire dans l'oeuvre de Kafka.* Geneva and Paris: Droz and Minard, 1961. Pp. 11-16.

The horror of the metamorphosis is constituted detail by detail through Gregor's eyes by means of inward sensory experiences. This nightmare enters the most banal of worlds with absolute naturalness. At the same time, the narrative mode indicates that the author is taking no pleasure in the shock–rather, he aims at distancing both himself and the reader from it.

There are signs of this intent in the overlapping of nightmare and reality. "The story is presented as a series of real facts, whereas for Gregor these facts appear at first to be only a hallucination; and even if later on it is no longer a question for him of hallucination, the transition occurs so imperceptibly that this partly explains his lack of amazement, rebellion, or terror, confronted with the destiny that overwhelms him" (12). Hence a discrepancy arises between the responses which we expect of Gregor and his actual responses–as in his reflection, after having been metamorphosed into a bug, that if it were not on account of his parents, he would have given the boss a piece of his mind; or in the exhortation he addresses to himself: "Just don't stay in bed being useless." There is an internal logic to these and other reflections, but as a whole they reveal a "total maladjustment. . . . He does not dominate his situation, while the reader thinks he himself does–spectator and judge" (12). The reader's distance, his sense of being in possession, is heightened again through such effects as the discomfiture of the arrogant office manager; at this point the story's initial mood of abasement gives way to a mood of amused satisfaction. A similar effect is obtained when the haughty manners of the three roomers are made ridiculous by the puppetlike symmetry of their movements. These events (to which others can be added) have in common the effect of surprising the reader, of "exciting the attention of the reader and making him aware of his privileged position" (13). In this position he feels his own superiority to the characters and is prompted to judge their responses–responses invariably made in ignorance of the real and complete situation that envelops them.

The analysis of other instances of Kafka's playfulness permits this conclusion: his playfulness bears less on the characters themselves than on his manner of developing the primary material of the story.

Thus the technique of the story does not aim solely at making the metamorphosis persuasive: its other intention is to "bring to light, through clear signs, the fact that [the author] disposes freely over his fictional material, that he is free to play with it when he wants to. The tale oscillates between seriousness and unseriousness" (14). At the same time Kafka's aesthetic distance from the story in no way robs the narrated events of their oppressive character.

It would seem important to decide whether Kafka's aesthetic distance and the oppressiveness of his themes do indeed exist in isolation or whether, to speak with **Adorno**, the force with which the text commands interpretation "collapses aesthetic distance."

It is also questionable whether Kafka's playful intention can rightly be called comical or humorous. (**Luke**'s essay goes some distance toward making this distinction.) Kafka's playfulness is absolutely distinctive of his poetic universe; and to define it precisely means to define the general sense of Kafka's project.

Meanwhile, the real achievement of Dentan's essay lies in his discovering moments of disparity between the narrator's consciousness and the consciousness of Gregor. This disparity contradicts **Beissner**'s thesis of the sheer coincidence in Kafka's fiction of narrator, hero, and reader. It makes necessary the fine adjustments of Kafka's point of view in **Henel** and in Martin Walser, *Beschreibung einer Form* (Munich, 1961).

34. **Derycke, Gaston.** *"La Métamorphose"* (a review). *Le Rouge et le Noir*, May 5, 1938.

Not seen.

35-A. Dietz, Ludwig. "Franz Kafka, Drucke zu seinen Lebzeiten. Eine textkritisch-bibliographische Studie." *Jahrbuch der deutschen Schillergesellschaft,* VII (1963), 416-57.

The interest with which Kafka's works were received during his lifetime has been generally underestimated; the number and volume of the printings of his works tell a different story. After the first printing of *The Metamorphosis* in the journal *Die Weissen Blätter* in October, 1915, it appeared in two different versions in the series called *Der jüngste Tag*—the first in 1915, the second, which is difficult to date, probably in 1917. Until 1963 the existence of this third printing of *The Metamorphosis* was not known. Brod's complete edition of Kafka's works prints the next-to-last version of *The Metamorphosis*, unaware of the existence of a final version. On the other hand, the third version of *The Metamorphosis* (that is, its second edition within *Der jüngste Tag*) contains so many typographical errors that it cannot by itself constitute an authorized version, though it reveals other variations from the first edition of 1915 which must be taken into account.

In March, 1915, if not earlier, Kafka sent Max Brod a copy of *The Metamorphosis* for forwarding to René Schickele, editor of *Die Weissen Blätter*. Kafka stated to Brod that it did not matter to him when it appeared and repeated the same thing to Schickele. But he was very concerned that it be published. When difficulties arose because of the story's length, Kafka proved very stubborn and would not voluntarily take it back. In spite of what Kafka called the "questionable character" of the story, he was bent on having his work published.[23]

In October, 1915, Carl Sternheim received the Fontane Prize and passed on the cash prize to Kafka; in the same month *The Metamorphosis* was published in *Die Weissen Blätter* and accepted for the series "Neue deutsche Erzähler" in *Der jüngste Tag*, the publishing venture of Kurt Wolff. In 1913 Kafka had proposed a book of novellas to be called *The Sons* (*Briefe*, 116) consisting of *The Stoker,* "The Judgment," and *The Metamorphosis*; he now proposed a novella collection to be called *Punishments*, consisting of the last two stories plus *In the Penal Colony*.

Neither of these projects was ever realized. Yet by 1916, after the publication of "The Judgment," all three of the works comprising *The Sons* had at least been published in the same format and under the same auspices of *Der jüngste Tag*. In 1918 *The Metamorphosis* appeared in a second edition; for this edition Kafka changed details of the text (but cf. **Dietz**, 35-C). Considerably more copies of the second edition were printed than of the first, showing clearly the degree to which Kafka had penetrated the consciousness of his time.

There are difficulties in the way of an exact dating of the second edition of *The Metamorphosis*, but probability speaks for late 1917 or (with better justification) 1918. This edition contains several blatant printer's errors and cannot have been carefully proofread. The kind and number of the significant variations nevertheless leave no doubt that this new edition was made with Kafka's knowledge and help. Wagenbach's special edition of Kafka's stories (*Die Erzählungen*, Frankfurt am Main, 1961), claims to be based on the first edition of *The Metamorphosis*; in fact Wagenbach has stumbled on a second edition and tacitly corrected most of the printer's errors while considering others to be acceptable. For the rest, he follows Brod's reliable reprinting of the first edition, only sometimes introducing corrections. This text is unsatisfactory.

The reappearance of *The Metamorphosis* in two new editions following its first printing in *Die Weissen Blätter* in each case prompted Kafka to undertake corrections. These changes consist of so-called editorial, not genetic, variants, for they seem to have been made in retouching the proofs. Particularly between the magazine version and the first book version of *The Metamorphosis* a genuine creative impulse appears to have entered into play.

Two-thirds of the variants concern changes in punctuation. Kafka's punctuation is informed by a double movement. The first movement can be understood, in Fritz Martini's words, as a "flowing together of sentences and ideas" ["Ein Manuskript Franz Kafkas: 'Der Dorfschullehrer.' " *Jahrbuch der deutschen Schillergesellschaft*, II (1958), 292]. Kafka's deviations from the norms of punctuation, Martini asserts, constitute a particular style and rhythm. This confluence of sentences and ideas, at least in the instant of creation, reflects the tight inner linking of conditions and expression, consequences and contradictions, and requires the effect of fluency and unity in the verbal mode; on the other hand, the conventional rules exact an overly clear articulation and distribution of sense through the logic of punctuation. This movement, Dietz continues, is fully present in the expansion of the instant of conception to the organized work. Kafka's language is frequently praised as clear and cool, precise, concrete, sober; but there is also something unclear in his language, not only in the punctuation, but present even earlier, in the sentence structure, which enables such an effect of flowing convergence; sentences spill into one another, and the rhythmic profile is levelled and blurred—an effect which later variations in punctuation can only mask but cannot fundamentally change. On the other hand, Martini is only partially correct in asserting that Kafka's use or avoidance of punctuation amounts to a "poetic formal structure" which is destroyed when the punctuation is normalized. As we pass from the first to the second and third editions of *The Metamorphosis*, we note increasingly vivid, definite, and profuse punctuation: commas are replaced with semicolons; semicolons with periods; periods with exclamation points. All of Kafka's changes point to normalization. This is the second movement informing his punctuation. His creative project tends toward an inner linkage in his poetic language, expressed in sparse punctuation which neglects commas altogether and prefers commas to periods and so attempts to blur even the outer contour of the sentence. Yet in the finished work this tendency is suppressed. Every subsequent revision uses increasingly heavier punctuation and with greater emphasis. Frequently in pursuing the norm Kafka in effect demolishes the native rhythm of his sentences; his revisions in punctuation cannot therefore amount to a creative process. Where this occurs, a critical edition of Kafka's works would be justified in defending Kafka the poet against Kafka the proofreader.

Dietz's introduction of a second movement informing Kafka's punctuation (toward a punctuation ever more profuse and emphatic) is justified only by the changes Kafka made between the first printing of *The Metamorphosis* in *Die Weissen Blätter* and its first appearance in book form. The changes in punctuation that appear between the first and second editions of the single-volume version of *The Metamorphosis* very frequently substitute commas for semicolons and omit commas altogether. It becomes obvious that Dietz must retract either his general thesis about the growing definiteness of Kafka's punctuation or his thesis that Kafka is himself responsible for the changes made between the first and second single-volume editions of *The Metamorphosis*. In 35-C **Dietz** does in fact retract the claim that Kafka could have been responsible for these changes.

35-B. Dietz, Ludwig. "Drucke Franz Kafkas bis 1924." In *Kafka-Symposion*. Berlin: Wagenbach, 1965. Pp. 85-125.

This article lists—as items 21, 22, and 34—the three printings of *The Metamorphosis* discussed in **Dietz**, 35-A and 35-C.

35-C. Dietz, Ludwig. "Die Autorisierten Dichtungen Kafkas, Textkritische Anmerkungen." *Zeitschrift für deutsche Philologie*, 86, no. 2, 301-17.

This article is based on the author's preceding two articles (35-A and 35-B) treating textual and bibliographical problems. Much of the ground it covers is not new. Throughout various printings of the same work, Kafka's changes in diction and syntax aim toward an effect of tightening rather than one of "flowing coalescence" (Martini). The sense is made plainer and clearer—never adorned. It is possible that Kafka helped to correct the second edition of *The Metamorphosis* and that he is responsible for the variants. However, there are more typographical errors in this edition than in any other, nor is this edition ever mentioned in Kafka's correspondence with his publisher Kurt Wolff (their correspondence has not, however, been preserved in its entirety). Other considerations raise the question of whether Kafka indeed ever knew about the second edition at all.[24] Certain corrections might well be attributed to Kafka's desire to write more "orthodoxly," yet on closer inspection most appear to be changes for the worse. Other printer's errors are so grievous that it finally becomes impossible to suppose that Kafka could have read these proofs himself. (It is known that Kafka did not correct the proofs of the first printing of *The Metamorphosis* in *Die Weissen Blätter*.)

36. Dutourd, Jean. "Préface." *La Métamorphose et autres nouvelles de Franz Kafka.* Monte Carlo: Sauret, 1955.

Not seen.

37-A. Edel, Edmund. "Franz Kafka: Das Urteil." *Wirkendes Wort*, no. 4 (1959), 216-25.

"The Judgment" and *The Metamorphosis* stand in a relation to each other of inner correspondence and antithesis. Just as the name Georg (Bendemann), the hero of "The Judgment," can almost be formed by twisting around the letters of the name Gregor, the relation of father to son is reversed in the two stories. The point is that for a writer of Kafka's range there cannot be only a *single* version of this fundamental conflict. It is true that, in the end, both stories deal with the same theme of metamorphosis—the metamorphosis of death. But the same "sign" has opposite meanings in each story, "which might be paraphrased, allusively, with the terms transfiguration for Gregor and damnation for Georg" (217). Georg's death is a catastrophe for him; "but for the father, as for Gregor in *The Metamorphosis*, the death means elevation and liberation—in Gregor's case, liberation from the prison of being an animal, in the case of Mr. Bendemann, liberation from the burden of judgment. In both cases death means liberation from the world through knowledge" (224-25).

37-B. Edel, Edmund. "Franz Kafka: *Die Verwandlung,* Eine Auslegung." *Wirkendes Wort,* no. 4 (1957-58), 217-26.

Surface and interiority in *The Metamorphosis* diverge. The surface arouses a sort of moral and aesthetic repugnance; but the narration conceals an event capable of transforming the aversion of the reader into accession, of drawing him into the power of the metamorphosis.

The opening of *The Metamorphosis* is typical of Kafka's fiction: it begins at the origin, in which the event is concealed from the space and time into which it will unfold. "What is essential has always already happened before the action begins" (217). The source is ineffable.

What is the meaning of the monstrous transformation of a self with which *The Metamorphosis* opens? Two passages from Kafka's *Diaries* provide clues:

> I want to torture myself, want to change my state perpetually, think I have a sense that my salvation lies in change, and think furthermore that through such little changes which others make while half-asleep but which I make summoning up all my intellectual powers, I can prepare myself for the great change that I probably need. In exchange I certainly get a dwelling which is worse in many respects (March 1, 1915. T 464-465; DII 116).

> I avoid people not because I want to live quietly but because I want to go under quietly (July 28, 1914. T 411; DII 68).

For Gregor the metamorphosis is "the great change" which his hopeless predicament requires. It is his most fundamental hope when no other way remains "of going under quietly."

The metamorphosis preserves its extraordinary character and connection with the human world by issuing into the form of an animal of extraordinary size. Its uniqueness indicates that a self remains concealed behind the horrible mask of the creature—that a self remains in this prison, unimpaired.

Thus what is monstrous about the bug is not its larger-than-life size; this continually points to the distinctiveness of the creature, indicating its constant connection to the human world. Its size must keep alive in the consciousness of the family the identity of brother, son, and bug. The continuity of self-consciousness in fact remains unbroken throughout the metamorphosis. The metamorphosis does not mean "the effacement of the clarity, acuity, and duration of Gregor's consciousness; it means the opposite: clear insight into the lonely, hopeless, suffering but enduring essence precisely of this unique person" (218).[25] To find himself transformed means for Gregor to be aroused to the consciousness of the distinctive form of his existence; as such, he finds himself in paradoxical opposition to his world. The family has hitherto confined Gregor to the circle of its narrow practical concerns.

Now Gregor is disfigured into the form of a bug in order to demonstrate the absurdity of the existence imposed on him. The discrepancy between the person and the bug's body represents the discrepancy between the life which Gregor's family has exacted from him and his authentic spiritual distinctiveness. The metamorphosis is no dream, no mere notion, no fact belonging to empirical causality, but the creation of a narrative consciousness, through which ordinary reality is put in a new and truthful light.

Gregor's enormous capacity for suffering and understanding leads to the conclusion that the singularity and isolation of his existence belongs essentially to the world of the spirit. "Through his metamorphosis, through the consciousness of his complete isolation, he is aroused, so to speak, to the extreme form of his spirituality, i.e. he can suffer, he can perceive, he can evaluate his perceptions, and . . . then go under" (219). The metamorphosis presents Gregor and his family with a critical form of their task: for Gregor, to gain self-awareness; for the family, compassionately to accept him.

Gregor's struggle to manipulate his insect body is a struggle in general with the misery of bodily existence. In striving in his contention with his body to be calm and reflective and rational, Gregor is led to a general reflection on the burden of his work, the family's debts, and his obligation to support his parents. The metamorphosis breaks this circle of material concerns. It is now Gregor who requires care and support from the family. But the family bungles this chance of a humane existence for themselves.

Except for Gregor, all the characters in *The Metamorphosis* belong to "the vital sphere of existence." "The resistance of his animal body is perpetuated for Gregor in the resistance of these human beings who in the end are made of the same stuff" (220). These others can realize their humanity only in penetrating the ugliness and helplessness of the metamorphosed creature and perceiving the individual essence hidden beneath the horror. The metamorphosis patently occurs at a point when the burden which Gregor shoulders for the family is no longer enough to provide him with a place in the family circle. Their resistance comes to light in the father's violence, the mother's impotence, and the sister's jealousy and deceit.

After the metamorphosis Gregor attempts to enter into play

with the family; when this opening is barred to him, he enters into play with himself: i.e., "his being represents itself to him with ever greater clarity. Thus the experience of his complete meaninglessness for the others, the condemnation to pure self-reference, makes futile his every effort and every attempt to break out, because precisely those to whom Gregor attempts to break out are his jailers" (221). The truly monstrous consequence of the metamorphosis is the transformation of the father into the tormentor and annihilator of his son. Gregor's father and sister are both at work, meditating the death of their son and brother. The mother's impotence–her breach of faith and memory–makes her guilty, in a deeper sense, of Gregor's suffering. The loss of the mother's care is for Gregor the loss of the past, while the father obstructs his future.

The parents do not undergo development; what has hitherto been concealed and hinted at in them comes to light. They cannot cope with the metamorphosis, and for this they are indicted for failure.

The sister's violin playing signifies to Gregor that she shares in the world of the spirit; but she fails Gregor, and her betrayal causes the final catastrophe. She is Gregor's counterpart; as Gregor's vitality sinks, hers blooms.

Her care for him is not the result of genuine concern. Not content with driving him under the couch, she opens the window for him to climb out, so as voluntarily to free them all of his burden. Her creating an aperture toward the outside world and simultaneously shutting the door to the common living room anticipates her final condemnation of him to death.

In spite of the mother's warning, she robs his room of its "Lebensraum," turning it into a cave, divesting it of all shape and of its accustomed dimensions. By converting it into creeping space, she degrades space into a plane; in taking away its third dimension, she takes away its specifically human dimension. "For height elevates surface into space and space into a human dwelling" (223). When Gregor defends the picture on the wall, the issue is one of being or not being a man; what is at stake is the specifically human dimension, the possibility of glancing upward. For Gregor the picture of the woman is the last frontier of the human.

The food offered to Gregor is for him a sign of congruity or noncongruity between the I and Thou, between the self and the world. "With the increasing experience of incongruity, Gregor's hunger disappears; . . . Gregor and his sister dwell in totally disparate domains" (224).

The "inconsiderateness" of Gregor's breaking out of his room and advancing into the living room shows his devotion to the world of spirit which opens up to him within the music, shows the force of his longing for a shared, spiritually ordered human world. Music is a sign of unity and closeness, the expression of the most inward congruity. But its sound proves ungenuine. Gregor's "sacred emotion" is incapable of binding the domain of art and spirit on this earth.

Although his sister fails to provide him with the nourishment he desires, she shows Gregor the way to a quiet "going under." Yet his death is a moment of acute separation; the family's mode of dealing with it is to reassert its vital interests and activities. With this, their own spiritual quality is condemned.

Through dying, Gregor rescues the unique form of his spiritual existence by thinking back on the family with feeling and love. Gregor shows the merciful love of wisdom for ignorance. "As being is divorced from nothingness, perfection from imperfection, spirit from nonspirit, Gregor and the family are divorced from one another according to a presumably superhuman order" (225). By his charitable love Gregor is elevated to a higher stage of fulfillment. He fasts in anticipation of his death, for the knowledge is killing that there is no salvation in the world from the world.

Gregor's death coincides with a moment of insight. His liberation announces itself under the sign of the new day and the new season. The shimmer of light, the onset of the brightening of the day accompany the moment in which a life burns through. Death elevates the accomplished life of the spirit into God's order.

Edel says all that can be said for Gregor as a hero of authentic self-consciousness. He makes this claim, however, at the cost of ignoring all the negativity which Gregor exhibits, even apart from his terrifying and sadistic appearance: his absent-mindedness, his lapses into bestiality, his vindictiveness. **Emrich**'s essay is a needful corrective to this view.

A more important criticism concerns the relation of Gregor's alleged authentic self-awareness and his Christian insight at the close of *The Metamorphosis:* "He thought back on his family with deep emotion and love. His conviction that he would have to disappear was, if possible, even firmer than his sister's." Edel is surely right to see that this intersubjective experience at the close is consistent with Gregor's self-reflection; but then it is important to note the bitter irony with which this experience is narrated and the fact that Gregor is seen here once again taking over as his own the ignorant desires of the Other. This must cast doubt on the genuineness of Gregor's self-awareness throughout the story. In effect, Edel's position is contradictory. He maintains at one and the same time that Gregor's nightmarish shape holds the meaning of his former life, in which he adopted as his own the self-seeking interests of the Other; and that he accomplishes his spiritual destiny as an intensely self-aware consciousness by once again adopting the interests of the Other. It is a troublesome oversimplification of the split into bug and human in Gregor to identify the bug with the "sphere of vital interests"–Gregor's past life in the family.

38. **Elkinton, H. W.** "*Metamorphosis*" (a review). *American-German Review*, XIII, no. 4, 33.

How serious was Kafka in writing *The Metamorphosis*? "[The story] is offered as a son-father pattern or a parasitic father-superindustrious-insectivorous-son relation with the inescapable animosity that develops between two such persons."

39. **Empson, William.** "A Family Monster" (a review of *The Metamorphosis*). *The Nation*, CLXIII (December 7, 1946), 652-53.

Empson takes issue with **Goodman**'s analysis of Gregor's animality as a description of all the ways at once in which men have conceived animals. The point of the story is that Gregor is not like just any animal but is a nauseating monster, who preserves a sweetness of temperament in spite of the loathing he inspires. Empson finds the piece clear-cut, with only a lurking touch of neurosis in a passage at the very close, where it is said that Grete looked healthy "despite the make-up [*Pflege*] which made her cheek look pale." After all, writes Empson, "she was dressed before she knew her brother was dead, but she had no need to pretend to be pale." Empson discusses this sentence at some length as a typical piece of Kafka's puzzle-technique, and he is at once perceptive and deceived, since the sentence is, in fact, the translation of a misprint in the second book edition; the line should read "in spite of all the troubles [*Plage*] which had made her cheeks pale."

Empson notes a number of minor inconsistencies in the story and concludes: "In the other major Kafka books one feels sure that the contradictions are intentional; indeed the more baffling they are the more carefully they seem placed; but this is a different kind of story and does not need them. Maybe he could never bear to read over the manuscript."

This latter supposition is untrue; Kafka read the manuscript in proof before its first appearance in book form (see **Dietz**, 35-A). And it is not necessary to assert that any of the details which Empson singles out are indeed inconsistencies. See "Explanatory Notes," *The Metamorphosis*, trans. and ed. by Stanley Corngold, Bantam Books, 1972.

40. Emrich, Wilhelm. *"Das Tier als befreiendes 'Selbst'"* and *"Der Käfer in der Erzählung 'Die Verwandlung.'"* In *Franz Kafka.* Frankfurt am Main and Bonn: Athenäum, 1965. Pp. 115-27. "The Animal as Liberating 'Self'" and "The Beetle in the Story 'The Metamorphosis,'" trans. by Sheema Zeben Buehne. In *Franz Kafka: A Critical Study of his Writings*. New York: Ungar, 1968. Pp. 132-48.

In the early story, "Wedding Preparations in the Country," Kafka reflects on the theme of alienation in terms which precisely anticipate Heidegger's distinction between the self and the "they" (*das Man*). Kafka defines the principle of the "they" as the "law," which functions especially through bureaucracy and alienated work. The law is a ubiquitous force, urging all things into the domain of anonymous, collective behavior.

The self in Raban, the hero of this story, has no basis, since he owes everything to the "office." All the events in his life, which do not finally belong to him, inspire him with a sense of strangeness and loathesomeness, even the preparations for his own wedding.

The tension between the self and the prevalent impersonal "they" is resolved in favor of the autonomous self in Raban's vision of himself undergoing beetle metamorphosis [see pp. 20-22]. Kafka associates the mode of existence of this self with childhood, the prehuman animal, and the dream. The self does not reflect in the ordinary way, and it shuns the body and practical reason, though it exercises control over things and others in a magical, effortless way. It shuns the "law," the "they," and the office.

The emergence of Raban's self, however, is only a vision; in fact he remains in a condition of unresolved tension. Yet this tension is made transparent as the opposition between animal existence and the rational world of work.

The beetle metamorphosis in *The Metamorphosis* is fundamentally opposed to that in "Wedding Preparations." Gregor Samsa does not welcome this transformation; he finds it incomprehensible and resists identification with it. Samsa's conflict between the self and the world of work is actually the same as Raban's, but unlike Raban, Samsa vacillates between these two orders. On the one hand, he curses his work; on the other, he considers the metamorphosis an awkward intrusion on his routine. Raban's metamorphosis is conceived as a dream by a waking subject; Samsa's, as waking reality by a dreamer. Despite the revelation by the metamorphosis of Gregor Samsa's real feelings about his job, he remains rooted in the domain of the "they"; the self is a burdensome bug whose reality he denies.

But Gregor's desire to escape work and responsibility oppresses him; it is at the root of his "unsettling dreams." Unlike Raban, Gregor Samsa cannot simply remain in bed; but neither can he "get rid of" the self, which in the form of the metamorphosis now invades Samsa's reality. It is no dream, no fabrication; it is the ultimate, inescapable reality of the personal life. The conflict between inwardness and the demands of the world—which in traditional literature, such as Goethe's *William Meister's Theatrical Mission*, is represented as a conflict at the level of reflection—is radicalized in *The Metamorphosis*; contemplative inwardness is alienated from itself. Kafka represents the two orders of the self and the "they" as an absolute antinomy; they cannot be reached or bridged by reflection or articulation. The "law" is invisible to modern man, and the self is hidden. This conflict may be subliminally felt, but Samsa is typical in supposing he can smooth it over by "calculations." What does Samsa know of the potential forms of existence he hopes to actualize when he has made "the big break"?

This, then, is the crux of the incomprehensible, alien, verminous creature which Gregor becomes: it is the form of the radically unknown self. In *The Trial* the predicament of the hero is the same: he is "arrested" by an absurd and incomprehensible court. In breaking through the empirical order of everyday reality, the self must manifest itself suddenly and as something wholly strange. That is because the self in modern society is not a familiar inwardness which is possessed and one's own.

A slightly different logic justifies the deformation of Gregor's free and instinctive animallike inner life into a hideous vermin; it is deformed by the very force with which he denies it. Raban's attitude is the opposite; and this accounts for the fact that his omnipotent dreamy beetle is like the fairy-tale imaginings of a child.

In their original form Kafka's animals have a positive, salutary significance. They stand for man's prereflective subliminal state, for his early prehuman soul. This is the self disowned by the calculating man of business.

Not only Gregor, but the entire Samsa family, refuse to recognize the metamorphosis, and this is the source of the horror of the story. "The self is what is absolutely strange, null, nonexistent not only in the world of business but also in the world of the family" ("Der Käfer," 122). Mother and sister do try at first to improve Gregor's condition; but what comes to light is that even the most tender relations between people are founded on illusions and cannot survive the rupturing of these illusions. No one knows what he is or what the other is. Gregor's former life, adjusted to bare necessities, in fact served to conceal, distort, and destroy his self, and this escaped the notice of his family. When the distortion becomes palpable, the family is at a loss; they experience their son as a "foreign body."

Gregor too was deluded about his family, who were not

content with his sacrifices. No one understands the secret calculations and compromises on which personal relations are based. The semblance of interpersonal order is shattered by the truth that comes to light through Gregor's transformation. Gregor's self-sacrifice has resulted in tangible self-disfigurement.

The truth revealed by the metamorphosis is not only the self-distorting side of Gregor's sacrifice, but also its utter futility; Gregor's parents never needed the sacrifice; indeed, they suffered because of it. There was more money in the household than Gregor supposed, and his father was always able to work. The harmonious life of the family was a lie; and so the monstrous apparition that threatens to expose the lie must now be exorcised. With his dying wish Gregor himself participates in this assertion of rampant falsity. This falsity masks the family's assertion of optimism at the close.

The assertion of falsity stands out sharply next to the evanescent positive meaning of the metamorphosis. As an animal Gregor is moved by music, drawn to an unearthly nourishment. And so the metamorphosis also expresses the intent toward an inexpressible freedom. "Thus the animal or rather the monster of this 'metamorphosis' designates a sphere which cannot be expressed, which cannot even be seen. . . . It would be meaningless to interpret the beetle Samsa as a real beetle" ("Der Käfer," 124). Kafka himself made this point explicit in his letters when he wrote that the insect cannot be illustrated. Here is evidence that Gregor's hypostatized dream is more than a dream, for dream images can be depicted.

Beetle existence is an inexplicable force which makes Gregor Samsa alien, unbearable, and repellent to everyone, including himself. He is coerced into this existence even though his consciousness maintains an attachment to the being he was and to the world around him.

He does finally escape empirical entrapment; he realizes his freedom as a longing for music and an affirmation of his death. Throughout his experience of "liberation," however, there is no explicit self-realization.

"This 'self' can no longer be understood psychologically as a determinate psychic state, intelligible as an order of feelings, wishes, hopes, dreams, strivings, and the like; it is not true that from the conflict with his professional work a series of 'inward' feelings, ideals, goals rise up in opposition to the world of work and family and that these depict, so to speak, Samsa's 'authentic' self" ("Der Käfer," 126). For even if we say that this self has been suppressed and perverted and must therefore come to light negatively, as a vermin, Samsa would have to come to terms with this self. He would be forced to take an attitude toward it; he would be changed by it. But "the 'metamorphosis' does not occur as a transformation of psyche or mind or character" ("Der Käfer," 126). This is the disarming aspect of the tale, distinguishing it radically from all other literature about the self.

It is only in a very limited sense that the beetle animal stands for the dreamlike, unconscious, instinctual order of man. There is no overflow from dream to metamorphosis. Characteristics of dream consciousness–freedom, instinctive certainty, immediacy –are not present in Samsa. Neither is Samsa's state a nightmare or tropism moving through rational everyday consciousness. His beetle state is dominated by everyday concerns.

In the end, "the beetle is and remains something 'Other' which cannot be accommodated by the human mind. This alone is its meaning" ("Der Käfer," 126). Kafka's remark that the insect cannot be illustrated tells us, not only that it cannot be pictured, but also that it cannot be grasped by a sort of mimetic interpretation. This mode of existence is truthful only insofar as it cannot be explicated, truth for Kafka being fundamentally inexplicable. In this sense the creature is a self, one that exceeds all notions of the self. "The creature is the absolute transcendence of the so-called human world, although it is nothing but man 'himself.' The gap between Samsa's world and his beetle shape is the gap between 'thinking' and 'being.' Because for Kafka what is beyond imagining lies in man himself, because there is no Beyond outside him, the 'parable' of this Beyond is necessarily an earthly image that is at the same time unearthly and cannot be 'drawn' " ("Der Käfer," 127). This is the reason why Kafka represents the irruption of the uncanny into the everyday in the form of animal images.

Raban, of "Wedding Preparations," saw the world from the standpoint of the "foundation of truth" (Kafka); hence he saw the world as revolting. In Samsa, who wishes to remain in the world, the tranquil self must come to light as something revolting. Together both beetle visions define Kafka's view of the world.

41. **Erlich, Victor**. "Gogol and Kafka: Note on 'Realism' and 'Surrealism.' " In *For Roman Jakobson: Essays on the Occasion of his Sixtieth Birthday*, ed. by Morris Halle and others. The Hague: Mouton, 1956. Pp. 102-04.

The Metamorphosis shares with Gogol's "The Nose" a particular use of realistic detail: it does not serve "as the subsoil of an autonomous yet reality-like world, but as a factor of contrapuntal tension, of ironic incongruity." The Gogol story does not have the character, as *The Metamorphosis* does, of existential disaster; but in both there is a central discrepancy between the apparent realism of the representation and the incredible main event. On awakening, Gregor finds that he is a monstrous bug; Kovalëv, that he is noseless; both discard the notion that they are merely dreaming. The familiar dreariness of Gregor's surroundings vouches for the actuality of the metamorphosis. "The regular human room," "the line of fabric samples" absorb Gregor's predicament into the everyday order of things as, at worst, an awkward nuisance. What Gregor minds most, as **Camus** has noted, is that his boss will be angry. The "lack of astonishment" which, according to **Camus**, Kafka exhibits before the most implausible events, is based on a view of the world as senseless. Everyday life, Erlich continues, is "an absurd chaos, a web of incongruities, a series of interlocking nightmares." Indeed, the plot of *The Metamorphosis* has a dreamlike logic. Only in a dream could such solidly pedestrian detail exist side by side with ontological incompatibility. "It is precisely in a dream that a thing can be both itself and its own opposite, . . . a bug and a sentient being." In a dream situation incongruities of this sort are absorbed without shock. It is, of course, crucial that the metamorphosis is directly preceded by a dream. "One is tempted to speak here of a false awakening, of an 'unsettling' anxiety dream."

Baioni argues against this parallel. The main idea in Erlich's article–that the shock is absorbed as a nuisance into the everyday order of things–is developed by **Hasselblatt**, and the idea that the metamorphosis is a dream or dreamlike is resisted by **Hasselblatt** and developed by **Fraiberg** and **Lecomte**.

42. **Falk, Walter**. *Leid und Verwandlung: Rilke, Kafka, Trakl und der Epochenstil des Impressionismus und Expressionismus*. Salzburg: O. Müller, 1961. Pp. 108-09.

Falk takes as his starting point the theory that all suffering desires transformation. Poetry and style are determined by the way in which the writer seeks to transform his anguish.

Kafka's art shows a loss of analogy: domains of experience confront one another in antinomian fashion, e.g. Gregor Samsa/bug; they can be connected only by being yoked together in a violent identification which preserves the antinomy. The structure and meaning of Kafka's art is shaped by the second domain–a constant source of disaster, "an experience of perpetual disaster." The direction of Kafka's metamorphoses is the otherness, the strangeness of animals, of beings antihuman. "The metamorphosis which Kafka's figures experience is accomplished by an unearthly . . . power [which] changes man from within so that he is no longer able to obtain a footing in the familiar order of things and falls prey to . . . exile, strangeness." Kafka asserts disaster–suffering it without reprieve, failing to overcome it. This, for Falk, is the hallmark of expressionism.[26]

43. **Fast, Howard**. *Literature and Reality*. New York: International Publishers, 1950. Pp. 9-12.

Kafka sits near the top of the "cultural dung heap of reaction." Kafka creates "a shadow world, a world of twisted, tormented mockeries of mankind." Though *The Metamorphosis* has a satirical intention, it differs from satires of the past in the literalness with which it makes its point. As a result, Kafka's satire, a mode en route to the disclosure of reality, falls into horror. Kafka's thesis is that there is a kind of man so like a cockroach that it is reasonable for him to wake up and find himself transformed into one. What is the intent of this nauseating story? The German petty bourgeois is not "a cockroach"; but for Kafka "man and roach are the same."[27]

The equation of man and cockroach is, in fact, part of a process by which a ruling class distorts objective reality. In separating himself from reality, Kafka contributes to the political debasement of modern man. Kafka's production cannot be justified as art on the basis of its stylistic precision or the emotional response it excites; it must be judged on its truth.[28]

44. **Foulkes, A. P.** *The Reluctant Pessimist, A Study of Franz Kafka*. The Hague: Mouton. 1967. Pp. 107-11.

Gregor Samsa is a forerunner of the hunger artist, isolated from the world and dying of starvation. Like Georg Bendemann of "The Judgment," he lacks life force, but this condition may be a truthful and appropriate one with respect to the nature of physical life. The main theme of *The Metamorphosis* is Gregor's attempt to live without his false façade. "The only course Samsa finds still open to him, however, merely confirms what his initial transformation had suggested: he was unfit for life." Gregor's second, more gradual transformation is to discover his positive distaste for life, his desire for death. He grows to detest contact with his family. Foulkes quotes Kafka's diary entry for April 8, 1912: "The metaphysical urge is only the urge toward death" and terms this "an absolute longing for death which has little to do with suicide as a way out of a specific unhappy situation."[29] The conclusion of *The Metamorphosis* links Gregor's longing for a truly nourishing food with his death, accompanied by the dawn breaking outside his window. From the time he receives his wound until his death Gregor seems to achieve an ultimate insight into life and death.

45. **Fraiberg, Selma**. "Kafka and the Dream." *Partisan Review*, XXXIII (Winter 1956), 47-69. Reprinted in *Art and Psychoanalysis*, ed. by William Phillips. New York: Criterion Books, 1957. Pp. 21-53.

Fraiberg cites the exchange between Kafka and Janouch–J.: "*The Metamorphosis* is a terrible dream, a terrible conception"; K.: "The dream reveals the reality, while conception lags behind That is the horror of life–the terror of art" (J 35). This confirms Fraiberg's view that Kafka is a poet of inner experience; the notebooks also reveal that a dream, a fantasy, or a piece of imagery becomes the starting point for a sketch or a story.[30] The incidents of Kafka's fiction were not conceived as allegories for his age. If they amount to satire or social caricature, it is because the dream is in itself a caricature of life–in a sense, allegory.

The events of Kafka's fiction cannot be grasped as "Freudian symbols" with determinate significance, as **Neider** maintains; psychoanalysis does not know any exact formula for dream interpretation. Even so-called universal Freudian symbols possess various determinants. Kafka was affected only by the highly personal dream and not by the universal dream symbol.

The texts of Kafka's dreams reveal a visually precise intimacy; the danger of such intimacy is the loss of connection to "the other world." "Kafka's writing was the bridge, the connection between the two worlds; it was the strongest of the bonds which united him with the real world" (*Partisan*, 50). Kafka establishes a human fellowship in his writings through the fraternity of the dream. His life was a tragedy of broken communication with "the other world"; but through the private dream his work creates a world of collective memory in which all men can share. The tension between the two intents of his fiction–between the story which is concerned with communicating, and the manifest dream which conceals and disguises its meaning–always excites interpretation.

Kafka's explicit and objective style is the means by which the dream or delusion obtains conviction in his hands. The uncanniness in Gregor Samsa's metamorphosis, say, is a property not of the metamorphosis, the unconscious experience, but of the ego, represented in Kafka's art by his prose style, sustaining logic and belief. The language which adopts the principles of unconscious mental processes cannot achieve the effect of the uncanny or cause the reader to experience the dreamlike narrative as a dream. Kafka's fiction departs from the fairy tale because in the latter the animistic character of the events departs from reality, and there can be no experience of uncanniness. Kafka's fiction does not require a *willing* suspension of disbelief.

Kafka erases the boundaries between reality and the dream. Kafka's dream technique suspends the "as if" character of the metaphor; it is not as if Gregor were a bug: he is a bug.

The following objections should be stated:

Adorno stresses that Kafka's metamorphoses, unions, trials are never depicted as interior events. The kinship between Kafka and Freud, the recorder of real traumas, is greater than Fraiberg recognizes.

The social-critical character of Kafka's fictions is not an invariable dimension of the dream which is their starting point; it emerges through poetic elaboration of this starting point.

In Fraiberg's view, Kafka takes the dream at once as the model for poetic composition and as a representation of unconcious experience. Few would now accept a view of Kafka's fiction as representative, as mimetic; Kafka's fiction constitutes experience which could afterward be used to structure another, an "unconscious" experience.[31]

Fraiberg rigidly pursues the psychoanalytical approach; she sees Kafka's literary intent as aiming to discharge through repetition the painful effects of memory. But this therapy does not work, writes Fraiberg, because the affects accompanying the image remain repressed. "Only in this way could he confront his specters without dread" (*Partisan*, 66). Fraiberg instances as such a detached scene, "The Whippers," in *The Trial*, but this scene is in fact full of terror (see **Adorno**, *Prismen*, 314). Kafka solicits anxiety.

The critic recognizes the abstract character of Kafka's figures but concludes that "they are human abstractions . . . exactly as dream people are." But surely the "abstract" character of Gregor Samsa and Josef K. and of their predicaments is at least in part that of genuine philosophical generality.

It is dubious in the extreme to claim that we cannot understand Kafka the writer without understanding Kafka the neurotic. Fraiberg quotes Kafka's alleged remark: "Art is for the artist an affliction through which he frees himself for a new affliction"; yet this does not support her claim that for Kafka "disease and art were united in a kind of morbid love so that neither could set the other free" and that Kafka attempted to *repeat* his neurotic suffering in his art.

One may call the representative of Kafka's ego in his work his objective narrative style; then how is it possible to conclude that "in Kafka's stories . . . the ego is submissive"?

46. Freedman, Ralph. "Kafka's Obscurity: The Illusion of Logic in Narrative." *Modern Fiction Studies*, VIII (Spring 1962), 61-74.

Kafka's heroes are in pursuit of self-consciousness as of a minotaur in the labyrinth of the modern world. Kafka's obscurity reflects the intimate character of this pursuit, the relation of the self to the world. Kafka's worlds are not exact allegories or coherent symbolic systems; neither are they objective depictions of the subconscious. His is an essentially realistic art into which is introduced a degree of significant distortion. This distortion conveys the absurd character of the struggle of the self to come to terms with the objects which condition it; but these objects are real, and the mind's engagement with them is real. The distortion is a deliberate device to profile the self in its typical activity of coping with the world.

Kafka's art has an important base in naturalism, which makes allowances for distortion, since investigations of reality are often slanted toward preconceived results. And naturalistic too is "Kafka's concern with the self's insignificance before a world of overwhelming, extra-personal forces" (63). Kafka's art shares with Expressionism the use of "distortion or stylization to reveal the essential character . . . of an object or world" (64). The expressionist hero is detached from time, place, and milieu, and his universe is reconstituted as a vision of reality. In Kafka, however, the energy which goes to free the object from its external appearances does not redound to the self of the protagonist; rather, he is eventually dissolved into his world in the course of his effort to clarify it. To sum up: Kafka represents a reality independent of the self, and distorts this reality so as to provoke the self into disclosing its true relations.

More precisely: The principle of Kafka's fiction is a distortion, a change, deliberately introduced into the world. This change generates consequences in a rigorously logical manner. The world thus transformed is confronted by a self which seeks to understand its antagonist. The metamorphosed world is, for the self, a problem to be solved. It proceeds by trials, the effects of which it investigates; the hero puts "to the test . . . his own capacity for understanding" (65). Each such trial, however, generates a baffling array of new and impenetrable relations. These relations–paradoxes, riddles–extend throughout the entire scope of human life.

This principle is exactly exemplified in *The Metamorphosis*. A distortion is introduced into the world of the Samsas by Gregor's metamorphosis; the story plots the changes generated in the hero and his world. These changes in the hero occur at first in response to a cognitive crisis: "Kafka's way of exploring the paradoxes Gregor confronts is therefore at first epistemological; that is, it is concerned with different ways of knowing reality, of exploring the shifting relations between self and world. From Gregor's point of view, the tragedy of 'The Metamorphosis' consists in the self's gradual reduction to its most vital center–its self-consciousness. In two stages–a more superficial change in spatial relations and a more central change in the consciousness of time–Gregor is finally reduced to a mere speck of self-awareness which is ultimately extinguished" (65-66).

At the outset Gregor's essential self appears to be unchanged, though his physical perspectives, mainly his perceptions of space, are changed. Then the transformations that afflict him begin to affect him more deeply. His voice degenerates into an animal squeak. His room and furniture oppress him; he prefers airlessness and dirt. This degradation is conditioned by the response of the family to his metamorphosis.

The bombardment with apples brings about a new relation between Gregor's self and his world. "The wound eats more and more deeply towards the center of his self, his human consciousness and memory" (66). At the end of the story, Gregor's self-consciousness fades and with it his sense of time.

The changes that take place in the world, paralleling Gregor's metamorphosis, are no less radical. The appearance of the three roomers typifies the oppressive intrusion of an alien principle. The world of the family is distorted, and as long as Gregor remains alive, this distortion is irrevocable.

A crucial feature of the metamorphosis is that it acts to preserve in Gregor a condition which the world had already exacted of him. As a salesman Gregor had suffered the constraints of an insect. The world continues to require that Gregor be an insect, as he is successively rejected by boss, father, mother, and sister. Gregor's condition at the close—his reduction to a "mere" self—emerges as "an *aspired* condition. He had been imprisoned in his animal existence which had been implied by his human life, yet freed from intolerable burdens, including the tyranny of time. In his death likewise he is both extinguished and set free" (67).

Gregor's life, under successive constriction, has become a burden to himself; his death liberates him from this bondage. Thus successive constriction and liberation mark the destiny of both Gregor and his family. Kafka's binocular vision focuses simultaneously on the self and its world. The liberation of the family at the close is a figure for the inexpressible liberation the hero has sought. "Grete's yawn of freedom neatly ties the story to the transformation of the beginning" (67). But in so doing it also creates a zero point of unintelligibility, because to this created and dislocated fictional world "contradictory solutions, like constriction and freedom, obliteration and awareness of existence, equally apply" (67).

47-A. Friedman, Norman. "Kafka's *Metamorphosis*: A Literal Reading." *Approach*, XLIX (Fall 1963), 26-34.

Friedman sets up a Freudian psychological reading of the metamorphosis identical with **Sokel** (105-A). Friedman then rejects this interpretation on the grounds that it is more suited to an analyst's couch than to the "artistic" intentions of the story. The interpretation that Friedman proposes in its place is a schematic version of the reading which appears in his later essay on *The Metamorphosis* (47-B).

47-B. Friedman, Norman. "The Struggle of Vermin: Parasitism and Family Love in Kafka's *Metamorphosis.*" *Ball State University Forum*, IX, No. 1, 23-32.

The circumstances of Kafka's life define the theme of his work: guilt. Kafka's relation to his father is the primary event in his life, the source of the feelings of inadequacy which distorted his soul. He was haunted throughout his life by the shame of never being able to measure up to the standard of manhood set by his father. "The attempt to come to terms with this shame . . . governed the entire course of his career. . . . [Though] he had intelligence enough to see that what was torturing him was completely senseless and irrational, yet he still could not free himself of it" (23).

Kafka's heroes are the inventions of Kafka's neurosis. "Kafka sees what is happening to the inner reality of our world—he sees the threats developing beneath the surface of our lives because they are closer to the surface of his life than of ours—and by means of the special catastrophes of fantasy brings them vividly to light" (26).

Kafka's "subtle and ironic attitude was a form of courage" (26). He sees many sides, "and in *The Metamorphosis*, for example, he is as aware of the need for family love as he is of its dangers" (26). The problem in this story is one of reconciling the need for society and the need for autonomy; the solution lies in a man's having the courage "to cast off a love which has enslaved him, or which he is using in order to enslave himself" (26).

The story has an hourglass pattern: until the metamorphosis the family members have been Gregor's parasites and as a consequence have fallen into psychosomatic torpor. After the event Gregor is reduced to the hebetude of a vermin, but the family recovers its vitality and prospects.

The Metamorphosis is fundamentally about family love and the dangers of dependency in this situation. The danger for the dependent person is weakness; for the stronger one, entrapment as a consequence of his responsibility. Before the metamorphosis, the family has grown stupid and Gregor has ceased to live a life of his own. Afterward it is the family which finds itself enslaved to the responsibility of caring for Gregor. The others are not freed until he dies.

Kafka scrutinizes and criticizes the threat to growth in a love in which there is dependency. To be dependent on love is to be a parasite, to inflict death in life on oneself and on the being one feeds on. Thus the misfortune of the metamorphosis is finally a happy one, for it dissolves a crippling love. "But it is a tragic redemption. Gregor still has a few human feelings left at the end, and we feel that his sacrifice is a cruel price to pay for his family's welfare" (29). Yet there were no alternatives. As provider or as vermin Gregor was scarcely alive, and until his death his family was condemned to moral degradation.

The specific way in which Kafka transforms his personal situation in *The Metamorphosis* is to represent—at least at first—the father as weak and the son as strong. "This reversal of roles makes the issue more universal and less personal . . . by showing that the dependency problem works both ways" (29). But Kafka's aesthetic transmutation of his situation functions as if to rob him of the power for practical change: he was never able to reject his father as in fact Gregor's father rejects Gregor. The crux is that Kafka envisions himself, and not his father, as a vermin.

Kafka's personal tragedy is that, although he could see the path to his freedom, he could not take it. "Although he wanted desperately to free himself from his dependency on his father, he could not surrender the comfort of his love for his father, a love which enslaved because it enabled him, in a twisted and neurotic way, to avoid self-reproach for his inadequacies of which he was sometimes too exquisitely aware and on whose bitter fruit he had to feed in order to live at all" (30). By loving his father, by endowing his father's judgment with immense importance, and thus by convicting himself of defeat in advance, Kafka could safely exempt himself from the task of succeeding in his own eyes. And yet the great art he made out of his predicament is, paradoxically, his success, although this was not a success he could permit himself to enjoy: thus he requested that his manuscripts be burned.

The point of *The Metamorphosis* is, finally, this: "Caring, which enables you to nourish your feelings of inadequacy instead of seeing that the other's love may be at fault, may be a cover-up for your fear of failure, for it allows you covertly to make the person you love responsible for your own inadequacies" (30-31). It is as if Gregor, perceiving this, chose unconsciously to be transformed into a repulsive vermin so as to free his family from their dependent love—their parasitism.

48. Gaillard, J. M. "Une Mythologie du désespoir: *La Métamorphose* de Franz Kafka." *Helvetia*, Bern (June 1961), 151-58.

Not seen.

49. Gibian, George. "Dichtung und Wahrheit: Three Versions of Reality in Franz Kafka." *German Quarterly*, XXX (Jan. 1957), 20-31.

The apparent reasonableness of the world of *The Metamorphosis* clashes with the basic absurdity of the situation, parodies our cautious everyday concerns, and profiles the horror of the metamorphosis. We have "a protracted process of gradual dying, a mixture of murder and suicide through lack of will to live." The interaction between father and son is expressed parabolically—for example, through such incidental parables as that of the lodgers, "who seem to be parasites established in the family through Gregor's fault and of whom the father can rid the family as soon as Gregor dies" (29).

The elements of fantasy, nightmare, and fear are strong in *The Metamorphosis*. "The horror of waking up transformed into an insect brings in its train all our subconscious fears of transformation (discussed among others in Freud's essay on *The Uncanny*)" (29). The world of *The Metamorphosis* is not that of everyday reality, since the failure of the family to question Gregor's metamorphosis is incongruous. The narrative suggests "that our own accepted world may be as unreal as that of the Samsas, and that painstaking reasonableness . . . may be as misplaced and vain as Gregor's and his family's. . . . *The Metamor-*

phosis moves from a beginning which ought to be a renewal of life (the awakening in the morning), but actually is moribund and catastrophic, to a conclusion which brings the death of the protagonist, accompanied by the promise of an improved life for the survivors" (30).[32] From Gregor's point of view, the development of the piece is a steady decline leading to extinction.[33] Through the eyes of the family, the event is a long struggle to contain and eliminate Gregor and the abuses he has brought about—the lodgers, the cleaning woman's attitude. This struggle is in the end successful.

The Metamorphosis has a much broader parabolic meaning than "The Judgment." "Some of the situations to which it can be taken to refer are: man and the state; man and his subconscious feelings of guilt and inadequacy in general; totemistic fears of metamorphosis; the Jew in a Gentile society; man and grace; or man and God. The mood of the story is precise, but the references made by it parabolically are multiple" (30-31).

50. Goldstein, Bluma. "The Wound in Stories by Kafka," *Germanic Review*, XLI (May 1966), 206-14.

The wound in Kafka's work symbolizes a rupture in existence. With the exception of the wounds in "A Report to the Academy" and "Prometheus," the wounds in Kafka's stories do not heal. Gregor Samsa's open wound is a highly significant element in *The Metamorphosis*.

Here, "the open wound . . . allows or perhaps even persuades the inflicted person to become introspective, to seek within himself that comprehension which could conceivably establish his *raison d'être*. On the other hand, precisely this possibility seems to restrict the person involved, isolating him from his environment, and . . . extinguishes the individual" (207). Gregor and the protagonist of *In the Penal Colony* die "because there is no way or opportunity for them to live out . . . their insight in the world around them" (207). The wound promises hope, a new beginning; but it is in fact that which the protagonist dies of.

The Metamorphosis is saturated with pain and physical suffering. Gregor's emotional predicament is bound up with the torments of his body. His pain is concentrated, at the conclusions of the first and second parts, in the blows which the father deals his defenseless son.

In the first section a link is established between the pain which Gregor suffers from having to endure an insect's body and "the injuries to the psyche which men suffer in their daily living" (208). The wounds Gregor receives in the first part hobble him and confine him and in this way repeat and intensify the restrictive effect of the metamorphosis. Gregor's loss of mobility is particularly grievous when we remember that movement is one of the few ways left to him to express himself. After the metamorphosis Gregor's self-consciousness remains substantially what it was before the change; his mind is rigid; yet occasional insights suggest a deepening change of sensibility. This movement toward a radical transformation of consciousness is to some extent realized after Gregor has been mortally injured at the close of Part II. He stops being obsessively concerned with the family's well-being at the cost of his own development. He can begin to express his resentment of the family and demand that it "treat him in a manner becoming a human being. . . . The change in Gregor is not merely an apparent . . . one. There are indications throughout the third part and especially in his response to the music played by his sister that his orientation has slowly and even painfully turned away from the outside world toward himself, his own feelings, his private reactions" (211). It is true that his response to the music mingles aesthetic and sexual intentions; these responses are nevertheless deeply felt, deeply personal. This moment is the first time that Gregor has ventured to express his own being. He speaks inwardly from the core of his existence.

Gregor's authentic moment is without consequences for life. The others will not allow him to enter their world. Neither can he hope any longer to live apart from the others in a condition of insight, for he is dying of the wound in his back.

Motif, image, and action throughout *The Metamorphosis* confirm the link between Gregor's mortal wound and his growing inwardness. It is the wound, for example, which moves the family to treat Gregor more humanely. They open the door to the living room: this allows him to hear his sister's violin and to attempt to express in their world of empirical concerns the self-insight which this experience provokes. The break in being, inhibiting this unity, is sharply defined in the image of the two rooms: "the family, sitting . . . apathetically in their bright living room, is always concerned with its economic and social situation; Gregor—badly crippled, almost blind, suffering intense pain, covered with dust and garbage, that is, as cut off from the outside world as is, outside of death, possible—lies silently in the darkness of his own room and his own self" (212). Gregor comes into self-consciousness at the cost of sacrificing the common world, though he never chose to make this sacrifice.

The metamorphosis thus makes manifest the division between the solitary self and the world of everyday concerns; but Gregor did not become conscious of this division until he suffered the fatal wound. For Gregor Samsa the experience of self-consciousness is just potent enough to destroy him precisely at the moment when he enters into the enjoyment of his own being. The description of Gregor's death conveys his genuine contentment, which he extends with simplicity and directness to his family.

51. **Goodman, Paul.** "Preface." In *The Metamorphosis*, trans. by A. L. Lloyd. New York: Vanguard Press, 1946. Pp. 5-8.

The bug Gregor behaves in all the ways in which men have ever conceived of animals as behaving: he acts like a man, like a bug in a situation full of human interest, and simply like a bug. That is because Kafka accomplishes in Gregor a totemic identification of man and beast. Men symbolically project into the beast their own unconscious conflicts, centering on destructive and devouring impulses; "but, literally, the beast is in his own person a true friend and communicant, another self." Indeed, he is a better self, for the bug Gregor responds to music with an elation that Kafka himself did not experience. In general the animal for Kafka means "escape from his ego into nature, freedom and community."[34] Kafka's projection of a beast is of a man acting out some animal identity within himself. Kafka frees himself in presenting the bug just as he is, for this is a creature "closer to guiltless nature" and released "from moral delusions and conventional defenses."

1. Goodman's assertion that in Gregor Samsa man and animal are identified is questionable. Other critics–such as **Falk** and **Tauber**–have stressed the antinomy of the two orders preserved within the identification. An assertion of simple identification blurs the distinction between Gregor's involuntary animal-like acts and other acts of his which are bestial.

2. **Neider**, 85-A (181) objects to Goodman's equation of animal and totem. The bug is Kafka, says **Neider**, and Freud has always conceived the totem as a father symbol. "In mythical symbolism children are represented by vermin." Furthermore, the notion of the bug fits Kafka's sense of his worthlessness before his father. The original sense of the totem is its double taboo against parricide and incest.

3. Gregor, writes Goodman, responds to music with an elation Kafka did not experience. Let us stay with the text. Gregor responds to music with an elation Gregor did not formerly experience. Before his metamorphosis he had no liking for music. Yet it is surely moot to assert that it is the bug in Gregor that "is laid open to this language of living feeling." Gregor's responsiveness does not arise immediately from his metamorphosis. It is itself a dialectical response to his reaching the low point of his abasement–that is, becoming most a bug.

4. Goodman writes that Kafka's animals are projections of man's animal identity. Yet at another moment when he is almost entirely a bug, Gregor is declared to be "absent-minded." In Kafka's earlier works–in the story fragment beginning " 'You,' I said . . . ," noted in his *Diaries* for July 19, 1910, and in "Description of a Struggle"–the moment of forgetfulness signifies a moment of greatest danger to the self, in which it betrays itself or in which the whole world vanishes. To argue that Gregor imitates the real animal substratum in man is to miss the moral terms in which, in *The Metamorphosis*, the struggle between animal consciousness and bug consciousness is couched. Gregor is most a bug when he is least aware that he is one. Being a bug is represented as a certain kind of consciousness, a privative mode of remembering–namely, forgetting. In a word, Gregor's struggle is not between some animal essence in man and his human essence; the struggle is between inauthentic and authentic self-consciousness. Thus the projection of the bug is very much a literary and philosophical strategy, an "alienation effect," designed to present a human predicament more sparely and vividly.

5. In describing the bug as a creature "closer to guiltless nature," Goodman overlooks the crucial fact that this animal is a monster; and if to create it is to liberate deep unconscious

impulses, it is by the same token to disparage and punish these impulses.

52. **Greenberg, Martin**. "Kafka's 'Metamorphosis' and Modern Spirituality." *Tri-Quarterly* (Winter 1966), 5-20. Reprinted with minor variations as "Gregor Samsa and Modern Spirituality." In *The Terror of Art: Kafka and Modern Literature*. New York: Basic Books, 1968. Pp. 69-91.

"The first sentence of *The Metamorphosis* announces Gregor Samsa's death and the rest of the story is his slow dying" (70). This death is not to be taken only literally, for what Gregor Samsa struggles against is the knowledge of his death in life. Unlike the struggle in Tolstoy's story, "The Death of Ivan Ilyich," Gregor Samsa's struggle is without redemption.

The reality to which Gregor awakens is the truth of his life—not his life as his ordinary consciousness has disclosed it to him all along, but the nightmare of truth: he is a vermin, cast out of the human circle. Try as he will, he cannot put off the change: "the human self whose claims he always postponed . . . has declared itself negatively by changing him from a human being into an insect" (*Terror*, 72). His past has been hopelessly arid, without love or decision or the expression of genuine feeling. He has lived a life of self-deception and self-denial; his relations to his family have been ones of deception and denial; and now all ends in horror.

The relation of Gregor to his family is marked by a fundamental incompatibility, that "between sickliness and parasitism on the one hand and vigor and independence on the other, between death and life" (*Terror*, 76). As Gregor wanes, his family thrives. But it is not his father and the rest of the family who have pronounced a judgment on Gregor; Gregor stands self-condemned as one who even before his metamorphosis has already locked himself inside his room. He is not helped by his mother, in whom shame and horror dissipate compassion and who with a terrible silence acquiesces in the death of her son.

"Gregor breaks out of his room the first time hoping that his transformation will turn out to be 'nonsense'; the second time, in the course of defending at least his hope of returning to his 'human past.' His third eruption has quite a different aim" (*Terror*, 78). It corresponds to his perception of having been finally cast out from the human circle. In grasping, now, the truth of his life as death in life, stemming from his banishment and self-banishment, he begins to perceive a positive possibility. He is hungry for a nourishment which could exist for him only in this outcast state. He is no longer prompted by the delusion of returning to his former place in the community. The possibility of relief can be approached only through solitude. This possibility manifests itself to him as music (he was formerly indifferent to music). Yet this becomes a possibility he betrays in refusing to recognize that his hunger is a sign of his spiritual development and not of his bestialization. An incipient reversal fails to take place.

Gregor dies, in the end, self-condemned. He dies without redemption, starving for the unknown spiritual nourishment he cannot live without.

Gregor's point of view pervades the narration of the events following his death—that unregenerate point of view which fails to grasp the sense of the metamorphosis as the moral condemnation of his family. In the end, mere vulgar life condemns the sick and the dead. Gregor Samsa, drawn once by the promise of a healing knowledge, cannot penetrate this mystery—"and he surrenders to the impossibility of living" (*Terror*, 88).

53. **Hasselblatt, Dieter**. *Zauber und Logik. Eine Kafka Studie*. Cologne: Verlag Wissenschaft und Politik, 1964. Pp. 192-205.

In this reading of *The Metamorphosis* only the text itself is taken into account, and everything extraneous, everything obtained through biography or depth psychology, is left aside. "Nowhere for the purpose of understanding shall we attempt to substitute for a fictional being (as for example for Gregor Samsa after the metamorphosis) some entity taken from another system of meanings. Our reading may only stress what is already there in the text. Once the analysis has been accomplished, it must prove superfluous" (192-93).

The Metamorphosis takes three sections (I, II, III), each around twenty pages long, to recount the confrontation of ordinary life with the extraordinary. The story is about the impossibility that the extraordinary can be maintained. With the metamorphosis—something unreal—an autonomous linguistic and poetic world is constituted. "Words like '*unruhig*' ['unsettling'], '*ungeheuer*' ['unnatural,' 'monstrous'], and '*Ungeziefer*' ['vermin,' 'bug'] have already attuned the first sentence of the text to the '*Un*.' This '*Un*,' which does more than merely negate, which can also be heard as an overtone in the '*ver*' ['trans'] of '*verwandelt*' ['transformed,' 'changed'], sets the tone of the entire story. *Unglück* [disaster], *Ungeheures* [the monstrous], indeed *Ungeheuerliches* [the atrocious], *Unfassbares* [the inconceivable], *Ungewohntes* [the unconventional], *Ungewöhnliches* [the unusual], and *Unordentliches* [the disorderly] have in some unintelligible way irrupted into the domain of the intelligible, *Geheure* [the normal], *Fassbare* [the conceivable], *Gewohnte* [the conventional], and *Geordnete* [the orderly]. The irruption of the unusual into the usual is accommodated through a corresponding model or symbolic form; and through the transformation of a human being into a bug, the monstrous is lodged in the sphere of the usual—the petty bourgeois family" (193). After Gregor Samsa's first reflection, quite as if Kafka knew from which quarter misinterpretation was most likely, Kafka declares—it is the first possible place for it—"It was no dream." This cannot be ignored; and nothing justifies diminishing the unusual to the innocuous level of the dreamlike.[35] In the next five paragraphs the metamorphosed hero's interior monologues lament and verify his unintelligible predicament. What has happened is genuinely inconceivable, but it does not seem inconceivable to the victim; it is at most awkward. "In the further course of the text these two ways of understanding the inconceivable will repeatedly arise. From the standpoint of the conventional, the ordinary, and the everyday, the inconceivable is a scandal, something incomprehensible, indeed a frankly undeserved disaster, a 'metaphysical' doom; from the standpoint of the victim himself, it seems something awkward, annoying, unpleasant, a 'metaphysical' breakdown" (194).

The rest of Section I recounts the confrontation of the ordinary, everyday milieu with the inconceivable. If it seemed awkward to the metamorphosed hero, it seems unconventional to the others immediately around him.[36] As Gregor Samsa attempts to reply to his mother's mild surprise, he is terrified by the sound of his own voice. What is extraordinary cannot be communicated to the ordinary. The hero's eagerness "to see how today's fantasy would gradually fade away" describes the attempt to explain away the extraordinary by the plausible. He is not successful. It is out of the question for him to call for help from the everyday; and so the monstrous continues to appear to the victim as "distress" *(Not).* Genuine distress would require help; but since he feels that help would not be appropriate, his condition cannot be one of distress. It is significant that all through *The Metamorphosis* Kafka avoids giving Gregor Samsa any name other than the conventional Gregor Samsa (with the exception of the crass name used by the cleaning woman). Thus the point of the story is not to describe some gigantic, grotesque animal–it would be easy then to give it a fantastic animal name–but to configure as a parable "the irruption of the extraordinary into the [domain of the] orderly and the ordinary" (195).

The extraordinary is afterward experienced privatively, as the absence and omission of the conventional and matter of fact.

Thus, Section I has treated the inconceivable, first as something uncomfortable, as an occasion for perplexity and distress, then as an irregularity and a lapse. Gregor's success in opening the door with his jaws allows for an immediate confrontation of the extraordinary with the conventional and its ultimate exclusion from the conventional. Gregor puts the monstrous on view before the everyday; his intention, of course, is to establish that he is not something atrocious. "But when the monstrous and extraordinary leaves its room–the environing space [*Um-Raum*], which is properly its own–it unintentionally makes room [*räumt sich ein*] again for an environing space for itself in the domain of the conventional" (196). His monstrous appearance inspires terror; as the wholly other, it has the effect of astonishing the others and driving them out. Not only in the spatial dimension, but in the temporal dimension as well, the monstrous undoes everything that had been well provided for. With the departure of the manager, the future is put wholly into question. The monstrous spells sheer terror to the conventional and the everyday and is expelled and driven back into its own room. The exclusive prerogative claimed by the extraordinary from the domain of the conventional and the everyday is answered with its being excluded and incarcerated in a domain for itself in which it is meant to remain.

Section II of *The Metamorphosis* describes the way in which the inconceivable appears to the everyday; its theme is the effort to take care of the monstrous. The sister's attempts to bring about an acclimatization are unsuitable; Gregor suffers shame; this shame corresponds to the family's sense of the painfulness of the situation. Gregor's shame arises from the impossibility of his identifying himself with his atrocious condition; the family's embarrassment arises from its continuing to ascribe the metamorphosis to a sort of unseemliness on Gregor's part. "Every attempt to acclimatize the extraordinary must fail" (198). The general cluster of problems is that of coming to an arrangement with the inconceivable; its inevitable consequence is the rearrangement of Gregor's room. The irruption of the family, however, into Gregor's living-space is followed antithetically by his outbreak into the family's dwelling. At the close of the second section the father–chief exponent of the domain of the conventional and the everyday–attempts not only to exclude the extraordinary but to annihilate it as well.

"The third phase (Section III) in the altercation with the inconceivable is the decision at least to tolerate it. The failure of the effort to maintain it is followed by sheer endurance" (199). The family's tolerance, however, soon passes into inattentiveness. The domain of the ordinary has to struggle to keep itself intact. The consequence of diverting its energy into maintaining the extraordinary leads to a sense of the misfortune of being struck by the extraordinary.

Hence the appearance of the cleaning woman who addresses the metamorphosed creature by names–names which it promptly resists. "Names which are translated and carried over from the domain of familiar experience to the unfamiliar are unable to designate the latter; here their evocative and characterizing power gives out" (200). The three roomers in their useful conventionality are housed, constituting a counterpart to the useless, extraordinary being who cannot be housed; they are fed, while he starves. The rented rooms are made livable at the expense of the living space of the extraordinary creature. The inconceivable is degraded into something inconsiderable. The violin music played by the sister suggests Gregor's true sustenance and habitation. "Elsewhere in Kafka music also fulfills the function of the authentic, the most appropriate, and also the barely achievable and unattainable . . . . In *The Metamorphosis* it takes over the function of the 'unknown nourishment' as well" (201). Of course Kafka does not actually speak of music in *The Metamorphosis,* but of "playing." Playing stands in unmistakable contrast to the grudging labor of taking care. "Has not Kafka wanted to say here, in passing, that the inconceivable can remain itself and be maintained as itself only through play?" (201). In the end, the inconceivable dies of a want of sustenance. The triumph of the ordinary succeeds the annihilation of all traces of the extraordinary.

"*The Metamorphosis* is a working out, in model form, of the structure of relations between the inconceivable and the everyday world as it is expounded in Kafka's piece 'On Parables.' The inconceivable is the wholly other; from the standpoint of the everyday, it is the un-usual, the un-comfortable, and finally the un-profitable" (203). These two dimensions are irreconcilable. The story is a progressive reflection on its origin: irruption of the extraordinary into the ordinary. The atrocious cannot sustain itself if it is not sustained by others. "And so, after the initial shock, deformity loses its atrociousness and is taken care of as something unusual with the aim of acclimatization, then despised as something useless and unprofitable, until finally the deformity–unsightly, insignificant, stripped of being, and bare of all atrociousness–is, as 'stuff,' removed like trash from the domain of the everyday" (204). The story successively bares the impossibility of sustaining the monster. The extraordinary is destroyed by the ordinary: "Kafka projects here in the model of an atrocious metamorphosis a parable of the narrow-minded deafness of the everyday and the hopeless homelessness of the extraordinary" (204).[37]

54. Hawkins, Desmond A. "Fiction Chronicle." *Criterion,* XVIII (1938), 506-08.

The meaning of Kafka's fiction is "all possible meanings which can be grouped within a single mood." What is peculiarly horrible about *The Metamorphosis* is the fact that Gregor, as a bug, remains man-sized.[38] But the horror can be endured because it is touched with "unreality."

The Metamorphosis should be grasped as the drama of all "spiritually alien men who unwittingly destroy the reassurances of use and conformity and custom." It does not matter if Gregor is really a lunatic who has the delusion that he is a bug; or the victim of a repulsive disease; or some other sort of gross misfit. The translation of this predicament into the objective symbols of fantasy avoids sentimentality, reducing and purifying the drama. Instead of producing a man "who excites a mood of *strangeness*," Kafka presents this strangeness as a material fact. But this is the only strangeness in the piece; everything follows the initial event with commonplace logic, and it is this that is truly terrible. Now the sense of the piece grows into the general horror "of any loss of one's identity in a conventional world of limited probabilities. Fundamentally it is the haunting, brooding fear of the *déraciné*, the unrecognized, the stranger, the one ignorant of loyal passwords, the inarticulate, the alien, the outcast, the lost man with no antecedents, man in the void, the man without a tribe."

55. Hecht, M. B. "Uncanniness, Yearning and Franz Kafka's Works." *Imago* (April 1952), 45-55.

"In the short stories animistic thinking processes appear . . . directly; [viz.] . . . dehumanization of the human in 'Metamorphosis.' " Archaic ideas are confirmed; Freud's definition of the uncanny is satisfied; and the sentiment of the uncanny is produced.

56. Heller, Erich. "Einleitung." In *Franz Kafka: Briefe an Felice*, ed. by Erich Heller and Jürgen Born. Frankfurt am Main: S. Fischer, 1967. Pp. 11, 24-25.

The Metamorphosis was one of the few works which Kafka explicitly asked Max Brod not to burn after Kafka's death.

The work is illuminated by a sentence from Kafka's letter to Felice Bauer: "Not to write was already to be lying on the floor, deserving to be swept out" (F 65). (See p. 24.)

57. Henel, Ingeborg. "Die Deutbarkeit von Kafkas Werken." *Zeitschrift für deutsche Philologie*, 86, no. 2, 250-66.

According to Henel, **Beissner**'s view that the world of *The Metamorphosis* is a delusion appears to come from a misunderstanding of Kafka's famous diary entry for August 6, 1914. The entry reads: "The sense for the representation of my dreamlike inner life has pushed everything else to one side." This does not mean that Kafka's art consists of immediate reproductions of Kafka's dreams; the passage means only that the writer in Kafka has flourished at the expense of the practical man in him.

Beissner's view of *The Metamorphosis* is contradictory; on the one hand the metamorphosis is supposed to be a delusion of the sick hero;[39] having only subjective reality, it must be represented from the standpoint of the hero if the reader is to believe it. On the other hand, **Beissner** is not convinced of the reality of the metamorphosis. It is a fact that Kafka's style steadily becomes more objective, yet, for **Beissner**, in Henel's words, "the subjective character of what is narrated and the subjective character of the perspective appear to go together" (253).

Beissner is wrong to speak of the identification of author and hero in Kafka's work and consequently of the identification of reader and hero. If Kafka were concerned with producing an identification of narrator and hero, he would have had to write in the first person.

But Kafka did not attempt to convert readers into heroes. The reader must make up his mind about the contradictory facts and inferences put before him. "In *The Metamorphosis* Kafka aims to represent a reality—the parasitical nature which Gregor conceals beneath his solicitude—and not a delusion" (254). Kafka uses the concrete image of the bug. He keeps clear of subjectivizing, psychologizing tactics. The subject of Kafka's works is not the hero's psyche: the relation that exists between author and hero is one of perspectival congruence, not sheer identity. As a consequence, the reader is not meant to identify himself with the hero.

58. **Hermsdorf, Klaus**. "Künstler und Kunst bei Franz Kafka." In *Franz Kafka aus Prager Sicht, 1963.* Prague: Verlag der Tschechoslowakischen Akademie der Wissenschaften, 1963. P. 97.

"Gregor Samsa, the metamorphosed vermin (1912), had still believed that he could find in art the 'unknown nourishment he longed for.' . . . Ten years later the artist is described [by Kafka] as one who will *never* discover his nourishment, as 'the greatest *hunger* artist of all times.' "

59. **Heselhaus, Clemens**. "Kafkas Erzählformen." *Deutsche Vierteljahrszeitschrift für Literaturwissenschaft und Geistesgeschichte,* III (1952), 353-76.

Kafka's stories fuse various dimensions: a naturalistic side; an element of fantasy and spookiness, which belongs to the atmosphere of "Bohemian" literature and visual art; the narrative forms of parable and legend from the Jewish tradition. It is possible to suppose that these elements are brought into unity by the poetic intent to "raise the world into the pure, the true, and the immutable" (DII 187).

On the basis of "A Country Doctor," Heselhaus develops the form of the *Antimärchen* (anti-fairy-tale). An extraordinary event breaks into the ordinary world, tearing it apart, endangering it; the ordinary world is transformed, derailed. This dream world of extraordinary events has a higher meaning; but the hero, who places the meaning of life in his way of life, cannot succeed in bringing into harmony with his way of life the extraordinary events which befall him. The reflective hero of the *Antimärchen* fails to achieve a correct relation to being and to the human world. And the *Antimärchen* reveals that the world cannot be endured without degree and relation.

Thus the meaning of the *Antimärchen* is not an immediate *donnée* but a pointing toward the truth. Its subject is the world as it should not be. The *Antimärchen* introduces a moral dimension in the course of "offending" the expectation of a naive moral; it is "the literary form of offended and disappointed self-consciousness" (357). The ugliness and brutality of Kafka's world represent the painful experience of the distance from the absolute in the tonality of self-destructiveness. The world is unmasked. But the possibility of truth is not disenchanted.

The Metamorphosis is an *Antimärchen:* the encroaching extraordinary element is the metamorphosis. At first the story appears to show only how Gregor Samsa, who still thinks and feels as a man, sinks more and more into the dullness of the brute (the family, which more and more neglects him, is partly responsible). There is no dearth of autobiographical relations: the name Gregor Samsa is to be understood autobiographically; the relation of the metamorphosed son to the father reflects Kafka's own father conflict; there is an allusion to the beginning of a sickness. Again, the story might symbolize someone's falling ill physically or mentally and becoming a burden on his family; Kafka's writing, which put him outside of his mercantile and active family, fits this description. But these autobiographical relations do not touch the core of the piece—its structural element.

Kafka leaves dark the reason for Gregor's metamorphosis as well as the nature of the metamorphosing power. The acceptance of the inexplicable is part of the world of the *Antimärchen*. This mystery is never solved in the story; its solution cannot be our concern. The problem is the metamorphosis itself; the problem exists more for the Samsa family than for Gregor, who after initial reflection comes to terms with it. The metamorphosis is an interpersonal task; as Grete says, how is it "possible for human beings to live with such a creature?" Gregor's own position is that it is impossible for a man to live with such people. The task of cohabitation implies another one. Could Gregor be metamorphosed back out of his insect state? This possibility appears to reside with Grete: Gregor dies only after his sister has abandoned him.

A familiar fairy-tale theme is that of the man transformed into a beast living with human beings. In this, *The Metamorphosis* reveals itself to be an *Antimärchen*, for Gregor's sister does not possess the power to break the enchantment. In her love for music she had the magic wand, but she let it fall; her concerns are the way of all flesh. As an *Antimärchen, The Metamorphosis* is a protest against modern life: it shows this life fulfilling itself but declares it to be garbage and vermin. It is a protest issuing from the absolute.

Can it be countered that the absolute is in fact negated by the degradation of a human being into a bug? As early as Hegel's *Aesthetics* the metamorphoses of antiquity were accounted a degradation of the human person and consequently a punishment. In *The Metamorphosis* the agency of degradation remains dark: either the father has the power of the metamorphosis, or it is a question of self-degradation and self-damnation. In either case, the Kafkan metamorphosis represents a punishment. The final negative overthrow in Kafka's *Antimärchen* takes the form of self-punishment. Projected into a poetic world where man and beast are all God's creatures—a poetic world in which changing shapes are the image of truths—the Kafkan man, Gregor Samsa, is a bug. The charge which Kafka's *Antimärchen* levels against the world is that there are no powers to negate and prevent the moments in which the self and all existence are damned. Yet in Kafka, as in other writers (Augustine, Dante), the poetic degradation of the human is not irreconcilable with the acknowledgment of the absolute. The poetic degradation does not nullify the human spirit; though Gregor Samsa falls more and more into the stultification and sleepiness of the brute, his human consciousness remains.

Thus the Kafkan metamorphosis is different from the metamorphosis of the fairy tale: in it the redemptive magic word is ineffectual. It is also different from the mythic metamorphosis because the process of metamorphosis is not depicted. "The Kafkan metamorphosis is neither that of the fairy tale nor of the myth: it belongs to a theological domain. I would characterize it as a *parabolic metamorphosis*; i.e. as phenomenon, as mere happening, it points beyond itself" (366). In Kafka's narratives the experience of man as a stricken, vulnerable, frail creature becomes "the gateway to the absolute, in that the symbolic character of the language, the imagery, and the narrative procedure—the relatedness of man to something higher, absolute—becomes palpable. The sensuousness and the symbolical character of Kafka's narrative style are indivisible" (366).

1. **Beissner**, 13-B, comments on Heselhaus' essay: "His definition of Kafka's narrative forms as *'Antimärchen'* . . . is not only terminologically clumsy but also methodologically wrong. Kafka's nothing less than 'simple' form cannot very well be related to the simple form of the fairy tale, as André Jolles conceives it; and since Jolles understands something quite definite by the *'Antimärchen'* (p. 242) it ought as a matter of course to be impermissible to apply the same term to a wholly different form (Heselhaus, p. 365f.) . . . .[40] Thus if Heselhaus' formulation should gain currency one would have to speak henceforth in discussion of the *'Antimärchen'* in Jolles' sense and under different circumstances in Heselhaus' sense!

"To say this quite clearly, for Jolles, of course, the *'Antimärchen'* is in respect of its origin, narrative mode, and all its other characteristics (aside from one, that of the unhappy conclusion) also a fairy tale. But does Heselhaus mean to call Kafka a teller of fairy tales?" (42-43).

2. A second, more substantive, critique of Heselhaus' article could also take its bearing from **Beissner**'s *Der Erzähler Franz Kafka*. For Heselhaus the metamorphosis is an interpersonal task. Concerned to show the likeness and difference between this story and the fairy tale, Heselhaus sees the essential meaning of the story in the task it lays on the Samsa family to break Gregor's enchantment through love. Now **Beissner** shows that up until the close, *The Metamorphosis* is narrated from the standpoint of a single subjectivity, Gregor's. This perspective is unique and unitive and has the effect, in **Pfeiffer**'s words, of making Gregor, the main character, dominate everything: "Any attempt to leave out of consideration the perspective which determines the fundamental meaning of the story and to transfer the center of gravity, let us say, to the family, disturbed and disconcerted by Gregor's transformation, amounts to an arbitrary construction" (299). It is difficult to agree with **Beissner**, 13-B, that Kafka's single-minded narration renders Kafka himself "subject and object of the [fictional] representation" (12). Kafka does not maintain perfect congruence between the intentions of the author (the

totality of intentions functioning in the work) and the conscious intentions of the main character. Nonetheless, our essential concern in *The Metamorphosis* is with a self and its predicament—a self basically constituting and reflecting on its own impasse—not with others independent of this self.

3. For **Politzer**, 91-A, Gregor Samsa's redoubtably commonplace character is the telling objection to Heselhaus' description of *The Metamorphosis* as an "anti-fairy-tale." Gregor is neither the enchanted prince nor the outcast pauper. In the metamorphosis "there is no tragic plunge from the noble and the unique. . . . Quite the contrary, the metamorphosis appears consistent and strangely appropriate to Gregor's thoroughly unheroic character. The beast into which this non-hero has been changed remains as nondescript as Gregor was" (80).

Moreover, Kafka never suggests the power which has metamorphosed Gregor. (Indeed, Heselhaus also makes this point.) But for **Politzer**, an anti-fairy-tale requires "this power . . . to appear in order to indicate the means by which it could be either placated or exorcised" (80).

Finally, if *The Metamorphosis*, as an anti-fairy-tale, had presented the world "as it ought not to be," it would also have had to suggest a desirable world order. This cannot be the epilogue of the story, however, because the health regained by the Samsas is merely physical; this conclusion seemed unsatisfactory to Kafka and it seems unsatisfactory to us.

4. Heselhaus stresses the parabolic dimension of *The Metamorphosis*, its power to point beyond itself to another order of meanings. This dimension is one which most critics have acknowledged. But for Heselhaus the parabolic element in *The Metamorphosis* attests to the absolute in a theological sense. This notion has to be countered by the stress of **Anders**' argument. The fact that Kafka is commonly referred to as *homo religiosus* testifies precisely to the bankruptcy of religious content in his position. Kafka's fundamental themes—for example, guilt, salvation, transcendence—can be explained in terms of secular desires and experiences. "Kafka's [religious] investiture took place in—literature: thus, at a level long since become irreligious or at least indifferent to religion" (71-72). Again, "Kafka was an unbeliever. But he did not have the courage of his own disbelief" (74).

60. Hillmann, Heinz. *Franz Kafka: Dichtungstheorie und Dichtungsgestalt.* Bonn: Bouvier, 1964. Pp. 138-39.

In *The Metamorphosis* a considerable number of hypothetical formulations and images reveal symbolic as opposed to descriptive meaning.

61. Holland, Norman N. "Realism and Unrealism, Kafka's 'Metamorphosis.' " *Modern Fiction Studies*, IV (Summer 1958), 143-50.

Kafka's strategy in *The Metamorphosis* does not fundamentally differ from the allegorical strategy of Spenser and Bunyan; he inserts an unrealistic element into a realistic setting. To grasp the allegorical dimension of Kafka's work, the reader must determine "the extra values given the realistic elements" by the unbelievable event or the allegorical name (143).

Looking first at the realistic element escapes the danger of reducing the sense of the unrealistic element to an alleged biographical experience or of reflecting pure abstractions back onto the realistic element.

If we put to one side the unreality of Gregor Samsa's metamorphosis, the core story is that of a man who feels sick and decides to stay home from work. Job, employer, employee are at the heart of the realistic situation as well as of the allegory of *The Metamorphosis*. The subsequent episodes deal with the attempt of the Samsa family to support itself, and structure the elements of employer, employee, and job.

The tenor of many passages in *The Metamorphosis* is ambiguous, even cryptic. The description of Gregor's boss might apply to the God of the Old Testament.

After the hasty departure of the office manager, "employers come in threes" (146): each of the Samsas now takes up for separate employers the burden that Gregor formerly bore alone; and the three roomers also employ the family. This shift to triads suggests the shift from the order of the Old Testament to the New which recurs in *In the Penal Colony*. The father exhibits the pride with which Gregor used to support the family; the mother deals with cloth, as Gregor did; and like the traveling salesman, *homo viator*, his sister trots to and fro.

When other realistic moments in *The Metamorphosis* are read imaginatively, they tend to support this extrarealistic structure: "Employers are like gods. Money suggests psychic resources; debts suggest psychic deficits or guilts. Traveling . . . suggests the need to serve an employer, an escape from freedom (sitting still). . . . Cloth and clothing are the badges of subservience; it is only in states of nightdress or undress that the inner self can emerge" (146).

Each of the realistic details is charged with a spiritual value; the spiritual concept is concentrated as a physical fact. Space does not allow for a total exegesis, but certain links are explicit. The taking of food comes to mean devotion or communion. The distinctions between bedroom, living room, and outdoors correspond to the distinctions between the private self, intersubjectivity, and obligations to others. Of course these distinctions are linked to the distinction between id, ego, and superego. Locks and doors mark the barriers between these areas of experience. (See **Starobinski**.) "Locks also symbolize Gregor's imprisonment in the body of an insect. . . .

"If, in every case, Kafka converts a spiritual concept down to a physical fact, then the transformation of Gregor to dung-bettle, of man to animal, must stand for the transformation of god to man, and, indeed, Kafka has given Gregor a number of Christ-like attributes" (147). He has taken on the parents' debts; the metamorphosis occurs around Christmas and ends with Gregor's death around Easter. Gregor is killed by the apple of Eden and mortality. In this divine comedy, the cleaning woman is a perverse "angel of the Lord."

Samsa is also linked to Samson, called in German "the Jewish Christ" (*Judenchrist*)–this further lends a "spiritual charge" to details of Gregor's growing blindness, his sacrifice, his manumission of the family from the yoke of the Philistine roomers.

Many of the incidental images of *The Metamorphosis* are charged with echoes of Chapter 52 of Isaiah. "*The Metamorphosis* satirizes Christians who are only distressed, angry, and, ultimately, cruel when a second Christ appears" (149-50).

The Metamorphosis is at one level, but only at one level, a parody of Christ's sacrifice. A rich sexual symbolism is also in play throughout.

"Gregor's transformation dramatizes the human predicament. That is, we are all blind, like Samson, trapped between a set of dark instinctual urges on the one hand and an obscure drive to serve 'gods' on the other. . . . Our only freedom is not to know that we are imprisoned" (150).

The integrity of this imaginative discussion does not emerge here, since many of Holland's insights have had to be omitted. His discovery of the play of religious symbols beneath the surface of *The Metamorphosis* is seminal. **Weinberg** has exhaustively developed this starting point. But for a perspective on Kafka's religiosity, fundamentally without religious belief, **Anders**' discussion (71ff.) is indispensable.

From the opposite side, however, Holland's approach is basically put into question by **Spilka** (252), who writes: "The comparison [between *David Copperfield* and *The Metamorphosis*] underscores what should be evident, that Kafka was not creating [in *The Metamorphosis*] a religious parable, but was working instead with social and familial themes like those in *Copperfield*. I emphasize this point because many critics (e.g. Scott, Madden, Tauber, Holland, Sackville-West) stretch this story onto the religious framework of the later fiction."

Spilka is surely right to claim that Kafka did not intend with *The Metamorphosis* to create a religious parable, since such an explanation fails to take account of the various kinds of themes and intentions present. On the other hand, Holland does not claim that *The Metamorphosis* is a religious parable. He claims that *The Metamorphosis* contains an unrealistic dimension charged with religious motifs. Holland's (and especially **Weinberg**'s) evidence makes this point indisputable.

62. **Honig, Edwin**. *Dark Conceit: The Making of Allegory*. New York: Oxford University Press, 1966. Pp. 63-68 and passim.

The allegory of *The Metamorphosis* is "a prose fiction inverting the elements of a beast fable with a mock-naturalistic narrative and framing a satire-eulogy on the suicidal Judeo-Christian conscience" (14).

The realistic milieu of *The Metamorphosis* "is really an emanation of the hero's own disabled consciousness" (64). Scene and character come to light through the focus of Gregor Samsa's inwardness. Samsa's punishment–his metamorphosis–enacts a self-condemnation.

The subject of *The Metamorphosis* is the relationship of a man to social authority, reduced to the relationship of a man to his immediate family. "Authority rests with the father and [with] the social injunction to work, which he represents" (64).

Gregor's metamorphosis issues from his crime, his apparently inexplicable lassitude; "he falls into an animal-like lethargy–i.e., he lies down on the job" (64). His punishment and the means to his illumination are one and the same–it is to be a monstrous insect with the consciousness of a human being.

The sleep from which Gregor awakens is the darkness of alienated, guilty existence. His new life is the terrifying prospect of a new awareness. By denying the work that has been imposed on him, Gregor denies a life of usefulness. "His dilemma is that he must challenge, grapple with, and seek protection from the judgment that society places on him for deserting his work, and at the same time accept the judgment, the guilt he actually feels, 'lying down' " (65). The insect shape is the physical correlative of internal metamorphosis and a metamorphosis in social relations–the expression at once of defiance and social repudiation.

The metamorphosis, being undeniable, bars Gregor from having a future. His response to it is to let his past come to consciousness. His yearning to be reassimilated evokes past disappointments. His effort to come to terms with his condition takes the form of his becoming exactly what each of the other members of the household takes him for. Though their responses are inadequate and absurd, Gregor's response to them generates "a cumulative and recapitulative sense which confirms his physical metamorphosis" (65).

To his sister, Gregor is an animal who feeds on garbage; to the office manager, he is the monster who breaks the rule of punctuality. Gregor's father punishes him with all the violence of the authority he does not exercise on himself. The mother does not understand her son. The boarders unify the family against Gregor; "it is as though the family needed first to have the goad of the boarders' social disapprobation in order to swallow its own distaste and personal chagrin, before finally expressing its own real feelings overtly" (65).

The metamorphosis begins as an act of consciousness; the story moves toward progressive physical transformation. Gregor's nightmarish shape defines him through the dramatic unfolding of the others' responses to him. In the end Gregor is overwhelmed by the metaphor of his condition, his metamorphosis.

Gregor's pursuit of affection and recognition gains him only his sister's shame, his mother's grieving incomprehension, and the repudiation of the institution he has labored for. He finds in his father, from whom he seeks guidance and support, a rival and an angry dispenser of justice.

Gregor's situation is a theater of opposing forces. But "since he cannot assert any actual sense of himself, he falls prey to those forces in himself and in others that have hopelessly mistaken him" (67).

But it is as if he knows one thing: that he is fundamentally dependent on the others and that the risk of his never finding the right sustenance is immense. The very consciousness of his fragility erodes him. "If the social dispensation, typified by the self-preservation of the family, is pre-eminent, who then is the individual alone? The story seems to answer the question by ironically posing another: Nobody?" (67).

The story describes a self impoverished not only by the reluctance of others to nurture him, but one *already* impoverished. In the last resort the failure is not the family's but Gregor's. Gregor can experience his dilemma because he has been unable to find his real self. In this sense the defective and stultified responses which Gregor provokes are further self-accusations.

This point illustrates the fashion in which the allegory of *The Metamorphosis* differs from traditional allegory. The latter begins with a personified attribute, with the intention of finding out the inner sense of the attribute within a preestablished moral context. The movement of *The Metamorphosis* is outward from an inward focus; everything follows from the hero's self-condemnation at the beginning. But as this inner focus is impoverished, the result of his relations to others is a dwindling: "instead of finding his many actual identities, he shrinks and is finally converted into nothingness. There is no moral closure in *The Metamorphosis*" (68).

"In *The Metamorphosis* . . . the world of concentrated purpose takes on the apparently fixed but vagrant characteristics of a dream. Freed from pressures of strict chronology and verisimilitude, the unfolding of basic oppositions is unusually fluent and persuasive. This suggests that the traditional dream artifice in allegorical narratives disguises deliberate intention in the form of a mystery or seeming irrelevances; and this quality invariably invites interpretation" (68).

"The same tone of baffled constraint [as in *The Trial*] pervades the description of Gregor Samsa waking to an unreal reality at the beginning of *The Metamorphosis*. . . . Such initial characterizations introduce the hero in immediate symbolic focus at the threshold of his experience. In Kafka, however, they often seem an ironical inversion of the dream induction. Kafka's heroes wake from a dream to a world which appears more illusory—more baffling and more demanding of inner consciousness, since it is the dream of 'real life'—than the sleep of the past from which they have just emerged. But the same inclusive relationship (symbol-dreamer-plight) is present in both the dream induction and its inversion" (74).

"The dramatized experience expressed in a series of actions depends upon an increasing integration of consciousness in the hero. Typical of post-medieval literature is a growing emphasis on the realistic portrayal of the hero's situation and surroundings. With this emphasis the judicial and antagonistic principles are often driven inward and only hinted at in the fictional process, rather than being externalized throughout. . . . The pattern of initiation is not manifested in simple moral actions but is implicitly worked out and modulated through psychological characteristics, as shown in Kafka's *Metamorphosis*.

"In Kafka's *Metamorphosis* the principal analogy, between the self-abandoned salesman and the giant insect, also has the power of a concentrative accumulation. The analogy combines aspects of the hero's physical, social, and psychic plight with all the connotations of rejection, worthlessness, contemptibleness, and the final voiding of the insect body. Throughout the story the analogy effects a wavering between the appearance and the reality: Is Samsa really an insect? Is Samsa really human? He (or it) is both" (128-29).

Honig writes, "It is as if Gregor negatively and inevitably 'self-awares' himself out of existence on learning how arbitrary his identity is" (67). Is Gregor's decline a function of his increased self-awareness? More questionable still: is Gregor's alleged self-awareness the fruit of an insight (into the arbitrariness of his identity); is it not rather a sheer trial of consciousness upon blindness and opacity? So mentalistic a description of Gregor's progress as Honig gives cannot account for a different kind of evidence in the story: Gregor grows increasingly vague, befuddled, and bestial without troubling himself about this development.

Furthermore, if Gregor had been struck, as Honig claims, by the arbitrariness of his new identity, we should expect from him a reflection on the questions: What have I become? Why have I become such a being? But such a meditation is, of course, missing from this story.

Honig also sees the cleaning woman's gesture of prodding Gregor with her broom as an expression of gratuitous malice. Her malice is the product of her situation, which differs from that of the others in contact with Gregor, since she alone has "no organized system of 'values' to propel her upward" (65).

Honig's reading is at variance with Spilka's (110-B, 80), who recognizes in the responses of this cleaning woman to Gregor a friendly acceptance without malice or bad faith. She brings to light Kafka's essential humor, "persistently transcendent," amounting to a "spiritual assertion."

63. Janouch, Gustav. *Gespräche mit Kafka*, expanded edition. Frankfurt am Main: S. Fischer, 1968. The earlier publication of 1951 appeared as *Conversations with Kafka: Notes and Reminiscenses*, trans. by Goronwy Rees. New York: Praeger, 1963.

Kafka wrote during his "terrible, sleepless nights," this way constantly aware of his "dark solitary confinement." Janouch reflects: "Isn't the miserable bedbug of *Metamorphosis* Kafka himself?" (*Gespräche*, 32). Kafka said that the source of *The Metamorphosis* was the times: "We are closer to the animal than to man. That is the cage. It is easier to relate to animals than to human beings." (*Gespräche,* 43). On another occasion he said, "The word Samsa is not a cryptogram. Samsa is not just Kafka. *The Metamorphosis* is not a confession, although in a certain sense it is an indiscretion. Is it perhaps nice and discreet to talk about the bedbugs in one's own family?" When Janouch said, " '*The Metamorphosis* is a terrible dream, a terrible conception,' Kafka stood still. 'The dream reveals the reality, which conception lags behind. That is the horror of life–the terror of art' " (*Gespräche*, 55-56).

64. Jarrett-Kerr, Martin C. R. *Studies in Literature and Belief*. London: Rockliff, 1954. Pp. 185ff.

"The survival of the imagination, as well as of man . . . depends upon hope." Kafka is admirable for his intellectual integrity; but the absence of hope in his work is oppressive. It is instructive to compare with *The Metamorphosis* the conclusion of another modern metamorphosis–Jules Supervielle's *Les Suites d'une Course*. Here the man-horse succeeds in venting his anger against the lover who betrays him and is restored to a human shape.

65. Jens, Walter. *Statt einer Literaturgeschichte*. Pfullingen: Neske, 1957. Pp. 76 ff.

Man likes to set himself as the measure, as lord and master of all existing things. Kafka's heroes take a different path, "a path that leads from speech to silence, from thesis to paradox, from deception to a truth which, in the moment of catastrophe–the soul sinking into namelessness–once again becomes visible" (76).

In Kafka's world the reality of the banal has grown threadbare; in familiar domains, monstrous things seem normal. The most staggering paradox is taken for granted.

Kafka's poetic work before "The Judgment" is full of dreams and miracles: thereafter his language is that of the protocol (see

Anders), yet it is no less paradoxical; indeed, the paradox gains in reality. His later fiction creates "a single space, ruled by the law of logic, of calculation and contrary calculation, of 'on the one hand'–'on the other hand,' consequence and paradox . . . .

"In the oxymorons of Musil and Kafka ('scalding cold'; 'I called without a sound'), their animations of things ('wailing window'; 'rotten light'), their piecing together of heterogeneous elements, . . . a process begins to define itself whose result is that the plane of comparison disintegrates: the word 'like' is abandoned for 'is,' the simile for the identification. . . . Gregor Samsa does not live symbolically *as* an insect; he has in reality been transformed into a beetle" (78).

66. **Kaiser, Hellmuth.** "Franz Kafkas Inferno: Eine psychologische Deutung seiner Strafphantasie." *Imago*, XVII, no. 1 (1931), 41-104.

Kafka's works are intensely and peculiarly suited to psychoanalytical investigation; in one respect they are like dreams, in another, like fairy tales and myths "for the self-contained character of their symbolic content" (41). The psychological elements constituting his works are unconscious.

What is the meaning of Gregor Samsa's metamorphosis? Kafka gives no reason for it; but some conclusion is possible on the basis of its effects.

In the five years prior to the metamorphosis, a steady development took place. As the Samsa family, except for Gregor, sank into a condition of lassitude and futility, Gregor's successes and ambition grew. Now he intends to send his sister to the conservatory.

After the metamorphosis, father and mother work; the family's financial prospects improve; the daughter matures into a beautiful woman. The father, in particular, is transformed into a vigorous official.

The metamorphosis is thus a turning point between two developments similar in kind though opposite in direction. Before the catastrophe, the father's degradation led to the son's assuming the dominant family position. After the event, the son's humiliation leads to the father's reassertion of authority.

In other words "the story depicts the struggle between son and father as it rises out of the oedipal conflict. . . . Viewed psychologically, the metamorphosis of the son does not signify an external event but an internal change in the direction of drive. It is a kind of self-punishment for his earlier competitive striving aimed against the father, a withdrawal from the exacting genital position" (55).

The word "punishment" seems odd; the son does not appear to have done anything reprehensible. Yet there is evidence of repressed hostility toward the father encoded in the depiction of the father's fury at the son after the metamorphosis.

The animal into which K. (Kafka's subconscious) transforms itself is conspicuously base, the sign of "a lower, more infantile level of development of the instinctual life" (56). It is significant that this creature feels no disgust; the level of its psychic development corresponds to a stage of infantility preceding even the repression of anal pleasure. The metamorphosis is thus a regression into the anal phase of sexuality.

It is noteworthy that as the son triumphs, the father grows unclean, and that this relation is reversed after the metamorphosis. "Uncleanliness, anality, is here conceived as a demon which, driven out of one person, must enter into another. The drives which are no longer allowed to take effect in one's actions are projected onto the partner, the 'adversary' " (57).

The metamorphosis is punitive also because it twice provokes the father physically to maltreat his son, at the conclusion of the first and the second sections of the story. "There are two scenes of maltreatment; in the first scene two injuries occur; in the second, two apples strike. The repeated occurrence of the number two strengthens the interpretation, in any case obvious, that the mistreatments are 'acts of castration' "(58).

The second section makes clear the sexual basis of the entire action. Mother and sister treat Gregor precisely as any well-intentioned family would treat a neurotic member whose regressive behavior has destroyed his last connections with reality. Gregor's response to these women's intention to empty his room is to protect with his body the picture of the aggressively erotic woman which hangs on the wall. He is defending his sexuality.

The oedipal character of this representation of sexuality is transparent at the conclusion of the second section, with its graphic allusion to the "primal scene," and the son's subsequent "paralysis of sight," which corresponds to the act of repression.

There is a third, crucial punitive moment to the metamorphosis—the masochistic. This is plain enough in the "startling and unbelievable" character of the pain Gregor feels upon being bombarded with apples. The "complete confusion" of all his senses is the confused mingling of pleasure and pain.

The fact that Gregor is punished from behind points to the connection of masochism with the anal sphere.

The psychoanalytic approach sees *The Metamorphosis* as a family drama which depicts a father-son conflict. It notes a detail of the story which in its perspective is extraordinary, namely that Gregor almost never displays any hostility toward his father. It concludes that the extraordinary degree to which this hostility is repressed in Gregor confirms that we are dealing here with a psychodrama peculiarly susceptible to Freudian analysis.

Common sense reverses this perspective by noting that filial hostility is an assumption of Freudian psychology; that the plain fact of the story is the absence on Gregor's part of hostility toward his father; and that the story consequently confirms, not the animus of psychoanalysis against literature, but Kafka's animus against psychology.

Kaiser finds a pattern in *The Metamorphosis* which seems a replica of the psychoanalytical truth about the development of the psyche. Yet the possibility of finding in a work of art "entities from another system of meanings" (**Hasselblatt**, 193) rests on special assumptions about the nature of the mind and the nature of literary language; and these assumptions are not obvious. We are asked to believe that Kafka has the basic sense of *The Metamorphosis* already "in mind"—however subconsciously—even before he writes the story. It would be more plausible to say that for Kafka, as well as for his reader, the meaning of *The Metamorphosis*, like that of the earlier story "The Judgment, is first constituted by interpretation. [41] *The Metamorphosis* simply cannot be admired as the mirror image of an existing meaning or decoded in terms of an available key. It reflects the intent to constitute meaning which does not yet exist; it aims to fill in an absence.

Thus the meaning of this story would have to be radically different from the meaning which Kafka naturally and immediately has for himself. It would stand in the same relation to his personality as the violin music which Gregor Samsa hears to the language which the others have, but he does not: the relation of an "unknown nourishment" to the food the others eat, but he does not. If the meaning of *The Metamorphosis* is psychoanalytical, then Gregor is deluded from the start, and the music he hears is only program music for a repressed oedipal trauma and a self-inflicted wound.

An approach which stresses the aesthetic autonomy and the unique origin of *The Metamorphosis* nonetheless shares an affinity with psychoanalysis, which distinguishes both from the seductive approaches of empirical psychology and sociology. For empirical psychology, *The Metamorphosis* reproduces the emotional problems which were troubling Kafka and of which he was aware: e.g. for **Baioni**, *The Metamorphosis* is the expression of Kafka's inability to love Felice Bauer. For the sociologist, *The Metamorphosis* reproduces the social problems of turn-of-the-century Prague, reflecting, for example, for **Sokel**, 105-A, the predicament of the worker under the Taylor speed-up system. The difference between these approaches, on the one hand, and psychoanalysis and autonomous aesthetic analysis on the other is that only the latter consider the work to embody a sense otherwise inaccessible to the writer; the source of this meaning is in both cases nonconscious. (And yet this insistence in the case of psychoanalysis is incomplete. Could not Kaiser have arrived at the same understanding of Kafka if he had had him as a patient to recount his dreams and fantasies?)

There is, however, a profound difference between the latter two approaches in the way that they define the nonreflective source of poetic language. For psychoanalysis, this source–the unconscious–is a compendium of affects abridged from random, mainly erotic, infantile experiences; these affects vary in their sense–their intensity and direction–from person to person, but the connections between them reflect the presence of invariable patterns. The source of the literary work is nevertheless the unique sense of the individual unconscious.

Autonomous aesthetic analysis, on the other hand, thinks of the source in the activity of literary language itself, "whose origin cannot be derived, but can only be understood as source, as a beginning which is its own foundation."[42] The ultimate origin of literary language is thus a nothingness, unlike the mere absence of some particular affect or of a situation in which a connection between affects could be instituted; for this nothingness could only be filled by "a beginning," an intent and not an object.

Thus the basis of literary activity is irreducibly general, unvarying from poet to poet, and inaccessible only in the sense that pure generality is inaccessible through any particular experience of writing or reflection.

67. Kassel, Norbert. *Das Groteske bei Franz Kafka.* Munich: Wilhelm Fink, 1969. Pp. 153-69.

The "playful arbitrariness" of the grotesque has enabled literature to actualize the "impossibility" of the modern world. Kafka's prose is characterized by the grotesque metaphor; if the classical metaphor is defined as a simultaneous seeing of similar things, in the grotesque metaphor incompatible things are seen simultaneously. The animal metaphor in Kafka is grotesque in the sense that it is an inadequate expression of something mental or spiritual. It may then function as a representation of anxiety or doubt or misery.

Metamorphosis in Kafka is a mode of the narrative realization of grotesque images in which the elements of suddenness and contradiction preponderate. Gregor Samsa's metamorphosis is a kind of ultimate in Kafka's art of the realization of impossibilities; for in him a shapeless monster has assumed sensuous form.

Metamorphoses have always abounded in fables—especially "degradation metamorphoses," in which a man is cast out into a lower or inanimate order of nature. Hegel has explicated this category of metamorphosis as a degradation of spirituality. The punitive sort of metamorphosis implies an acute attack on behalf of the spirit against nature. Sometimes these metamorphoses are traceable to a crime committed by the man metamorphosed. In others there is no such trace, but in them the condition of being an animal still emerges as a misery and a humiliation. Gregor Samsa suffers a fairy-tale metamorphosis in the form of a degradation.

Grotesque metaphor and metamorphosis are linked in this story in the following way: the characteristic feature of the grotesque metaphor is its "tendency toward the absolute animation [of a literal meaning]—which can lead to the transformation of one thing into another, into something strange; metamorphosis, as in *The Metamorphosis*, is the most logical form of a grotesque animation of this sort" (156).

The opening of the story is typical of Kafka's story-telling: an extraordinary event is reported in a sober and unmoved tone. The factual, objective, realistic character of the metamorphosis is stressed when Gregor "finds himself changed"—that is, when he is confronted with the metamorphosis as an accomplished fact. There is no introduction for the reader into this unintelligible event. The sense of brute reality engendered by the factual character of the report prevents us from conceiving the metamorphosis as an aftereffect—a dreamlike event or hallucination—of his "unsettling dreams." The grotesque, which is first incorporated in the figure of the monstrous vermin, is present again at a stylistic level in the contrast between cool, factual reportage and the repulsiveness and monstrousness of what is being described. The course of the story shows how Gregor comes to terms with his metamorphosis: not, of course, by means of a knowing response including the emotions of despair and terror, but by the transformation of his initial skepticism under the compulsion of "coming to terms realistically with the new bodily and existential *données* of an animal existence" (159).

He remains grotesque, however; for his empirical existence as an animal contrasts with his inner, mental existence as a human being. But this distinction is not absolute: just as, in the first section, Gregor evidences uncertainty about his ability to orient himself in the external, empirical world, he gradually begins to doubt the constitution of his own inwardness. He wonders, for example, whether his sensibility has not grown blunter and is surprised at his readiness to forget the whole of his human past. We are moved to assume that the roots of his psychic degradation are in himself, hence, "that a metamorphosis of this kind into animal existence is determined by his own behavior" (163).

The central theme of the story, however, is that of interpersonal relations. It is the behavior of Gregor's family that seals his fate; as he is more and more deprived of interpersonal contact, he more and more sinks into the torpor of a brute. It is his destiny to have a family. Perhaps at the root of his situation is his concealed guilt for having neglected his family in every truly human way. At any event, his metamorphosis becomes a task in human love for his family—a task they wholly fail. Paradoxically, in the condition of the metamorphosis Gregor is first able to see his family clearly; his customary human perceptions disappear, but an inner and more penetrating perceptiveness takes their place.

This movement is paralleled by Gregor's rejection of ordinary food and his sudden longing for an "unknown nourishment." This moment is the turning point of the story and calls to mind similar passages in fairy tales; but now the contrast of Gregor's spiritual longings with the animal-like behavior of the roomers does not lead to Gregor's deliverance. It leads, instead, under the compulsions of reality, to an unredemptive end. "His sister's music is the medium of the interpersonal; here, in the possibility of his being accepted once more into the human domain of the family, the redemptive fairy-tale act should have been found. . . . But the happy wish dream is destroyed by crass reality" (168).

To sum up: *The Metamorphosis* bares in grotesque fashion the problem of interpersonal relations within the family. The perspective of the grotesque is crucial; "for example, the behavior of the Samsa family toward the metamorphosed Gregor cannot be judged by the same real and conventional standards as its behavior, let us say, toward a nonmetamorphosed Gregor. Thus, in the light of the grotesque happening, the meaning of the story cannot lie in an answer to the question of value judgments of guilt and innocence" (169).

Though the story is narrated mainly from Gregor's perspective, other evidence reveals the presence of a reflective narrator. First, the various adverbs indicating time; second, the narration which continues after Gregor's death; third, certain places in the "enacted discourse" (*erlebte Rede*) of Gregor's soul when key questions are put—for example, "Was he an animal, that music could move him so?" Here the narrator is speaking as well as Gregor and not out of some fictive innocence; here we have a crucial moment of the story as a whole. This question goes out to the reader; it is a question which the reader puts to himself.

In the grotesque outcast Gregor the problem of spirituality is exhibited in a negative mode. The longing for redemption is constituted as the problem of intersubjectivity. The essence of the intersubjective is put into question by the narrator Kafka in allowing his hero to go to his ruin as a consequence of the failure of the intersubjective. "Here lies the aesthetic function of the grotesque and the spiritual meaning of the metamorphosis image of the beetle Gregor Samsa" (170).

It is difficult to understand how the essence of the story can be at once Kafka's critique of intersubjectivity for its failure to provide salvation; and on the other hand, the representation of an "impossible" predicament in a grotesque metaphor, not to be judged by "real and conventional standards . . . , [by] value judgments of guilt and innocence" (169).

68. **Kayser, Wolfgang.** *Das Groteske: Seine Gestaltung in Malerei und Dichtung.* Oldenburg and Hamburg: Stalling, 1961. Pp. 160, 221.

Kafka's stories are types of the "cold grotesque." In them a distance has been interposed between narrator and reader to a degree that is unique. His mode of narration is wholly new. The newness does not lie in the fact that in *The Metamorphosis* Kafka tells the story from the perspective of the main character or that the narrator-hero does not possess a complete grasp of the action or the ability to interpret it. "But the Kafkan narrator . . . alienates himself from us by reacting emotionally in a way other than we expect. It is oppressive that in *The Metamorphosis* Gregor accepts his animality with such composure and that the narrator reports on it so coldly and impartially" (160). The satirical tone at the end of the story suggests where Kafka's meaning and sympathy lie; but the diaries reveal that Kafka, evidently just on this account, was dissatisfied with the ending.

69. **Landsberg, Paul L.** "Kafka et la 'Métamorphose.' " *Esprit,* LXXII (Sept. 1938), 671-84. Reprinted in *Problèmes du personnalisme.* Paris: Editions du Seuil, 1952. Pp. 83-98. "Kafka and 'The Metamorphosis,' trans. by Carolyn Muehlenberg. *Quarterly Review of Literature*, II, no. 3 (1945), 228-36. "The Metamorphosis," in *The Kafka Problem*, ed. by Angel Flores. New York: New Directions, 1946. Pp. 122-33.

Kafka's prose is classic, characterized by an "absence of sentimental variations of tone" (*Esprit*, 672).[43] Kafka's moodless intellectual style reflects the paradoxical construction of his world; his style seeks reality, it resists imagination and will, but it must disclaim everyday reality to achieve it. Yet "the transformation suffered by accustomed reality in Kafka's writing is not simply a diminution. . . . His writing treats the question of change–change of a type foreign to our knowledge of reality" (*Esprit*, 672).

What we mean by reality is a certain cohesiveness in our experience, its similarity to past and present events. The metamorphosis shatters our assumed knowledge of reality, but the genuineness of the reactions of Gregor and his family to this event moves us to accept the event as real.

In sleep it is literally the case that our bodies and ourselves are transformed. "It is by means of a certain and peculiar process that each morning we take up our body and soul again and readjust ourselves to the surrounding world. . . . But in our customary certainty of the identity of our self and the world in general, there is just enough artificiality, will, and fragility, so that Kafka's fiction touches an anguishing reality, nourished from sources deeper than those of rational reflection and scientific knowledge" (*Esprit*, 676). It is on awakening from an "unsettling dream" that Gregor discovers his metamorphosis.

"The metamorphosis of a civilized man into, first, a colopteron, perfect example of an instinctive and almost automatic being, and finally into a simple bit of matter, portrays in successive stages up until the end the death instinct, the desire for a return to the inorganic, the power of which Freud has shown in the human subconscious" (*Esprit,* 676). The metamorphosis brings to light the desires and the aura of anxiety with which the subconscious acts against life. It names the loss of the conscious will and the satisfaction of pent-up desires–a satisfaction so gross as to inspire the feeling of guilt which haunts the man transformed into a bug. Samsa sought to flee the intolerable role of civilized man, to desert humanity: this knowledge is painful as is his helplessness to justify himself. The father exercises the right of life in firing the apple at Gregor: "the culprit instills horror into those who surround him because he calls attention to the universal possibility of the crime" (*Esprit*, 677). The death of this fugitive–his return to brute matter–brings relief to the world around him and a still keener joy to himself. "The inevitable struggle between the misfortune of being born, and of wanting to return to nothingness, the misfortune of being responsible and of not wanting to be, has only the saddest solution in Kafka's moral universe" (*Esprit*, 677-78).

We are temporal beings, engaged in perpetual metamorphosis. Consciousness of this predicament comes to us only at particular moments and fills us with anguish. The oblivion in which we hold the experience of change originates finally from a fear of death. This anguish inspires us to maintain the identity of our being through ritual and repetitive acts. To the Samsas, Gregor's metamorphosis connotes the ultimate metamorphosis of life into death, an insight which they must hate and fear. What is at stake is the preservation of a world in which they can continue to live oblivious of change and free from the fear of death. In this work, anguish is defeated, order wins—an order "in which death is passionately excluded and with it the true life of every person.

"The terrible apple which the . . . father . . . throws into the back of his poor son expresses the foolish and inevitable revolt of the likely against the unlikely, of the *uniform* against the monstrous, of custom against the exceptional, of triviality against the explicit nightmare, of an artificially sweetened, slowed and comfortably falsified life, the life oblivious of death, against a true life which progresses resolutely towards its final catastrophe" (*Esprit*, 679). The father's act of hostility has metaphysical sanction.

Gregor's change is marked—but this change is primarily physical; implicated is the affirmation of an abiding moral personality. As vermin he remains "morally identical with his former self, . . . sweet, timid, and amiable . . ." (*Kafka Problem*, 130). This self is nonetheless not autonomous. Radical physical metamorphosis makes it radically vulnerable. Witness poor Gregor's loss of language: "He resembles Kafka's other heroes, refined Talmudists surrounded by corporals, superb reasoners in a deaf world" (*Esprit,* 682).

The abyss which opens up between Gregor's logic and the logic of his peers (who are his equals though they resist this knowledge) suggests the isolation of madness, of schizophrenia. Kafka's poetic universe contains states which would probably have induced real schizophrenia if his art had not exorcised them. "If Gregor Samsa himself had told his story, it would be the sincere confession of a schizophrenic. By creating the main character and telling his story in the third person, Kafka is liberating himself of an obsession" (*Esprit*, 683).

The transformation into a cockroach can symbolize innumerable disasters. It is the condition of the minority—of the Jew, of the poet as well, in a world sworn to hate and fear his authentic insights.

70. **Lawson, Richard H.** "*Ungeheueres Ungeziefer* in Kafka's *Die Verwandlung.*" *German Quarterly*, XXXIII (May 1960), 216-19.

Gregor Samsa is transformed into an "*ungeheueres Ungeziefer.*" In this phrase *Ungeziefer* is regularly translated by Kafka's English interpreters and critics as "insect." But Kafka has not used the word "*Insekt*" in *The Metamorphosis*. "*Insekt* is too cold a word, too scientific, and incapable of bearing the negative, hence unpleasant connotation in *Ungeziefer*. . . . It lacks its emotional impact, its disgusting unpleasantness." On the other hand, the alternative "vermin," which is frequently used, is vague, since it can, according to *Webster's New International*, refer to such animals as mice and owls. "*Ungeheuer*" is translated in various ways, but "monstrous" seems right, since it expresses both "unpleasant dimension and unpleasant quality. . . . Kafka's German deserves to be rendered in sympathetically accurate and connotative language. In plain yet connotative English, Gregor Samsa became a monstrous bug." Lawson supports this translation on the visual evidence of a portfolio of illustrations of *The Metamorphosis* made by Otto Coester and published in 1929 by Dobré Dílo at Stará říše in Moravia.

This evidence is irrelevant, since Kafka specified that the bug was not to be drawn. See his letter to Wolff, Oct. 25, 1915.

71. **Lecomte, Marcel.** "Note sur Kafka et le rêve (*La Métamorphose*)." In *Rêve*, ed. by André Breton. Paris: 1938. Pp. 61-62.

The opening of *The Metamorphosis* suggests that Gregor is only half-awake and still dreaming. The passage contains themes stressed in the earliest treatises on dreams, themes which are explained by the position of the sleeper; familiar, too, is the phenomenon of the "hardening" of the body. The deeper sense here is that Gregor is continuing to play with the *données* of his dream; the game is singularly prolonged. Gregor "digs deeply" into his dream. He is able to imagine himself transformed into a bug, all the while remaining lucid.

How would Lecomte explain the line "It was no dream"?

72. **Lockemann, Fritz.** *Gestalt und Wandlungen der deutschen Novelle: Geschichte einer literarischen Gattung im 19ten und 20ten Jahrhundert.* Munich: Hueber, 1957. Pp. 359-61.

At the outset the world of Gregor Samsa, ostensibly innocent, suffers a magic intrusion. This apparently meaningless intrusion amounts in fact to a challenge to Gregor's family to heal a shattered order. They do not respond to the challenge: "judgment does not ensue; the law has summoned in vain; men remain deaf, tangled in their chaos."

What Kafka's reader might suppose to be the intrusions of chaos mean the appeal to men made by divine law. An event seems to men a metamorphosis, a distortion of reality; the sense of the event is the appeal for a restitution of order. Kafka's representation of the tension between chaos and order is dualistic. The divine order has the character of a law exacting absolute obedience, even when it is unintelligible.

The presumption here seems to be that the everyday world, apart from the dislocation of the metamorphosis, is a divine order. Nothing could be further from the intent of *The Metamorphosis* or from Kafka's spirit.

73. **Loeb, Ernst.** "Bedeutungswandel der Metamorphose bei Franz Kafka und E. T. A. Hoffmann: Ein Vergleich." *The German Quarterly*, XXXV (Jan. 1962), 47-59.

"The unattainability of a heaven is only the reflection of . . . the 'undiscoverable' because hopelessly divided self" (54). In

Kafka the simultaneity of the two domains—the world of truth and the world of experience—is intensified into the complete equivalence of parallel lines. The apparent point of juncture is disclosed as an optical illusion. Paradoxically, it is precisely through this illusion that the hope of a real coincidence, even if in the domain of the "infinite," is kept alive. This parallelism is perpetuated in the figure of the bug. It is only in this way that Gregor's uncanny equanimity can be understood—the fact that upon awakening he is seized, not by terror or amazement, but by a ravenous hunger, and he finds himself unable to repress a smile (55). **Sokel**, 105-B, sees the metamorphosis simply as the manifestation of a wish to flee the duties of the bourgeois through parasitism, but with this he misses the tragic fact that after the metamorphosis Gregor remains unknowingly and unknowably divided.

In Gregor human and bestial impulses dwell side by side. The Kantian opposition of duty and inclination is taken up and reversed; it is the world of duty which categorically bids Gregor lose his self; his protest takes the form of the metamorphosis into a creature and leads him into a world of inclinations more proximate to his being but which does not effectually comprise a human world.[44] The existence of the two parallel and irreconcilable directions of Gregor's being after the metamorphosis confirms **Emrich**'s thesis that Gregor's metamorphosis into a condition of greater authenticity is not a matter of bringing to the surface a hitherto suppressed or buried "inwardness" but rather of disclosing a dimension of authenticity which remains radically new, strange, unassimilable. Gregor's love of music is wholly new and completes a metamorphosis which is progressive and passes through stages of loss of language and blurring of vision. In this scene music does not unveil existence but incarnates the tantalizing of the unattainable, a torture heightened by the detail that the "longed-for nourishment" remains unknowable. Gregor's experience of music is accompanied by a desire for erotic possession of his sister: at this point the juncture of the parallels thought to be near is again lost in infinity. Gregor's fantasy represents a high point of erotic self-knowledge: once he had loved the fur-coated lady in a picture and indeed had been ready to defend her precisely against his sister. But at the point of highest experience the abyss of his beastliness opens up: the transference of his erotic daydream onto his sister reveals the unsuspected reverse side of his self-righteous façade of brotherly love and unselfishness. **Tauber** is only partially right in maintaining that Gregor perishes of his concealed (or no longer representable) humanity—or that his family fails the test of love. At the bottom of this impossibility for Gregor of showing his humanity is the fact of his division: "Samsa 'is' not only the beetle which he appears (outwardly to the others and at times also to himself); he 'is' also no longer Gregor, which he appears (inwardly to himself and in the first instance to others too)" (58). The fact that the father is the last to cease considering him as Gregor and actually asks the question, "If he could understand us?" (E 134) reveals an apparent comprehension which is farthest from the truth. His sister constitutes the opposite extreme: at the beginning she was closest to Gregor; but the fact that at the close she can consider him only as a beetle (grotesquely, in the interest of honoring his memory) still leaves this memory intact, while in the father's unconscious the suspicion of malicious dissimulation continues to fester. But both are far from the truth and prevented from penetrating the surface of things by concern for their own peace of mind. For Kafka, authenticity becomes a value which the writer can record but neither interpret nor realize. Gregor never disentangles the incomprehensible experience which assails him; but in grasping that something similar to this could also happen to others, he is able to experience the "onset of the general brightening" (E 136). In this, the experience of the abyss is reflected as the creature's intuition of a concealed meaning. Yet this brightening remains a personal experience. It is general in the sense that it is a possibility for all, but it can be experienced only by the individual. The world of family and business cuts itself off from this possibility and digs itself more deeply into the concealing appearance of familiar things.

In Kafka there is no longer a way which leads from within the self to the outside. "Being, grown questionable to itself, withers undetectable in what is obtrusive and merciless in the everyday world of appearance" (59).

74. **Ludwig, Richard**, and **Perry, Marvin B.**, Eds. *Nine Short Novels*. Boston: Heath, 1952. Pp. xlii-xlvii.

Kafka's work invites autobiographical interpretation, though this dangerously predetermines the intentions of his work. *The Metamorphosis* is rooted in a guilt complex. The story originates in the description in "Letter to His Father" of the fight between vermin which not only bite, but at the same time suck the blood on which they live. According to the editors, Kafka's dispassionate description of Gregor's physical state and the drab reality of his room produces a contrast.

Erlich argues that the familiar drabness of the room vouches for the authenticity of Gregor's metamorphosis, absorbs and dissipates the shock. Whether or not the metamorphosis and the reality of the bedroom are fused into a single continuum, Ludwig is right to stress the mood of incongruity which arises from a monster chiefly concerned with pleasing his former manager. The source of Gregor's responses is not the new and actual enormity, but habit. The mind pretends to adjust to its shock but is unable. Ludwig is not right, however, in asserting that "once Gregor does adapt, he lapses into the complete insect state" or that "Grete never forgets that this insect is her brother."

75. **Luke, F. D.** "The Metamorphosis." *Modern Language Review,* XLVI (1951), 232-45. Reprinted in *Franz Kafka Today,* ed. by Angel Flores and Homer Swander. Pp. 25-43.

The Metamorphosis, the longest of Kafka's stories, is one of the few works which Kafka finished, published in his life time, and never wished to have destroyed. It illustrates the virtues of Kafka's prose, a balance of fantasy and naturalism, tragedy and humor. *The Metamorphosis*, along with "The Judgment" and *In the Penal Colony*, elaborates one of Kafka's central themes: "the punishment fantasy associated with an extremely primitive father-image" (*Franz Kafka*, 26). Like "The Judgment," it is a family catastrophe.

In both stories the sons are guilty of "the unforgivable offense of self-assertion" (*Franz Kafka*, 26). Gregor has replaced the father as family provider; indeed, after the son declines, the father recovers dramatically. In *The Metamorphosis*, however, Gregor's sin of usurpation is scarcely alluded to, and the metamorphosis is not made manifest as punishment or self-punishment.

A work of art embodies a self analyzable on two levels: the primitive or infantile level (corresponding to the id and primary process) and the adult level (corresponding to the ego and secondary process). It is at the second level that we make aesthetic and moral judgments. **Kaiser**'s essay on *The Metamorphosis* richly explores the id material of the story and deserves to be augmented.

The metamorphosis is meant to be taken literally, as a real event. Not a symbol of someone's derangement, it is an object reflecting disparate intentions, which have to be kept apart. On the one hand it is the object of Kafka's poetic imagination; on the other, its intention is inscribed in its consequences within the story world. "Within the story it is *the metamorphosis* (literally an impossible event) that represents objective reality for Gregor and his family . . . ; whereas it is *their behavior* that is strange, dreamlike, incongruous, inappropriate, and for this reason life-like—the ordinary behavior of humanity confronted with the ugliness of fact" (*Franz Kafka,* 28-29). The family acts toward the metamorphosis as if it were a natural event to which it could adapt; Gregor, for his part, acts at first as if the event had never occurred. All are nightmarishly estranged from the truth.

The Metamorphosis has a humorous dimension and a comic dimension. The first expresses, through indirections, a tragic-humorous intention of the author, the latent protagonist. The comic aspect of *The Metamorphosis* is a function of Gregor's and the others' behavior.

Two categories of the comic suggest themselves in this story: effects derived from the physical metamorphosis and effects derived from the moral response of Gregor and the others to the metamorphosis. In the first category are such effects as Gregor's inability to get out of bed: "he is at the disadvantage of being (like infants and young animals) unacquainted with his own anatomy" (*Franz Kafka*, 30). There is also his automatism—for example, the unwilled, automatic loss of speech and other ways in which Gregor is shown to be unable to "*help* acting and reacting in many respects like an insect" (*Franz Kafka,* 31). He now lives at a biologically more primitive level. These effects are frequently "combined with comedy of contradicted expectation," as when Gregor's moral responses are followed by instinctive insectlike movements. Gregor's new habits—"the interest in dirt, the pleasure in crawling, and the further habit he develops of taking food into his mouth merely 'as a pastime,' spitting it out again hours later—all serve to emphasize the *infantile* character of the degraded state to which Gregor has symbolically returned; thus strengthening the latent aspect (adult-infant) of the implied comic comparison (human being-animal; living creature-automaton). . . . Only one change in Gregor's tastes (his new appetite for music) is not similarly regressive" (*Franz Kafka,* 32).

The moral comedy in *The Metamorphosis* is based on the incongruity between what the responses of the characters ought to be and what these responses are. The entire work is informed by the strategy of obliquity and understatement. The latent impact of the metamorphosis is communicated through the incongruous effect it provokes. "This disparity can be described . . . as a defense mechanism involving reality-denial and affect-displacement, and thus as analogous to . . . (1) the abnormal mental behavior of psychotics . . . and (2) the behavior of the mind in dreams" (*Franz Kafka,* 33). *The Metamorphosis* is saturated with "dream logic." On awakening to the metamorphosis, Gregor "automatically *displaces* his attention onto inessentials, onto peripheral details of his situation, distributing and reducing his manifest emotion accordingly" (*Franz Kafka*, 33). There is a disparity between the quantity of emotion generated in the reader by the experience of the metamorphosis and the quantity of emotion in Gregor's response: "empathy is first stimulated, then rendered superfluous, and so discharged in the form of laughter" (*Franz Kafka*, 33).

This disparity is also the source of intense tragic irony. "Gregor is shown clinging to the belief that his metamorphosis is a dream or other hallucination, while at the same time thinking and acting . . . on the basis of a fear . . . that it is real and could be perceived by other people. . . . That he should have lost his human shape is not tolerable, 'therefore' not true" (*Franz Kafka*, 34-35). The first section of the story is informed by Gregor's resistance to knowledge of the metamorphosis; henceforth "Gregor is presumed to abandon . . . his forlorn pretenses, and achieves a certain pathetic resignation" (*Franz Kafka*, 35). Now the psychic functions of displacement and repression (in the service of self-protection) reappear in the bizarre acceptance of the situation by the family. In Kafka's world the criterion of reality is not allowed to apply.

The Metamorphosis is riddled with arguments inspired not by logic but by fear and desire. Hence "the comedy of unwitting self-contradiction" (*Franz Kafka*, 37). There unfolds through Gregor's ruminations a series of disparate explanations, all pathetically irrelevant to the fact of the metamorphosis. In this case "the desire to exonerate oneself overrides with *automatic ease* the law of contradiction" (*Franz Kafka*, 38).

The comedy of Gregor's behavior throughout the story is the comedy of primitiveness. Yet a tragic dimension adheres to this–the fact that his is the primitiveness, not of genuine innocence, but of monstrous regression. Gregor's speeches are unintelligible as the language of human beings; "Gregor's processes of thought have sunk below the level of organization and synthesis, and it is to this *intellectual* degradation . . . that the physical loss of his human shape and voice is parabolically equivalent" (*Franz Kafka*, 38).

In *The Metamorphosis* the humorous object is "the manifest protagonist, Gregor. Gregor is (tragi-) comic but not himself humorous; the (tragic) humor of the story is an aspect of the attitude of the author (towards himself and mankind)" (*Franz Kafka*, 42).

Sokel, 105-A, offers the following objections:

"In this comic discrepancy between the actual situation and Gregor's rationalizations, Mr. Luke has seen a satiric parable on the irrationality of human mental processes; Gregor's transformation into a subhuman creature is for him the external correlative to the atavistic, irrational nature of his thinking. However, it is less faulty logic than a psychic compromise which lies at the basis of Gregor's self-deception—a compromise between the satisfaction of an aggressively rebellious impulse and a duty-bound conscience that demands submission. The function of the metamorphosis is to allow the compromise" (208-09).

"Mr. Luke has seen in Gregor's specious pleading [at the outset of *The Metamorphosis*] the deterioration of his rationality, an inner correlate of his external transformation into a subhuman creature. But the pleading is a failure of nerve rather than a failure of logic. It is the compulsive effort to deceive himself and the others about the truth . . . " (211).

76. Madden, William A. "A Myth of Mediation: Kafka's Metamorphosis." *Thought*, XXVI (Summer 1951), 246-66.

Kafka is positive, in the sense that his style elaborates a dialectic of spirit and matter, meaning and nonsense, order and anarchy. Kafka's lesson in the metamorphosis is of life without hope yet shored up by "the myth of mediation."

Our first concern is not with the cause of the metamorphosis but with the reaction it produces in Gregor and his family. The chief horror here is that no one considers the metamorphosis "impossible": everyone adjusts.

The contingent worlds of Gregor and his family have an inexpungeable reality, resisting allegorization.[45] Kafka's concern in this piece is for a "symbolic" representation of a fundamental human situation, but at bottom "Franz Kafka's relationship with his family and society is the real theme of *The Metamorphosis*" (255).

Madden asserts that Gregor's metamorphosis is brought on by "self-knowledge [in] circumstances favoring self-scrutiny";[46] that the sense of the animal transmogrification is his affliction by guilt; finally, that the cruelty of the family is merely a further confirmation of Gregor's guilt. "Kafka, like Kierkegaard, sees all of 'Christendom' reflected in the destiny of the individual person" (257). Yet "Gregor remains ignorant throughout of the true cause ['of the spiritual rupture of man from his true destiny'], and he does not display the least desire to find an explanation" (258).

Madden quotes Kafka's aphorism, "The state in which we find

ourselves is sinful, quite independent of guilt,"[47] and comments: "Gregor Samsa represents the fructification of an inherent maladjustment which tethers man to the idiosyncratic whims of a hidden God" (259). The second "metaphysical principle" that emerges from the dialectic of *The Metamorphosis* is "that men could not unite in their search for the truth, that every solution is finally a private and personal one" (261). The third principle, the myth of mediation, is something that may only be spoken of darkly, because it is dark in Kafka. "Though it defies logic, there is a faith indispensable to man, a myth of mediation or of a bridge which exists *because it must exist*, based on a logic superior to the logic of this world" (265).

The only evidence Madden adduces to support the assertion of such a faith in *The Metamorphosis* is the fact that Gregor, on the verge of death, "thought of his family with deep emotion and love."

Von Wiese notes that though Madden takes Kafka's realism seriously, he nonetheless offers a symbolic interpretation. In a similar vein, **Pongs** remarks that the vision of the metamorphosis extends far beyond that of real cockroaches: "More decisive than the kind of insect Gregor is is the terror which his change diffuses" (267).

77. **Maione, Italo**. *Franz Kafka*. Naples, n.d. Pp. 49-50.

The drama of *The Metamorphosis* is that of a man and his destiny which alienates him from society, from traditional values, and from preferred occupations. The piece explores with irony the genuinely human responses of a variety of actors faced with this misfortune. Everything develops as in the normal ambience of this world–yet within a mythic framework.

78. **Margolis, Joseph**. "Kafka vs. Eudaimonia and Duty." *Philosophy and Phenomenological Research*, XIX (Sept. 1958), 27-42.

The way in which *The Metamorphosis* treats morality is an implicit critique of Plato's *Republic* and Kant's *Foundations of the Metaphysics of Morals*. Kafka's story "dramatizes the isolating, restrictive, and paradoxical conditions under which the human being exerts his particular freedom" (27). It rebuts all oversimplified moral systems; it creates a sense of the variousness and complexity of the circumstances of life from which principles and models are constructed.

The works of Plato and Kant confidently advance solutions to the problem of moral responsibility; *The Metamorphosis*, on the other hand, stresses its sheerly problematical character. It does this by exhibiting through the narrative a sure grasp of the basic issues of moral philosophy. Gregor Samsa–in some sense the beneficiary of the two most important moral doctrines of the Western tradition–cannot bring together or understand eudaemonism or the philosophy of duty. He moves between these two viewpoints; he abstracts from each the philosophical puzzle involved but cannot solve it. He dies in the mood of a higher concern, but this concern is the dialectical outcome of a critique of Plato's and Kant's moral views.

Section I of *The Metamorphosis* shows Gregor insisting that his change is a hallucination and terrified of being unable to resume his usual habits and obligations. In Section II he acknowledges the change and explores the character and tastes of his new body. A new life style is imposed on him–but he remains loyal to his old business obligations and to the family pattern. The human world he remembers and his solitary life as a bug split him in two "and contradict his every motivation. In III he is reconciled to the permanence of the change and comprehends the futility of his monstrous isolation as well as the crippling burden which his continued existence places on the family" (35). Having accepted his new life, he decides to disappear; and, indeed, immediately after he dies, the family shows new signs of life.

The metamorphosis is to be taken seriously, and this means not literally. The image of the bug "is, fundamentally, an image of self-examination–of the contempt for, and misery of, self that follows the first truly searching doubt of the meaning and worth of one's actual existence" (35). Gregor's career has hitherto been successful–but virtually automatic. The metamorphosis reveals to him profound dissatisfactions at the bottom of his soul. The bug-human split corresponds roughly to the split between rational and irrational components of man in classical moral theory.

The metamorphosis signalizes in a manner of speaking the beginning of Gregor's pursuit of "the rational direction and coherence of the moral life of the *Republic* or of the *Foundations*" (36). Until now he has regarded himself (in the Kantian perspective) as the mere means to an end, an instrument for paying off the debts of his parents for the sake of a remote independence. He has permitted (in the Platonic perspective) aggressive and appetitive powers of the soul to enslave his reason; he has dominated his family. This interpretation should not, however, lead us to the conclusion which Kafka specifically denies, "*that the mere exercise of reason could have anticipated or disposed of the present evil*" (36).

Gregor attempts to understand how he has brought about this predicament. In the end he relieves his guilt by assuming full responsibility–by dying to liberate the family. Though at the beginning and the end of the piece he has a sense that his career has been an error, he does not correct it, and he does not "manage to formulate principles on which he could have met his obligations or fulfilled the promise of his nature" (36). He has implicitly accepted the ordinary standards of common morality as seen by Kant and Plato, but he cannot develop them in a general way. The conclusion is an imaginative leap; but before he achieves it, Gregor raises the fundamental problems which the later stages of Kant's and Plato's arguments are obliged to address.

Platonic categories clarify the development of Gregor's self-awareness. In Section I, he is ignorant of his true nature; in Section II, he gradually becomes aware of his own hybrid character as a being of rational powers and insect appetites. In Section III, he grasps his new nature as the integral fact of the sheer incommensurability of his being and the moral commonplaces with which he began. Kantian categories stress that the commonplace duties which Gregor earlier assumed grow self-evidently perverse as Gregor realizes that he had become a merely compulsive instrumentality. In Section II Gregor intends to bring about a *modus vivendi* with the family but cannot find a harmonious solution. In Section III both Gregor and the family come to realize that the moral motive of family duty has grown futile, and all regard themselves as exempted from duty.

"There is an instructive difficulty of moral decision as we move from Plato to Kant to Kafka . . . . Kafka's hero appears to be contemporary man, motivated by both happiness and duty but victimized in a world that is incoherent with respect to both" (37-38). Happiness and duty cannot be fulfilled: the moral enterprise reduces to the affirmation of its precondition—that the world is such as it is. Perceiving that his death is inevitable, Gregor accepts dying; the love which he directs toward the others is the consciousness that in dying he is enabling the others to be moral beings. In this attitude, however, there are no "moral principles that can insure either happiness or right duty; its confidence is religious, not moral. Gregor Samsa is reduced to endorsing the moral effort of man, but he has no instruction to offer except that it may be confounded by the discovery of crippling forces within oneself" (38).

The implications of Gregor's predicament tend to converge on the problems of the discrepancy of individuals and the incommunicability of intentions. "Kafka seems to teach that confidence in the personal search for happiness or in the progressive fulfillment of one's duties depends on a conformist society in which one seeks to adopt and maintain through regular and predictable habit a highly standardized role; correspondingly, moral judgment regarding self and others becomes disordered, indeed paralyzed, when the habitual pattern is challenged by the suddenly apparent discrepancy between its offerings and requirements and the radical capabilities and needs and limitations of a specific human individual. The discovery is spontaneous, neither one's self nor others can be insured against it" (38).

Gregor discovers that his early conceptions of happiness and duty are in error. The condition of the moral life is life among others: precisely this bond makes morality impossible for him, for to break with others is to break with the coherence that makes the pursuit of happiness or duty possible. The shock of recognizing his otherness with respect to society leads Gregor "to pass completely beyond the rejection without challenging it" (39).[48] Gregor accepts his death with a view to reconfirming the conventional order within which his family can pursue moral activity. His family recognizes this in excluding him from this order rather than condemning him within its terms. The outcome of Gregor's moral seriousness is his dying to respect "the adequacy of the original conventions for the rest of the family" (39-40). The equanimity and love with which Gregor dies suggest "the preconditions of any moral act that Gregor might commit, though he cannot now commit a single act or even contemplate one" (40). Before the metamorphosis Gregor sought the welfare of his family, an effort which entailed their loss of self-respect and his personal impoverishment. He now seeks their welfare once again through the only adequate act—suicide. "Similarly the family is forced to support what, in moral terms, would amount to murder" (40).

Kafka does not dismiss reason, but reason discovers—helplessly—a permanent source of unreason in man, ruining moral effort. Opposite to Plato and Kant, Kafka "claims in effect to have isolated a profound and neglected ingredient in human morality, . . . an ingredient of sudden and unaccountably evil changes of nature and fortune, of the appearance of the irretrievably hateful and monstrous, of whatever exiles one permanently from an intimate community of men, of insolubly evil and crippling dilemmas, paradoxes, ambiguities, and desires" (41).

Marill, René. See **Albérès.**

79. **Marion, Denis.** *"La Métamorphose* par Franz Kafka" (a review). *La Nouvelle Revue Française,* CCXCVII (June 1938), 1034-37.

"Kafka's work has only one theme—the absurdity of existence" (1034). Though this theme is not new, Kafka's relation to it is. "He neither complains of nor rebels against this situation, which instead inspires in him a perpetually renewed astonishment" (1034). He constantly experiences new proofs of this absurdity, at the same time contriving more and more subtle notions in an effort to explain it away. "Despite the utmost patience and ingenuity, he never succeeds in discovering a weak spot in the indomitable antagonism between thought and the world" (1034-35). In his attempt to reveal to others the intolerableness of their condition, his strategy is to put his protagonists into situations which are clearly absurd, then to show them behaving in exactly the same way that we ordinarily behave.

Kafka's heroes are not particularized; they can be defined only by their metaphysical anguish. *The Metamorphosis* conveys man's terror at his secret inclinations, a terror for which there is no remedy.

"The actual implausibility of the postulate which underlies each of his narratives is dissolved by the tranquil tonality of the story and the detailed realism with which the events are described. After a few pages of *The Metamorphosis* we no longer doubt that Gregor Samsa has been changed into a sort of monstrous louse, and it never occurs to us even to ask how such a thing could have happened: the authenticity of the themes and events narrated is so obvious that the point of departure indirectly gains a provisory credibility" (1036).

Moreover, Gregor Samsa does not question his transformation any more than we do, and he is not aware of an inner change. If he suffers from his condition, it is as if from a sickness or a blemish: he never considers that he is essentially transformed. "He would not have acted any differently had he always known that he was a louse, always managing to keep from himself the knowledge that this reality is revealed in his appearance. This feeling causes a malaise to weigh on the reader which is not due to the given circumstances but to the idea that each of us is vulnerable in this way: that our most secret nature might be revealed to those near to us and their affection destroyed by a revulsion which they could not control" (1036).

Kafka establishes the parallel between his fictional universe and everyday reality by developing his stories at great length through episodes without intrigue; there is little or no dramatic progression, "since the essential characteristic of the protagonist is incessantly to mark time in the face of the contradiction which he has come up against from the start and not to have advanced an inch by the time of the *dénouement*" (1037).

80. Martin, Peter. "The Cockroach as an Identification; With Reference to Kafka's *Metamorphosis.*" *American Imago,* XVI (1959), 65-71.

A patient freely associates his own predicament with the bug Gregor and in this way interprets *The Metamorphosis*. "I'm like a child. . . . I attach myself to a person. I make him God. Then I feel like a parasite. *I feel completely unworthy. The feeling of being like an insect is the feeling of being inferior.* I couldn't move in the dream. When a demand is made upon me, I become like that. I become sluggish like a bug. In *The Metamorphosis*, he had all the responsibility of the family. He should have hated them. He turned into a bug and *retreated* all the way to the other extreme. . . . Living frightens me. I don't want to go on. I want to sleep and push all activities away. As long as I don't move, as long as I stay in bed, I'm safe." Martin comments, "The identification with a cockroach represents a feeling of being . . . *weak, inferior and unworthy*. The cockroach is a symbol of inadequacy." Crucial, too, are "the feeling of being unloved and rejected by the important parent figure and an inability to conceive of an evaluation of self not based on some other person's attitude. . . . Every fibre of this type of patient is directed toward another person, placing the decision for life or death in the other person's hands and thus making of rejection a deadly weapon."

The final comment of the analysand is acutely perceptive for a psychological reading of *The Metamorphosis*: "Physical paralysis is the fear of going mad with hate for not being loved."

81. **Müller, Robert**. Review essay. *Die neue Rundschau*, II (1916), 1421-26. Cited in Jürgen **Born**, "Franz Kafka und seine Kritiker (1912-1914)." In *Kafka-Symposion*. Berlin: Wagenbach, 1965. Pp. 147-48.

Gregor Samsa awakens as a gigantic bug with the soul of a Christian and the weak spirituality of the good man who cannot even be astonished. These were precisely Gregor's qualities before the metamorphosis. The family, terrified at first, takes care of its grotesquely lost son until its natural egoism asserts itself. Gregor's predicament is not so much a problem as an experiment for the sake of telling a story. Yet the hypothesis of the metamorphosis is unsuccessful; the conceit is ingenious and flawlessly thought out, but we are, after all, asked to swallow too much.

82. **Muschg, Walter**. *Tragische Literaturgeschichte*, 2nd ed., revised and enlarged. Bern: Francke, 1953. Pp. 343-44.

Kafka is "the sole truly initiated writer of the present era"; "he has experienced in his own flesh the metamorphosis of man into a vermin, this most awful fact of the twentieth century."

83. **Nabokov, Vladimir**. "An Interview with Vladimir Nabokov" by Alfred Appel, Jr. In *Nabokov: The Man and his Work, Studies*, ed. by L. S. Dembo. Madison, Milwaukee, and London: The University of Wisconsin Press, 1967. Pp. 42-43.

In answer to the question, "What kind of beetle, by the way, was Gregor?" Nabokov replies: "It was a domed beetle, a scarab beetle with wing-sheaths, and neither Gregor nor his maker realized that when the room was being made by the maid, he could have flown out and escaped and joined the other happy dung beetles rolling the dung balls on rural paths."

84-A. **Neider, Charles**. *The Frozen Sea: A Study of Franz Kafka*. New York: Oxford University Press, 1948; republished as *Kafka: His Mind and Art*. London: Routledge and Kegan Paul, 1949. Pp. 77-78, 180-81.

In *The Metamorphosis* Kafka portrays himself as a gigantic bug. The work registers the masochistic self-hatred liberated by his relation with Felice Bauer. Gregor Samsa, though a philistine, is a fanatically good son. The family's parasitic dependence on him "is a wish projection of a Kafka depressed by his economic dependence on his father" (77). The attacks on the elder Samsa are attacks on the self disguised by reversal. Though a horror tale, *The Metamorphosis* is full of felt truth, "consisting especially of the universality of disaster and the fear of the unknown" (77). This metamorphosis is symbolic of more dreadful transformations which are actual and possible. "There is implicit everywhere the neurotic's horror of losing control, and there are hints of fear of the lower depths of sleep, night, and dream, and also of existence in death without the release of death–a mythical echo of Tantalus" (77).

84-B. Neider, Charles. "Franz Kafka." In *Short Novels of the Masters*. New York: Rinehart, 1948. Pp. 44-47.

The Metamorphosis has a personal significance, reflecting Kafka's sense of personal insufficiency with respect to his father and his traumatic experiences at the ages of two and three when infant brothers died.

Kafka conceived woman as the symbol and means of salvation. His meeting with Felice Bauer led to an important breakthrough in his work, to the writing of "The Judgment" and *The Metamorphosis*.

Gregor's way of dealing with his unintelligible metamorphosis is to protest against his former existence. The job fixation is Kafka's own. "Gregor's complete transformation, both mental and physical, saves him from realizing the true nature of his tragedy"–that is, his familial and economic servitude. Gregor's "mental inadequacy or ignorance" permits Kafka to tell his story directly. "Gregor's responses are purely behavioristic: he acts as he must in his bug state; every effort is toward self-preservation. . . . Whatever Gregor is, he is totally that: totally the insect, the commercial traveler, the faithful son. . . . It must have afforded Kafka no little pleasure, ambivalent as he was, to write of a character so steadfast in his duty and his conception of duty."

85-A. Oliass, Heinz-Günther. "Die Märchen von der verwandelten Existenz: Metamorphosen von Ovid bis Kafka." *Die neue Zeitung* (Munich), CCXXVII (September 26, 1952), 4.

Not seen.

85-B. Oliass, Heinz-Günther. "Schwarzkäfer und Fuchsdame: vom Wandel der Metamorphose." *Frankfurter Allgemeine Zeitung*, XV (December 15, 1954), 8.

The metamorphosis in Kafka's story is singular–unlike the classical metamorphosis in Ovid in which "punishment, refuge or elevation always occurs through the hand of higher destiny" and unlike the fairy-tale degradation of man into a beast, which appears to be dictated by moral law.

Gregor Samsa is "struck by an evil omen that makes him impure and suspicious" and casts him out of human society. It functions as a Job-like visitation for the family. "But there is not a single sentence to indicate a trace of the guilt of this creature who, to judge from his deformity, is very probably not without guilt. Gregor himself does not know of any guilt; indeed, he does not even meditate on the question of guilt. The metamorphosis is inflicted without a reason, and the animal shape imposed on him remains even after his death."

The agency behind the transformation shows no signs of grace; it can neither be seen nor even intuited. "This sad fate cannot be grasped under a mythical, magical, or religious head. This metamorphosis lacks a metaphysical superstructure establishing connections, the manifestation and hence the possibility of an awareness of the supremely powerful and sublime adversary. An act of law occurs without law and legislator."

Gregor becomes an "it," "stuff." A man is robbed of his self and does not contest the loss, does not contend "because in his situation the being no longer exists with whom he might contend. . . . Even the powers of understanding appear to be taken from him: the black beetle ventures to consider his situation but not to think on past it. The odyssey goes on–without Odysseus."

Even Gregor's patient acceptance of the animal shape does not lead him to any state of inner purity.

86. **Ollivier, Albert**. "Miroirs de Saint-Just." *Les Temps Modernes*, no. 6 (1946), 1008.

"In Saint-Just, as in Kafka, the metamorphosis, the degradation of a man into an animal, comes to testify to the misery of the human condition and the ineffable and subtle connections which link him to the cosmos through certain bodily forces."

87. **Parry, Idris F**. "Kafka and Gogol." *German Life and Letters*, n.s. VI (Jan. 1953), 141-45.

Kafka's technique—even the essence of his art—is not new. Gregor Samsa's predicament at the opening of *The Metamorphosis* is not essentially different from Kovalëv's in Gogol's *The Nose*. [See **Erlich**.] "Kovalëv . . . also wakes up . . . in the same place (bed) and at the same time (early morning) to find that his nose has disappeared overnight. . . . The place and time are significant. For Gregor Samsa and Kovalëv are awakening, not from a nightmare, but, reversing the normal process, *into* a nightmare, the nightmare world which is always just below the surface" (141). From the psychoanalytic viewpoint, this world of dreams is our real truth; these characters are therefore really finding themselves.

Kafka preserves the pedestrian surface of life, but his starting point is a proposition of pure imagination, which the reader is obliged to accept. "Kafka's absurdity is . . . an assault on the periphery of our conscious minds" (143).

Gregor Samsa's cockroach form perfectly expresses his personality—he is a creature of fear and inadequacy. In this formula Kafka mirrors his own work, which is "an expression of fear" (143). This formula is confirmed by the passage in "Letter to His Father" in which Kafka has his father describe him as a "noxious insect, which not only bites, but also sucks blood for its own preservation." "Samsa/Kafka," writes Parry, "is the noxious insect, unfit for human life, a pathetic and (some would say) pathological confession of human inadequacy" (144). Gregor has put aside his human mask; he stands spiritually naked. But he will wither as the father regains his economic and emotional ascendancy, "for this insect does not suck blood; it is a failure even as an insect. It dies because it is dependent—in the last resort dependent on the father" (144). This mirrors Kafka's own predicament. He lacked personal certainty; his life was a nightmare of vacillations.

At the same time, in the man-bug Gregor Samsa Kafka has created "a symbol for the whole of life, including that other realm of consciousness which lies behind appearance" (145). Rilke believed that there are gaps in our sensory awareness; hence our anxiety: we fear what we do not know. "It is to these gaps that Gogol and Kafka lead us" (145).

88. **Pasley, Malcolm**, and **Wagenbach, Klaus**. "Versuch einer Datierung sämtlicher Texte Franz Kafkas." *Deutsche Vierteljahrszeitschrift für Literaturwissenschaft und Geistesgeschichte*, XXXVIII, 2 (1964), 154.

The manuscript of *The Metamorphosis* is privately owned. On the basis of Max Brod's notation in his diary (on November 24, 1912, Kafka read aloud at Baum's "his splendid novella about the bug"), the authors date the composition of *The Metamorphosis* as "probably immediately prior [to the reading], but in any case not before October, 1912, since in several places in the manuscript 'Karl' is written instead of 'Gregor.' " [Kafka began writing the final version of "The Stoker," whose hero is Karl Rossman, at the end of September 1912.]

Since the publication of Kafka's *Briefe an Felice (Letters to Felice)* it is known that Kafka cannot have read the whole of *The Metamorphosis* at Baum's on November 24, 1912: *The Metamorphosis* was not yet finished. Kafka began writing *The Metamorphosis* on November 17, 1912, and finished on December 7, 1912.

Perry, Marvin B. See **Ludwig**.

89. **Pfeiffer, Johannes.** "Über Franz Kafkas Novelle 'Die Verwandlung.' " *Die Sammlung*, XIV (June 1959), 297-302. Reprinted as the third part of "Dichterische Wirklichkeit und 'weltanschauliche' Wahrheit, erläutert an Novellen von Hans Grimm, Thomas Mann und Franz Kafka." In Pfeiffer, *Die dichterische Wirklichkeit. Versuche über Wesen und Wahrheit der Dichtung.* Hamburg: Richard Meiner, 1962. "The Metamorphosis," trans. by Ronald Gray, in *Kafka, a Collection of Critical Essays,* ed. by Ronald Gray. Englewood Cliffs, N. J.: Prentice-Hall, 1962. Pp. 53-59.

The Metamorphosis is a parabolic story in the following sense: what is narrated is transparent to a background of meaning deepening the narrative at every point. The relation of depth to surface is not that of a conceptual starting point to its subsequent elaboration in sensuous form, from which it could then be abstracted. Meaning in *The Metamorphosis* is communicated through an imaged reality to the imagination which glimpses it as in a vision.

The story is divided into three parts of approximately equal length. The interval between the first and second sections is one day. Between the second and third sections the interval is of indeterminate length. Each of the three sections concludes with a catastrophe increasing in intensity. The first leads to a "deep, comalike sleep"; the second, to unconciousness and serious injury; the third, to death.

The balanced structure has its counterpart in the exactness with which spatial relations within the story are determined and in a sort of magic realism representing objects with such density and sober precision that the whole becomes unreal or surreal. "The physical nature of the monster is conceived from within, and the outer world is built up entirely from this bodily identity" ("Über Kafka," 297). The rooms of the apartment and the objects in them are never given as a complete picture from the start, but there is an oppressive and suggestive slow manifestation of spatiality strictly as it comes to light from the point of view of the metamorphosed creature.

The metamorphosis itself is presented as something normal, matter of fact, having the character of everyday reality.

The inner movement of the story is marked by Gregor's persistent efforts to act as if nothing more were at stake than a slight indisposition. "Cast out of human society by his enigmatic transformation, he does not realize the radical truth of his new position" ("Über Kafka," 298). But at the same time that he attempts to conceal his true condition from himself, a sort of instinctive clairvoyance bares it to him in all its inescapability. He notes how he is left to his own devices and how more and more he grows into his new role. The alienation and indifference of the others increases. Gregor becomes an "it"; "what the cleaning woman says and does after Gregor's death is basically what all the others think" ("Über Kafka," 299). It is only that she says it without inhibition, for which she is promptly fired: the family feel their own hidden impulses bared by her behavior. The same sort of bad faith is at work when the family marches on the roomers. At the close, life throws off the nuisance of the metamorphosis and, relieved, affirms itself once more—"a conclusion full of merciless, if not to say cynical, coldness which apparently dismisses us into the domain of the wholly indefinite and undefinable" ("Über Kafka," 299).

Apart from the last five pages the perspective is entirely Gregor's. This perspective determines the basic meaning of the story; it would be a mistake to transfer the center of gravity to the shattered family.[49]

The narrative resists making any express references to the background which lends the story significant depth; in a sense, then, this background is left blank. The main clue is perhaps the episode of the violin music; music gives a sign of that unknown and unknowable dimension which could satisfy Gregor's longing for liberation, redemption. One of Kafka's diary entries gives us a sudden insight into the novel's background: "From a certain point on there is no return. This point has to be reached."

The action of the piece is this: As a consequence of the metamorphosis a man drops out of normal life. He proceeds to exhaust himself in attempts to maintain his connection with this life. Gradually he resigns himself and goes to his ruin. As long as he considers the metamorphosis as a piece of bad luck, the possibility contained in the longing for some unknown nourishment remains uncomprehended. This possibility is one of "breaking through the constraints of life, the existential imprisonment which is our fate, of coming to know the primordial guilt of involvement in existence, and this way becoming free, free to return to authentic, true, absolute Being" ("Über Kafka," 301). As in all of Kafka, the way to this possibility lies closed; there is, however, a remote glimmer of the grace surmised as a possibility.

To put it differently: the mystery of being cast out contains glimmers of damnation and grace. In the parabolic form of an extreme situation man experiences his irremediable solitude: this solitude is rooted in the fact that he does not belong to the illusory world of everyday concerns and points toward an ultimate destination–what is sheerly Other, absolute and infinite. Two of Kafka's apothegms define this basic tension: "Life is a continual distraction which does not even let us reflect on that which it distracts us from." The second apothegm begins: "A first sign of the beginnings of awareness is the wish to die."

Kafka configures Gregor's radical extremity, then, in such a way that access to freedom remains closed to him: though the significant background is left blank, we are nonetheless indirectly given the feeling of it. The work is not merely negative or pessimistic, since it "structures an original and essential vision which, purely as such, signifies a spiritual conquest of the world" ("Über Kafka," 301).

There still remains the troubling reservation that a small part of the work is inspired, not by a desire for truth and salvation, but by an aestheticism concerned only with the success of an experimental narrative in the service of a secret delight in torment.

90. Poggioli, Renato. "Kafka and Dostoyevsky." In *The Kafka Problem*, ed. by Angel Flores. New York: New Directions, 1946. Pp. 102-04.

The unexpected metamorphosis creates a new destiny for Gregor; because his life until now has centered around habit and routine, his new life is his "true life and . . . real destiny." The metamorphosis forces on him a life of wakefulness and insomnia;

Gregor awakens into conscience.[50] His metamorphosis is a notion—of having been converted into an unclean animal. The miraculous metamorphosis "canalizes" the existence of Gregor into "one logical track, . . . tight-packed with consequences, necessities and habits, which in and of themselves are banal, natural and common." Gregor "must submit to the crude exigencies of animal and vegetable life." Gregor has become an underground man, judged and condemned for eternity.

He has been transformed into a bug because the sense of sin and of eternity reveals to man his bestiality; "and because only to a cockroach can a room, a wall or a bit of furniture seem infinite." The whole of Kafka's artistry aims at *not* suggesting that the metamorphosis occurs through an act of magic or enchantment; in this way he does not suggest the possibility that Gregor's soul will be changed through the catharsis of the miracle. (See **Angus** and **Heselhaus**.) Gregor's metamorphosis is an "irremediable internal catastrophe," an incarceration by conscience. Kafka's work "describes without pity the hard prison of our logic, a prison from which has never been heard the echo of a prayer nor the song of a prisoner."

91-A. Politzer, Heinz. *Franz Kafka, Parable and Paradox*. Ithaca, New York: Cornell University Press, 1962. Pp. 65-84.

The question of Gregor's guilt—the why of the metamorphosis—is not explicitly posed; yet, as in an analytic tragedy, the reader is drawn into this pursuit.

"If [the insect] was intended to serve as an allegory of Kafka's own existence, this intention is continually disturbed by Kafka's insistence on the insect's *being* Gregor in addition to *representing* him" (65).

The story has a schematic, triadic structure. The first part relates Gregor to his profession, the second to his family, the third to himself. And yet in another sense the story is endless and the actual conclusion only an unconvincing addition.

The first part is dominated by the image of the alarm clock, suggesting the closed, yet endless and irrevocable temporality of

Gregor's professional life. "With uncanny and inhuman regularity, reflected in the incessant ticking of the clock, business moves in to reclaim the fugitive" (66). The metamorphosis appears to be a device to escape the straitening job. But the fact is that Gregor has stayed on the job for the very human reason of paying off his parents' debt to the firm: paradoxically, the attempt to flee compulsion through the insect metamorphosis means the loss of Gregor's humanity as well.

Gregor is the victim of paralyzing contradictions. Though he has recently been promoted, "he shrinks back from the progress which would lead him closer to his long desired freedom" (67). Gregor wants success and at the same time flees from it; his life's motion is perpetual and circular.

The metamorphosis cannot represent an escape from reality: Gregor remains attached to himself and pleads, though an insect, to be kept on as a traveling salesman. He continues to go round in circles: "The circle of time, described by the hands of the alarm clock, is repeated in space by the insect's desperate gyrations" (68).

In the second part time dissolves. Particular temporal articulations are replaced by indefinite adverbs of time, such as "soon" and "later." The metamorphosis continues in the loss of a distinct rhythm to a shapeless vagueness. Gregor's experience is that of an invalid, a prisoner; as time goes on dissolving, space contracts all around him: his room becomes his cell.

Gregor's solitude is unalterable. The way in which the rest of the family comes to terms with this solitude is the mark of its humanity. When the finances of the Samsa household are bared, we grasp that the father has exploited Gregor's sense of duty and his ingrained submissiveness. "If Gregor's change into an insect was meant to dramatize certain parasitic traits in his character, we realize now that these traits are inherited" (70). Grete, for her part, is at first the only one to interpret Gregor's metamorphosis as a disaster for Gregor and not merely for the family. "She serves as a provider to the animal in addition to being his nurse, messenger, interpreter, and an expert in all his dealings with the family" (71).

Various passages in *The Metamorphosis* invite psychoanalytical speculation. But in this work Kafka "was still playing with psychoanalysis as a child plays with fire and, like the child, he was not so much interested in the fire as the play" (74).

Gregor does not turn inward. Abandoned by his sister, who gives over his charge to the charwoman, Gregor could make a breakthrough into an understanding of human failure. But he spoils the opportunity with displays of resentment and true beastliness. His earlier reactions and reminiscences were hold-overs from his life as a man. Now all his thoughts are superficial, with the exception of the realization to which he comes in Section III: that he cannot be satisfied by earthly food.

The rhetorical question, "Was he an animal that music could move him so?" affirms that Gregor keeps and possibly has always kept his human identity. Yet the lapse of his enchantment with the music into a crude desire to possess the musician shows that he remains what he has always been. "We feel the icy breath of an existence fatally gone astray" (77). A whirl of unanswerable questions arises about the depth and source of Gregor's guilt—the guilt intensified through images of solitude and dirt.

Politzer opposes **Emrich**'s view that Gregor's final mood of forgiveness amounts to a "liberating cognition" or a "reconciliation of Gregor with himself and the world." Gregor's final meditation is vacuous; he submits. "The metamorphosis has failed to change him. He dies, as he lived, a thing" (79).

But this does not permit the moralizing view that Gregor has been transformed into a heap of useless matter as a consequence of his lifelong preoccupation with things. Gregor never has the opportunity to choose another course, to atone, to resist. He is condemned by a power outside the scope of empirical experience—cruel, arbitrary, incomprehensible.

Kafka asked that Gregor be represented only through the total darkness of his room. "This complete darkness is the proper description of Gregor's fate as well as of the animal shape into which he was transformed. The un- [of *'ungeheueres Ungeziefer'* —'monstrous bug' or 'vermin'], the dark, the void, are the only designations Kafka could find for the mystery at the center of the tale. Gregor's metamorphosis is the image of his own negative possibilities as well as of the incomprehensibility of the power that changed him into an insect" (82).

91-B. Politzer, Heinz. "Letter to His Father." In *Franz Kafka Today*, ed. by Angel Flores and Homer Swander. Madison: The University of Wisconsin Press, 1964. Pp. 221-37.

The famous passage in "Letter to His Father" in which Kafka has his father liken him to vermin is anticipated by the self-involved daydream of the beautiful beetle in "Wedding Preparations in the Country." This image lies dormant until awakened by an incident concerning the Yiddish actor Löwy with whom Kafka identified himself. "The letter [to his father] records how the father compared the actor, 'without knowing him, in a terrible manner, which I have already forgotten [*sic*], with vermin' " (230). To this daydream, and this insult, Kafka brought the shock of self-recognition. "The Yiddish actor whom his father had called vermin, represented for him something he had been longing for all along, and something he would never be able to attain: the artist integrated in life, in community life. . . . He himself had been offended in Löwy, his own weakness had been discovered and punished by his father's word. In the hour of his defamation Löwy became Kafka, as Kafka became Samsa, . . . who in turn became what the father had called Löwy: an insect" (230-31). The father's curse transforms the son into a noxious bug. At the same time the curse falls on yielding soil: the son had long ago formulated and accepted this verdict.

92. Pongs, Hermann. "Franz Kafka–'Die Verwandlung,' zwischen West and Ost." In *Dichtung im gespaltenen Deutschland*. Stuttgart: Union, 1966. Pp. 262-85.

More terrifying at the outset than the metamorphosis itself is the coldness of the eye which registers the scene. *The Metamorphosis* departs radically from the animal stories arising from a world of love for animals. There is something inhuman in this narrator.

What deepens the terror is the metamorphosing force which debases a man to an unexampled degree yet does not reveal itself. The consequence of the metamorphosis is grave and terrible:

Gregor cannot articulate language as a man. He can no longer "form the sounds of language which for others cohere into meaning. With this, Gregor loses . . . the instrument of the inner form of language" (263). The substance of Gregor's consciousness derives from the inauthentic role he used to play. Without the possibilities of communication, the everyday world of the inauthentic self dwindles to nothing at a terrifying rate.

Gregor is divided. He is a man, yet because he has become an insect he cannot make himself understood. And he is an insect, but because he is also a man, he does not possess the primordial instincts with which he could be at home in the world. His one possible mode of life is to register his own proscription.

Kafka shows man in a condition of division, man's destiny in this epoch. (The extraordinary fame of *The Metamorphosis* suggests a world of fascinated readers caught in the trial which their age has prepared for them.) This division penetrates so deeply that it ruptures the relation of man and animal and disjoins language at its interior.

Western (non-Communist) interpretations of *The Metamorphosis* (for example, those of **Emrich** and **Muschg**) assert that the story dramatizes the fact of modern alienation–the division between self and world, between unconscious and conscious. The question to be posed to these interpretations is this: Is self-alienation the structure of modern existence in general or only the structure of Western interpreters who view the world through Kafka's eyes?

A corrective to these views is furnished by East German critics. For Lukács, Kafka's view of the world is not generally binding: Kafka stands impotent, blind, and panic-stricken by his anxiety in the face of the real world. True, continues Lukács, the world of contemporary capitalism is a hell, in which the human element is impotent. Nonetheless, there is a dimension missing from Kafka's world–the intersubjective, the social. Kafka's representation of the world is as a whole distorted by anxiety; his craft in representing concrete details leaves room for the "allegory of a transcendental nothingness" (Lukács).

Hermsdorf's book on Kafka (*Kafka–Weltbild und Roman*, Berlin, 1961) continues in the tradition of Lukács, stressing the debasement of the hero of *Amerika* through the inhuman treatment to which he is submitted. His disintegration is not far removed from Gregor Samsa's metamorphosis; as "The Boy Who Was Nevermore Heard Of" he is like Gregor, whose cry for help no one hears anymore. "In general the East views the metamorphosis into a bug as a symptom of decadence extending throughout the whole of Western art" (265). The Western overvaluation of Kafka's art as the source of the structure, the general myth, of our century is itself a product, perhaps, of the division between East and West.

In short, have the forces which debase Gregor Samsa objective validity, or are they symptoms of disease in Kafka? For **Anders**, Kafka does not create symbols, because in him all connection to a divine or worldly basis is missing; Kafka shares with the world only its language; from this source there issue not symbols but metaphors. Gregor's metamorphosis arises from a metaphor about bugs, rooted in language; but could certain terrifying metaphors in language legitimately originate the general myth of the twentieth century?

In fact, **Anders** continues, Kafka's style–the language of the protocol–arises from total isolation. All of Kafka's figures speak in the same idiom; there is no reflection of various moods, of the nuances of life. The fundamental tonality of Kafka's world is ambiguousness, irresoluteness, to a point of paralysis–"hence," for Pongs, "division which extends down into the sources of life, as far down as the source of language" (267).

Again, is the self-debasement in Kafka's world the result of a universally valid, modern condition or the "diseased symptoms of Western decadence, which find in Kafka their most condensed poetic form?" (267).

At the basis of the story, according to Kafka's conversation with Janouch, is a terrifying vision of reality, with which must be reconciled the fact that Kafka has transformed his own family into "bedbugs." However, we have to do here with an image signifying more than real bedbugs.

Gregor's metamorphosis is born in the interval, the dislocation, between his conscious and unconscious self. The hardness of the narrator's protocol style transforms the inconceivable into the suggestion of reality. Through this style unconscious tensions are operative. Gregor's fundamental ambivalence comes to light: he is revolted by his profession, he is rebellious toward his boss, but as the servile employee he is fundamentally terrified of oversleeping. The story assumes a disquieting comic dimension, transcending the category of the grotesque, as Gregor himself smiles at the thought of his calling for help. Gregor's conscious intent may be to pacify the manager, to remain submissive; but his opposite intent, at least unconscious, is to terrify the manager and in this way be rid of all responsibility as an employee.

It must be borne in mind that Eastern (Marxist) critics keep stressing Kafka's apothegm: "Writing is the reward for service to the devil!" (see p. 26). The terror which Gregor strikes into the manager is an objective expression of the diabolical polarization and intensification of Kafka's imagination, which permits him to register with the inhuman coldness of the protocolist "nightmarish visions as satanic realizations of self-destructive urges" (270). This is for Eastern critics a decadent art. In his own preoccupation with the "dark forces" of the unconscious, Kafka himself saw evidence of vanity and pleasure-seeking.

"What impelled Kafka to translate his nightmarish vision of the bug so radically into the being of a traveling salesman damned to act upon his world like a manifestation of Satan?" (270). In now having rid himself of his responsibility as a salesman, Gregor succeeds in effectually uprooting himself, in destroying himself. The conflict between father and son comes to light through various details—a conflict situated in the midst of the conflict in Gregor between conscious and unconscious. At the close of the first and second sections, Gregor's relinquishment of the role of provider, his shapelessness, defenselessness, and clumsiness goad the father into dominating, violent acts. In Gregor (as in Georg Bendemann in "The Judgment" and as in Kafka himself, according to his diary entries) innocence and guilt are intimately fused. Gregor seems innocent in the patience with which he endures his growing estrangement, but devilish in the way he punishes the family with the nightmarish form of his metamorphosis. The devilish and unconscious side of Gregor grotesquely eroticizes his ostensibly innocent family feelings. "In Gregor's doom we experience the self-abolishment of the human in the terror of existence purely and simply" (272). In a word, the devilish side of Kafka's art is the dislocation of human existence into hopeless situations linked to a self-destructive division between conscious and unconscious. This division reaches the depth of destroying the inner form of language.

Kafka's breakthrough in *The Metamorphosis* in the nightmarish vision of the bug destroys inhibitions at the cost of the radical negation of human values in general. Everything that follows the metamorphosis in this story remains, in the words of the Marxist critic **Hermsdorf**, "a hectic marking time." The action paralyzes, the style freezes. The effect of the conclusion of the piece is not that of a purging tragic pity but an all-leveling twilight of values. "The grotesque, scurrilous, absurd has leveled the authentic 'reckless despair' [of Thomas Mann's *Doctor Faustus*] into ambivalent banality. . . . The effect that remains is the aesthetic fascination which arises from the desperate tension between the language of the protocol and the nightmarish vision" (277-79). This fascination is operative only in the West, however–and rightly so; it is senseless to claim Kafka's style as a poetic norm, to adjust contemporary man to the model of Kafka's figures.

93-A. Rahv, Philip. "Franz Kafka: The Hero as Lonely Man." *Kenyon Review*, I (Winter 1939), 60-74.

In Kafka's hands the myth is an experiment, a mode of procedure, quite opposite to myths as products of history. Kafka's myths are circular; they return to their point of departure, which is uncertain and unknowable. "Origin and culmination . . . fuse in our minds into a single mystery" (62).

Kafka's sense of guilt was inordinate. "Plainly autobiographical, the protagonist of his fictions is coerced by extra-natural powers who are continally justified and exalted even as they are made to manifest themselves in the guise of a menacing and arbitrary bureaucracy" (63).

To the degree to which Kafka underwent literary influences, "he inclined toward purity and naturalness; above all he prized the exact accounting of experience–hence his admiration for Goethe and Flaubert" (64).

Criticism of Kafka cannot do without psychoanalysis which reveals Kafka's compulsion neurosis. "*The Metamorphosis*. . .

represents objectively the emotion of exclusion from the family and, beyond that, the estrangement of man from his human environment" (67). The insect symbol has another, a subjective meaning. Dream analysis shows that "dreams usually symbolize brothers and sisters as small animals or insects" (67). Now in this story the metamorphosis of Gregor is accompanied by a metamorphosis of the sister who at the close displaces him. If we take into account the sibling rivalry that must have existed between Kafka and his sister (keeping in mind the dream techniques of displacement and condensation), then the story reveals both wish and guilt thoughts. "Samsa wishes himself into the coveted and responsible position of family provider, thus lowering the father to the humiliating state of chronic dependence which in real life is his own; the guilt-compulsion, however, hastens to annul this imagined pleasure by compelling him to suffer himself the grotesque fate (transformation into an insect) which he had prepared for this sister" (68).

The acts of Kafka's heroes are never unmotivated; their situations are. "Phenomena are known . . . but relations are inexplicable and fantastic" (69). His men are on trial, not because they have failed in their heroic designs, but because they have failed to mark out their place in the social community.

Kafka is a religious writer in a quite particular sense: "his religious feeling was of a pristine nature, essentially magical and animistic: and he attempts to re-materialize the soul thousands of years after religious thought had de-materialized it" (71).

Kafka's works are informed by loneliness and exclusion. He inverts the tradition of Western individualism. In him this tradition "regards itself with self-revulsion; its joyous, ruthless hero is now a victim; he who once proudly disposed of many possessions is now destitute, he has neither woman nor child; in his conflict with society he has suffered an utter rout, and his fate no longer issues from his own high acts but from the abstract, enigmatical relations that bend him to their impersonal will" (73).

1. Selma **Fraiberg**, herself a psychoanalyst, asserts that there is no generally valid symbolic key to dream imagery. The insect in my dream may signify my sister; the insect in Kafka's dream may signify something else.

2. Within Kafka's work there is a cogent internal evolution of the image of the insect. The insect allegorizes developing possibilities of self-consciousness (see p. 20-22).

3. *The Metamorphosis* is a conscious elaboration of consciously apprehended psychic materials. Its analogy with dream work is accidental.

4. For a further critique of Rahv's article, see **Scott**.

93-B. Rahv, Philip. "Introduction." *Selected Short Stories of Franz Kafka*. New York: The Modern Library, 1952. Pp. xi-xii, xix-xx, and passim. Reprinted in *Literature and the Sixth Sense*. Boston: Houghton Mifflin, 1969. Pp. 186, 191, and passim.

With Gregor Samsa's metamorphosis Kafka does not mean to put the laws of nature into question. He means, rather, to suspend the convention that the laws of nature have to be observed in fiction. "The clerk's metamorphosis is a multiple symbol of his alienation from the human state, of his 'awakening' to the full horror of his dull, spiritless existence, and of the desperate self-disgust of his unconscious fantasy-life, in which the wish to displace the father and take over his authority in the family is annulled by the guilt-need to suffer a revolting punishment for his presumption" (xii).

The Metamorphosis "is the very embodiment of that quality of the exigent and the extreme, that sense of a human being hemmed in by his own existence and absolutely committed to it, which touches us so deeply in Kafka because it is at once method and content, entreaty and response, the goal and the way" (xix). In creating *The Metamorphosis* Kafka experienced a fundamental breakthrough to repressed material. The story is the outcome of the fusion of Kafka the artist and Kafka the neurotic.

For **Pfeiffer**, Kafka does not represent as "the goal and the way" the existence depicted throughout most of *The Metamorphosis*, but rather the recognition of the primordial guilt of involvement in this existence. Certainly a distinction has to be maintained among the various modes of existence which Gregor adopts–as animal, former family member, and, for a moment, outraged angel in pursuit of music.

Another question is the degree to which Gregor is "committed" to these modes of his existence. Rahv's first point is that Gregor's metamorphosis emerges as a kind of revenge of the repressed. To what extent can one be committed to what one has repressed?

94. Reiss, H. S. *Franz Kafka: Eine Betrachtung seines Werkes.* Heidelberg: Lambert Schneider, 1952. Pp. 37-41.

The Metamorphosis conveys the horror of the annihilation of a particular self, who is subject to "a false religion, a monster-machine or an abstract idea, the state or an industrial concern or the selfish material interests of his family" (37). The terrible allegory of an insect metamorphosis completes the alienation and makes intelligible the persecution of Gregor Samsa, wretched image of everyman.

He assumes all the physiological characteristics of the insect and comes to accept his filthy surroundings. At the same time he retains his human intellect and desperately wants to be part of the human world. His metamorphosis marks "the abrupt beginning of a decisive spiritual crisis" (38).

Hitherto Gregor was the victim of the business world and of his family (who are at the same time dependent on him). "Gregor's problems are Kafka's own problems" (39). Gregor cannot individualize his existence, cannot enter into a free and independent relation with others. Kafka is familiar with the indifference enveloping Gregor as he goes to his ruin–an indifference that does not take to heart one's fellow man because it lacks all comprehension, all insight.

Before the metamorphosis Gregor lived a life of repression and servitude. In the condition of the metamorphosis his spirituality is profiled: he maintains a sense of life, craves music, remains attached to the objects of his past. The isolation of the metamorphosis is a natural consequence of his previous life as one defeated and robbed of his prerogatives. "Such a life of deepest denial is wicked and perverse. . . . But the writer never asserts whether such a destiny is deserved or undeserved: it is simply a destiny remote from any grace" (40).

The metamorphosis is a crisis situation for everyone; but only in Gregor does it lead to the heightened awareness that was lacking in his previous humdrum life. His crisis leads in the fullest sense to a metamorphosis and radically endangers the possibilities of happiness. "Gregor's metamorphosis is the symbol of authentic self-awareness, of the coming into consciousness of the spiritual situation which is primordially one's own, truly a turning point in life" (41). Gregor's metamorphosis has been caused by his revulsion for his former life and by the repression of his own personality.

95. Richter, Helmut. *Franz Kafka: Werk und Entwurf.* Berlin: Ruetten and Loening, 1962. Pp. 112-19.

The narrative form of *The Metamorphosis* is the same as that of "The Stoker" and "The Judgment": epic recounting from the perspective of the hero. The central problem of the story is the transformation of Gregor from a useful member of society into a bug condemned to parasitism. The criterion of the epic is the inner truth and inevitability of the action; has Kafka made Gregor's transformation the inevitable aesthetic expression of the reality he depicts?

The reason behind Gregor's relative indifference to the metamorphosis, as well as its significant function, lies in Gregor's initial reflections: he hates his job and secretly craves to give it up. As a result of his reflections, something decisive happens: he is late for work, and this apparently excusable failure in fact consummates a series of failures which have shown Gregor's unfitness for his profession and his irresponsibility toward his family. The function of the metamorphosis is to assign an appropriate form of existence–that of a disgusting, parasitic bug–to a man who has failed in his human function. The way in which his family behaves toward him is therefore justified. Their disgust turns to tortured friendliness before hate breaks out openly for Gregor's incurable and compromising inferiority. Kafka does not blame the family for its behavior toward Gregor: Gregor is a bug.

There is a dimension of social reality in this image of the man "afraid of work": Gregor is viewed with the eyes of a world which determines the value of the individual solely according to the material advantages which can be obtained from him. In fact, it is hard to conceive that Gregor had ever been able to provide for his family. After Gregor's transformation, the family members discover their own potentialities; they have never needed him. With his death, a new life begins for them. His apparent successes meant only stultification for the others.

The fact that Gregor also loves his family makes his failure particularly serious. His failure is to remain the lonely weakling, whose work could not become the substance of his life, although he had a task to fulfill which required all his strength and responsibility. He convicts himself through an action, skipping work, to which he has gradually worked himself up. In compelling him to prepare to die, Gregor's father comes to the conclusion to which Gregor has already come.

The Metamorphosis describes a moment of failure which leads to death. The failure is not due simply to Gregor's incompetence, but arises from an objective predicament. Gregor cannot continue working because his job threatens to stultify him as a human being. Furthermore, Gregor's all-out effort to do well at work threatens to destroy the whole of his family life because it nullifies its humanity. But Gregor's attempt to save his own existence from a job that demands its sacrifice leads to a dereliction, "neglect of his natural duty of assuring his family a decent living" (117).

The root of Gregor's predicament is an objective social situation, the inhuman demands made on the individual by bourgeois acquisitive life under imperialism. The ensuing contradiction enters into the life, not only of society as a whole but of each individual family. "The demand that a man . . . satisfy both the human and social claims on him remains abstract as long as it fails to take into account the latent opposition of men to the forms and laws of everyday bourgeois life" (117).

But a definite element of Kafka's presentation of the plight of the hero under capitalism suggests a negative judgment on the hero—the judgment of his personal inferiority and unfitness for life. To capitulate to life-denying working conditions is not in itself automatic proof of incompetence, but Kafka makes this charge with great severity. He does so despite his sympathy for the unfortunate hero and despite the fact that the incongruously cruel sentence laid on the hero suggests the *objective* conditions giving rise to his guilt. The genuine problematic of an objective impasse comes to light despite Kafka's (personal) impulse to mask it. Kafka's stories depict not abnormalities, but the distress of men desperately searching for a way. "Their effort is desperate because there does not appear to be for them any life forms other than the bourgeois, because they do not recognize that these forms must necessarily collide with the claims of a truly human way of life. From the same bourgeois standpoint Kafka can see in his figures only unnatural exceptions, who have not fulfilled the human norm and have thus condemned themselves to solitude and to death" (118).

Thus *The Metamorphosis* tends to be the mere reflection of a dogma, maintaining the perspective of the individual problem and neglecting the conditioning social reality. "Kafka does not consider whether and to what extent the hero's situation is influenced by contradictions in reality, since he is bent on explaining all antitheses and catastrophes by means of the anomalousness and weakness of his heroes" (118).

96. Rohner, Wolfgang. *Franz Kafka*. Mühlacker: Stieglitz, 1967. Pp. 49-52.

Realistic everyday life is dislocated into a mythic dimension, which is described in precise sensations. All images, events, and reflections in this work constitute a unity bearing on the central figure of the traveling salesman. We are not asked to unpuzzle the significance of the sequence of images. "Its only function is to belong to the optic of the main figure and to characterize it." In *The Metamorphosis* Kafka represents the life of a salesman from the latter's own distorted perspective. "Gregor experiences his encapsulation with respect to the rest of the world as a 'metamorphosis' into a beetle whose body is armor-plated all around." But Kafka does not write the words "as" a metamorphosis. Psychic reality is no longer experienced through an "as" or "as if" in works just before the First World War. Gregor's perspective is preserved even after his death: "one must place the center of the personality at a point beyond living and dying." Kafka's task is to describe the way in which things appear in Gregor's perspective and to describe this perspective, not to maintain the conventional distinction between what is real and what is not.

97. Russell, Francis. *Three Studies in Twentieth-Century Obscurity*. Kent, England: The Hand and Flower Press, 1954. Pp. 52-54.

The Metamorphosis shows the relation of the author to his family in 1912. Gregor Samsa is "only a thinly veiled autobiographical figure." There is only one reversal: in *The Metamorphosis* Kafka makes his family dependent on him.[51]

98. Sackville-West, Edward. "*The Metamorphosis* of Franz Kafka" (a review). *Spectator* (July 23, 1937), 152.

The struggle in Kafka's works of the individual versus authority is unjust; "nothing in poor Gregor Samsa's blameless life could have justified his being arbitrarily metamorphosed into a bug. Yet the really terrible thing is that . . . the victim gradually comes to believe more and more deeply in his alleged guilt."

99. Schlingmann, Carsten. "Die Verwandlung–Eine Interpretation." In *Interpretationen zu Franz Kafka: Das Urteil, Die Verwandlung, Ein Landarzt, Kleine Prosastücke*. Munich: Oldenbourg, 1968. Pp. 81-105.

Faced with the metamorphoses recounted in primitive myths, in the *Odyssey*, and in modern ironic works, the reader is able to discriminate precisely between the fictive metamorphosis and empirical reality. Faced with *The Metamorphosis*, the reader is at a loss. Here the impossible metamorphosis and a depressingly real family drama are intimately linked, and their consequences are described in a direct, serious, and unsentimental tonality.

Various autobiographical details appear transmogrified in *The Metamorphosis*; but it would be a false tack to interpret the story as a coded autobiographical document. "It appears as if Kafka himself only subsequently attempts to comprehend his life with the help of his literary works, a fact which has led in his diaries and letters to every conceivable exaggeration and distortion" (83).

The first sentence of *The Metamorphosis* situates the really incomprehensible dimension of the story before its origin—a principle which informs Greek tragedy—*Oedipus Rex*, for example. The opening sentence of *The Metamorphosis* is itself a sort of invocation of the epic action. The story arises from the "unsettling dreams" from which Gregor Samsa awakens; Gregor is not only the main character, but aside from the somewhat dubious conclusion, he is the form through which the story manifests itself. By virtue of its point of view, the technique and the content of the narration are virtually the same. Story and main character originate in the condition of the metamorphosis. But as soon as the reader has accepted the first sentence and the domain of the metamorphosis, he is dismayed to find himself confronting a recognizable empirical reality. The metaphorical "monstrous vermin" is rapidly concretized as a huge bug. Hearing that Gregor was lying on "his" back—not "a" back—as hard as armor plate, we conclude that Gregor is identical with the "monstrous vermin." The realism of Kafka's language is to be understood, not as representing external realities, but as an aesthetic device to articulate an inner reality. The insect cannot be drawn because "a drawing of him could only show him from the outside, . . . he would become an object of curiosity, from whom the reader could inwardly distance himself. But precisely this would contradict the spirit of this story" (86).

Though not a first-person narrative, *The Metamorphosis* is narrated almost entirely from the perspective of the main character. Gregor's thoughts are frequently reproduced in the form of an inner monologue, which passes on occasion into the so-called enacted consciousness (*erlebte Rede*). This mode of representing Gregor's consciousness fuses an intimacy of inner experience with the character of the objective report. With only rare exceptions, everything we learn about the Samsa household until the close could have been reported by Gregor.

We are given, not Gregor's body as such, but his body as he experiences it. This is also the qualifying condition of Gregor's room, and indeed of his entire family: everything that exceeds Gregor's perspective is given only as a surmise. The center from which the story as a whole is oriented is in the metamorphosed Gregor Samsa. A personal narrator is virtually absent from the story, which is void of reflections and judgments. The reader cannot find any other point in the story around which to orient himself except that of the vermin; hence he must attempt to ward off this identification, ward off the story.

The conclusion, of course, in which the family celebrates its release from Gregor, provides a new place from which the reader can shake off the metamorphosis as a bad dream. But the conclusion, as Kafka himself realized, does not work. The reaction of the family consists of crudities, banalities, and poses. An indication of the flatness of the conclusion is that Kafka no longer speaks of father and mother but of Mr. and Mrs. Samsa.

Gregor is not a man in a beast's body; he is identical with the vermin, but it is dubious whether he can know this. Gregor sees the transformation as if from the outside; the habituation of his sensibilities as traveling salesman forbids a spontaneous expression of horror. Gregor's automatic thought—he must pack his bags and leave for his road trip—is so powerful that it represses his consciousness of being a vermin up until the flight of the office manager. But his true condition penetrates his consciousness and testifies to itself in elliptical and distorted ways.

Gregor's ambiguous behavior cannot be construed only as an attempt to evade the truth of his predicament, since it is simply not possible for him to act other than he does. Finding himself, after a second birth, in a state unknown to him, he must attempt to find himself out through trial and error.

Gregor's life prior to the metamorphosis was itself informed by ambivalence and contradiction: this is especially apparent in his relation to his job, which was only "purchased with repressions," only a pseudorenunciation, assuring him "protection against the trials of life" (97); and it is apparent in his flight from any lasting relation to women.

The fact that the metamorphosis occurs just as Gregor is due to go on the road again after having spent eight days at home, and that on the morning of the metamorphosis Gregor oversleeps by several hours, suggests that his own intentions are the source of the metamorphosis. He who was once a useful member of society is now as useless as can be: a vermin. "His abused nature, in secret accord with his longing for a life style opposed to his present one, restores the balance of forces through a powerful metamorphosis. His true being takes shape as a vermin–i.e. the distortions of his nature hitherto scantily covered over by his professional successes now themselves become nature. His inner nothingness is turned into external uselessness" (102).

It is true that, at the close, Gregor makes peace with the idea of his disappearance as the only possible solution: but this is not the same as saying that he has grasped the sense of his metamorphosis. His predicament is ghastly; but it is kept in balance throughout by the irony–indeed, the comedy–of its representation. The work in which every realistic element is put into the shade by poetic invention attests finally to a superiority of the human spirit.

100. Schneeberger, Irmgard. *Das Kunstmärchen in der ersten Hälfte des 20. Jahrhunderts*. Munich, 1960. Pp. 30-33.

Unlike Raban of "Wedding Preparations in the Country," Gregor Samsa is wholly a captive of the world of purposeful work. He really wants to remain part of this world. "His metamorphosis does not arise as a wish fulfillment but assails him as something terrible and mysterious and wholly extraordinary" (30). Yet animal metamorphosis has a primordially positive meaning in Kafka. It is a sign of nonpurposive inwardness. This is the meaning which Gregor denies; he shuns the recognition which might amount to his salvation. His concern is for business, for the world of the "they."

101. Schubiger, Jürg. *Franz Kafka: Die Verwandlung, Eine Interpretation*. Zurich and Freiburg i. Br.: Atlantis, 1969. 103 pp.

This monograph of 103 pages is divided into five sections which discuss, respectively, the difficulty of interpreting Kafka;

the place of *The Metamorphosis* in Kafka's life and works; the general meaning of *The Metamorphosis*; the meaning of special aspects of the story, such as Gregor's body and his relation to others; and finally, characteristics of Kafka's language and style in *The Metamorphosis*.

1. In the last three or four decades the literature on Kafka has assumed enormous proportions. The work itself is tangled in interpretations especially of a theological and psychological kind. The failure of literary critics and historians to mark out a clear path into Kafka's work is notable; but the work presents enormous difficulties.

"A poetic text is intelligible to us when we divine the direction in which it or one of its main characters is tending" (10). We grasp the sense of an action when we understand the future toward which it is striving–a future which may already be inscribed in the past. However, in Kafka's stories and novels we know little or nothing about the characters' past. Kafka is probably unique as a writer in orienting himself so little with respect to the past, to what already is. His originality is radical. His characters find themselves at the outset in an uncanny situation in which it is impossible for them to find their way. Gregor Samsa loses even the ground most familiar to him–his own body. In this uncanny state no future can open up: the paths to it are unknown. These characters have lost their destiny to others. There is only the impotent nostalgia for something to which all paths are barred; for Gregor, this is the unknown nourishment he had longed for. "The way, the connection of the present to the future, is missing: the future, like the past, is cut off from the present" (12).

In Kafka's stories, there is an abundance of gestures pregnant with significance; language itself seems to originate in gesture. Gesture in Kafka is the concretization of multiple meanings, "the expression of that which retreats from language into silence" (15). The disjunctive relation in Kafka between truth and language is what makes his works so difficult to interpret.

Kafka's ambiguity is a consequence of the peculiar temporal structure of his work; when past and future are infinitely remote, the present ceases to have sharp definition. Possibilities abound, they are unlimited. Because the present is isolated and uncanny, it appears to have profound significance.

The sense, however, of an inner direction guiding the work is provided by the wholly particular perspective through which the world of the work emerges. The narrator is a captive of his main character. The world of the work is further defined by its atmosphere of depression, expressive of the anxiety and mistrust of the central figure, his eye for what is menacing. Corresponding to this narrowness of perspective and attention is a world that gradually closes itself off.

Kafka's works show a tangle of relations: the critic runs the risk either of ordering all their elements under a single heading, in which case he lies; or of describing all their relations, in which case his work becomes itself a tangle. The present interpretation aims to approach the literal sense of the text from a variety of positions.

2. *The Metamorphosis*, composed between November 17 and December 7, 1912, is Kafka's first complete work following the breakthrough he achieved by writing "The Judgment" on September 22, 1912. Before the end of the year Kafka had also gotten as far as the seventh chapter of the novel *Amerika*. Max Brod, Kafka's literary executor, is correct in seeing the encounter with Felice Bauer on the evening of August 13, 1912, and Kafka's subsequent attempt to marry, as crucial to this creative spurt. The possibility of marriage leads Kafka to renewed and heightened self-reflection in the urgent need to take hold of himself and to an acute concentration of positive and negative energies, the outcome of which is the consciousness of a great deficit, a sense of shortcoming.

"The concentration on one theme, that of marriage, gathered together his distracted nature . . . under the single heading of 'guilt' " (22). The degree of his concentration is evident in the intricate unity of the stories that follow. In Kafka's state of urgency and harrassment, his world closes in on him, its contours clear. Now his stories unfold with just that coherence which he feels marriage would threaten. For his writing Kafka needs the purity of undistracted self-consciousness, freedom from others.

The encounter with Felice Bauer focused the themes of solitude and writing for Kafka. But a life of solitude was as impossible as a life of social responsibility. Like his heroes, Kafka stood bewitched by impossibilities. The approach to the biographical background of *The Metamorphosis* might focus equally well on Kafka's relation to his father or to his job: the outcome is the same. Whatever route we take, we arrive at the same basic motif of paradox.

3. *The Metamorphosis* is structured around Gregor's steadily diminishing sphere of action; "his death is only the conclusion of a progressive loss of the world" (27). He is reduced to living in a single room, and as his door is locked, his connection with the world is merely an acoustic one. Opposing this movement of straitening and circumscribing is one in which all limits are dissolved. As the work proceeds, such terms as "soon" and "each day" replace precise temporal discriminations; this dissolution of time is matched by an expansion of Gregor's spatial limits at the close, when the door to the living room is opened. But this is only to open a dark emptiness to him: he has already virtually withdrawn from the world. Gregor's greater "range" at the close is really only an extension of the boundless monotony of a being reduced to its own nothingness.

Two dimensions of the situation of the opening sentence must be stressed: first, Gregor's passivity–he "finds himself" metamorphosed; second, the motif, important in Kafka, of the man startled out of his dreamy abstractedness. Kafka called the moment of awakening the riskiest of the day, the moment in which a man risks falling out of his everyday passivity into a condition of at once dawning insight and abrupt mystification. The instant of awakening can be one in which the world is suddenly revealed as it is: what was hidden becomes open.

Awakening is precipitated by others; the disclosure to which one awakens is degrading (think of Gregor's body); it bares the nullity of a life of solitude. "The truth . . . is so terrifying that it can no longer be fruitful in any way for the man awakening. It radically puts into question the dreamer's private existence as a whole. Perplexed, he stares around him; the truth which he glimpses cannot find a place in his life, as it turns his life into nothing. He is afraid of the waking world, which holds such a truth in store for him; and in his fear he populates it with all the phantoms of his inner life. In this way the truth itself leads him back again into the benightedness of the dream. Now menacing objectivity is nothing more than the actualized [*verweltlichte*] anxiety of the dream" (30).

Gregor's room, like Kafka's room at home, is only a sort of connecting space through which the Samsa family communicates. It has the anonymous public character of the hotel rooms he sleeps in on the road. The room is barred, quite as the bachelor is barred from life. Gregor's solitude and defensiveness are also reflected in the image of his body armor, just as the infantilism of his former hobbies is reflected in the bug's dependence on the family and its opinions. The peculiarity and uniqueness of Gregor's destiny are tied to his former neglect of his distinctiveness and his anonymity as a traveling salesman.

It is consistent with Gregor's character that he does not take his metamorphosis to heart. However much he would take flight in fantastic, conditional reflections, he has to return, again and again, at the outset, to the starting point which his situation forces on him. The hopelessness of his situation comes to light in all its horror through the repeated failure of his attempts at flight.

In the second part of the story we see Gregor retreat more and more deeply into a cavelike darkness. By and large the narrator keeps the perspective of the beetle, but we see him again and again withdraw in disgust from his creation.

Kafka himself regarded "filth" as a creative element and an irreducible part of his personality; but in his solitude and poverty Gregor can do nothing with his filth. At the time of his death he is covered with garbage. He is in every sense of the word an untouchable. Because Gregor responds to the disgust of the family with shame, he becomes virtually "invisible" as well: draped in his bedsheet, he is only as visible as a ghost.

The care which Grete provides Gregor in his predicament has the effect of constantly defining Gregor as an animal. Gregor, for his part, expects so much from his sister in making her the object of his diffuse craving for salvation that she must disappoint him. Gregor's death is empty—the mere expiration of an insect. What has he still to lose except life in the biological sense? In one way the metamorphosis is already a death: it means the impossibility of a meaningful existence, an impossibility expressed in the concealed form of an unreal possibility.

4. When we put together all the details of Gregor Samsa's shape and function, we do not have a coherent whole but rather "an inventory of behavioral possibilities, the bodily basis for the various acts and intentions of the bug" (56). These body data are not facts but "body-imaged questions and answers in the bug's dialogue with the environment" (56). For Kafka the body is a language of gestures, of symbols; thus there is an intimate connection from moment to moment between Gregor's bodily identity and life style. The fact, for example, that it would have taken two able-bodied persons to tip him out of bed indicates his "heavy," melancholy mood. This point, however, should not be an invitation to subjectivize what Kafka describes as objectively given. Kafka's method is meaningful: Gregor himself experiences everything as objectively, invariably given, as oppressive external reality which he cannot resist or fathom; this is true even of his own body. In its callousness and its cringing and groveling character, Gregor's body is the clearest possible expression of his fundamental mode of being. All his nicks and wounds, for example, are a bodily expression of the "painfulness" of his situation. Yet he does not experience his body as a language but rather as a problem. "The entire story can be grasped as a representation of an extraordinary relation to 'corporeality' " (62-63). This relation is contradictory and mirrors Gregor's predicament. If he surrenders to his body, he loses his dignity and delicacy; but if he puts distance between himself and his body, treating it as a foreign body or as an instrument, he comes up against the insurmountable barrier of his "corporeality" which bars his access to human possibilities. "The loss of human corporeality, of a language of sounds and gestures, of professional competence, of the money that creates intimacy, and of generally valid temporal perception makes Gregor a unique being who cannot share immediately in anything and in whom nothing can immediately share" (66).

Gregor's body is an expression, and not the cause, of his inability to connect and to love. He wears armor, as it were; turns his back on others; hardens himself against them. "Gregor's body has the temperature of a bug" (67). His coldness and sullenness have, of course, their good reasons: each time Gregor ventures to cross the threshold into the family living room, he returns injured.

5. Peculiarities of Kafka's syntax express, so to speak, its constant urge to make up for things unsaid and to anticipate things still to be said. More: as the story is marked by an alternating movement of constriction and endless expansion, so Kafka's style exhibits a corresponding tendency toward absolute intimacy and absolute distance. This movement is illustrated in the story by the change in Gregor's *Lebensraum*, which is diminished from "the rather colorless space of a business area" to a dim corner of his room—and then, at the close, expanded into the vague immensity of the darkened living room. The corresponding stylistic movement is shown in Kafka's tendency to objectify and spatialize inwardness; for example, the distinction in dignity between boss and employee is objectified as the distance which the boss assumes by sitting on his desk while talking to his employees. The most remarkable examples of the movement toward intimacy in Kafka's language are his taking metaphors literally and his way of sinking the narrative perspective into the unreliable immediate consciousness of the disoriented hero.

Gregor's life is hampered and hemmed in by a myriad external circumstances: this situation is reflected in the prevalance of circumstantial adverbs in Kafka's prose. A host of negating and depleting verbs conveys the sense of a constriction of life.

Gregor's inclination not to face his situation is reflected in the many restrictive expressions which characterize his language. He tries to diminish into minor qualifications the events which confine him, with the result that he never attains even the dignity of a clear perception of his fate. His language trivializes his predicament.

The heaping up of modal verbs and adverbs contributes to the veiled atmosphere of the story, the sense of a darkness and absence at the heart of experience, of the world experienced through shadow hopes and fears. The prevalence of the subjunctive mood directly reflects Gregor's situation: his is a world of impossibilities. "Whatever he plans and aspires to must remain optative, since the preconditions of their realization no longer exist. . . . The conditional contrary-to-fact in our story can be characterized as the grammatical form of the lie: with its help Gregor denies the reality of his situation, and the family uses it in order to deceive itself" (96-7).

This essay, a delicate and scrupulous examination of the text, faithfully follows the critical precept of the Swiss professor of German literature, Emil Staiger ("Do not explain: describe!"). Unlike Staiger's work, however, this essay does not reveal a literary historical awareness, though it exhibits a shortcoming characteristic of Staiger's method: an *apparent* eschewal of interpretative or ideological superstructure which is in fact implicitly present in the description. In Schubiger's case, the chief interpretative schema is provided by Ludwig Binswanger's philosophical anthropology.

It is, in fact, doubtful whether Binswanger's conception of the mind-body relation can be equated with Kafka's; and this discrepancy stands behind an internal inconsistency in Schubiger's essay which is fundamentally troubling. He writes:
"In the 'Metamorphosis' the body metaphor is, so to speak, absolutized: Gregor *is* a bug. His body remains, it is true, . . . a symbol of his existence" (78). But also: "He has the body of a bug and in addition retains the wishes and goals of a traveling salesman" (96). However base we may be inclined to judge the soul of a salesman, it is still not reducible to the wishes and goals of a bug.

Through this inconsistency Schubiger enables us to grasp the important point: Gregor is at times purely his body, at other times "symbolized" by his body, at still other times wholly the traveling salesman at heart. Kafka incessantly shifts the relation of body and consciousness in this unique being, with the intent of putting his creation outside the order of metaphorical explanations. But precisely this destruction of the univocal body metaphor runs counter to the monistic assumptions of the philosophical anthropology which Schubiger employs.

102. Schuddekopf, Jürgen. "Rätsel der Faszination: Zu Franz Kafkas Erzählung." *Athena* (Berlin), II (1947-48), 40-43.

There is a discrepancy between Kafka and the critical literature on Kafka. "Nothing could be further from Kafka than the credulous abstractions of the most sublime analysis. For he had his monstrous image of reality before him with a unique compactness and recorded it in sentences of an almost primitive clarity." Kafka's special quality is a function of the displacement of the narrative perspective; it has changed from one comprising the totality of a wide panorama to the "cellular 'moment,' fleeting past impressionistically."[52]

> **103. Schulze, Hans.** "Anwärter der Gnade: Franz Kafka." *Tagebuch V* (1955), Veröffentlichung der Evangelischen Akademie Tutzing, VI. Munich: Höfling, 1956. Pp. 25-34.

Kafka's story is an anti-fairy-tale in the following sense: it treats the familiar fairy-tale theme of the metamorphosis of a man into an animal; but whereas in fairy tales the transmogrified figure is redeemed by the love of a fellow human, here, in the Samsa family, no one furnishes redemptive love.

"The basis of the deformation is not Gregor Samsa's culpability. It has the character of destiny: as a traveling salesman, he has been debased into a cog in the machinery of existence" (33). All human connections belong to the business world; man is a mere functionary of impersonal power structures; he has become an insect.

But now human nature revolts against its mechanization. Gregor protests both against the business world and against the lovelessness of his parents. For their crippled response to him is a sign of their incapacity to love. One gleam comes from the sister's violin playing; even so, Gregor is disappointed in supposing that this is a sign of an exceptional ability to love. She betrays him, just like the others.

"Gregor must perish because neither human being nor animal can live in an atmosphere of lovelessness. But life goes on uninterruptedly; guilt, repentance and love vanish into collective existence; everything sets itself to rights" (34).

104. Scott, Nathan. "Franz Kafka: The Sense of Cosmic Exile." In *Rehearsals of Discomposure*. New York: King's Crown Press, 1952. Pp. 37-39.

The Metamorphosis is more than the "mixture of wish and guilt thoughts" which **Rahv** holds it to be. "It is in fact a comment on the eventual and inevitable loss of life by him in whom conscience knows no alarm . . . when he suddenly awakens for the first time to self-recognition." Until the metamorphosis, Gregor was bent on total domination over his family. The spiritual bases of his life were pride, complacency, and self-assertion. "His only worries have been those of a traveling salesman: he has not measured his ego against its divine foundation, and so his has been an easy conscience." The meaning of the metamorphosis is the loss of support for his superficial existence and the acute sense of estrangement. Here Kafka projects the crisis into which the human spirit falls when it opposes God. "The tragedy of Gregor is the tragedy of the autonomous man as he becomes insecure in his autonomy—which is, indeed, the presiding theme in the whole of Kafka's work."

1. If God is claimed as the source of the metamorphosis, then He is an unintelligible void. See **Politzer**.
2. **Pongs** argues cogently against the view that *The Metamorphosis* is a tragedy, although the latter view is upheld, with more evidence than Scott provides, by **Sokel**, 105-C, and **Von Wiese**.

105-A. Sokel, Walter H. "Kafka's 'Metamorphosis': Rebellion and Punishment." *Monatshefte,* XLVIII (April-May 1956), 203-14.

Gregor's relation to his job is crucial; when he wakes, metamorphosed, he reflects more about his job than about his ghastly change. We learn of the feelings of resentment he harbors toward his work and about his old thoughts of rebellion. The first function which the metamorphosis fulfills, then, is to rid Gregor of his job. "At the same time, it relieves him of having to make a choice between his responsibility to his parents and his yearning to be free. The metamorphosis enables Gregor to become free and stay 'innocent,' a mere victim of uncontrollable calamity" (205-06). Gregor's falling sick would not have served the same purpose as the metamorphosis, because absent from it is "a condition vital to Gregor's metamorphosis—the element of retaliation and aggression against the firm" (207). The terrifying effect of Gregor's monstrous appearance on the office manager satisfies his secret wish to humiliate his superiors in the firm.

Gregor manages to vent his aggression against the office manager in such a way as to avoid responsibility for his acts and desires. He supposes, consciously, that he pursues the manager in order to get him to put in a good word for him at the office. In fact, his threatening gestures have a quite opposite effect. Here the metamorphosis reveals its character as a compromise formation for two contrary unconscious impulses: the desire to be aggressive and the desire to be innocent of aggression, to pacify "a duty-bound conscience that demands submission." If Gregor remains innocent of any knowledge of his aggressive intentions, his family and, of course, the office manager do not. "What the metamorphosis does is to make Gregor's suppressed desire visible. It turns him inside out, as it were. (Here, of course, we see the technique of expressionism)" (209). The metamorphosis is a structure akin to the accident as Freud describes it. (This point is developed in 105-C, 85-86.)

As a self-inflicted accident, the metamorphosis has another function: "it expresses Gregor's guilt and the punishment for this guilt. . . . This sense of guilt manifests itself in a panicky need to prove his innocence, and this need in turn plays a vital part in bringing him to ruin" (210). In his agitation to defend himself and reveal to all his good will, Gregor loses control of his voice and, swiftly, of all further possibility of communication. Thereafter, Gregor knows an almost total isolation: "this is, of course, Gregor's agonizing tragedy: that he feels and thinks as a human being while unable to make his humanity felt and known" (211). Yet he is himself responsible for much of this tragedy, through "his panicky urge to conform to what is expected of him, while . . . his real desires [are left] unacknowledged even when they work havoc with him" (211).

We know his real desire: he longs for leisure and freedom. Yet his conscience cannot admit his wish, and in Gregor's ineffectual efforts to satisfy his conscience by demonstrating innocence and inoffensiveness, he only succeeds in worsening the natural effect of the metamorphosis–isolation and helplessness. On the other hand, "the antidote to the metamorphosis"–the text hints– "would be Gregor's yielding to his guilty desire" (212).

"May we not infer from this that the metamorphosis itself is such a treacherous appeasement of a sense of guilt which in demonstrating innocence and helplessness actually invites punishment and destruction?" (212). If, as evidence suggests, Gregor is a sort of giant cockroach, then his appearance "perfectly expresses the two aspects of the metamorphosis, aggression and helplessness, and the order of their importance" (213). Actually the menace in his looks is only apparent, while his helplessness is real. Thus the ultimately important function of the metamorphosis is to punish Gregor.

"In conclusion . . . , the metamorphosis accommodates Gregor's conflicting needs, the need to rebel, and the need to suffer punishment for this rebellion. Above all, by being an unconscious process, the metamorphosis protects him from self-knowledge" (214).

Sokel interprets a work conspicuously bare of wishes, intentions, and motives through a Freudian psychology of intention and desire. What Sokel neglects is the work's steadfast objectivity, its distance, and the fact that Kafka has adopted the standpoint of an indifferent world, in the spirit of the aphorism: "In the struggle between you and the world, second the world" (H 44; DF 38).

The idea is odd that Gregor's panicky desire to defend himself is responsible for his loss of language and communication with the world. With a little extra discipline, Sokel suggests, Gregor could have nullified the "essential aspect" of the metamorphosis. This is not persuasive psychoanalysis: the power to undo neurosis does not exist in the neurotic as an unconscious wish or antiwish; as Gregor is in truth a vermin, so the neurotic is his neurosis. Sokel implies that the loss of language (through panic nervousness) effectually brings on the metamorphosis in all its horror; rather, the fundamental conception of the metamorphosis as total strangeness and total solitude entails the loss of language from the start.

The metamorphosis cannot be understood regressively in terms of Gregor's normal and familiar desire–his inwardness–whether conscious or not. The metamorphosis is the origin of the work, the absolutely irreducible origin of Gregor's behavior and of the behavior of the others. For an elaboration of this argument, see **Emrich** and **Loeb**.

105-B. Sokel, Walter H. *The Writer in Extremis: Expressionism in Twentieth-Century Literature*. Stanford, California: Stanford University Press, 1959. Pp. 45-48.

Gregor's metamorphosis is "an extended metaphor, a metaphoric visualization of an emotional situation, uprooted from any explanatory context" (46). There are no divisions in this universe between the interior of the self and the external world. *The Metamorphosis* is Expressionism's peak achievement.

Kafka makes certain that the metamorphosis cannot be taken for a hallucination, since Gregor's parents inspect his carcass after his death. There is no basis for doubting the physical, objective reality of the event. "Thus he creates a universe of his own which, exactly like the dream, exhibits similarities with our empirical world but is governed by at least one special law of its own" (46).

In the early novel fragment, "Wedding Preparations in the Country," Raban imagines himself transformed into a bug who would stay in bed and wallow in irresponsibility. But "Raban was many things beside his wish for irresponsibility and parasitic withdrawal from an active and mature way of life. Samsa, however, has become identical with his wish" (46). The empirical self disappears into the empirical event which expresses perfectly his genuine self. "Gregor Samsa has been transformed into a metaphor that states his essential self, and this metaphor in turn is treated like an actual fact" (47).

The metamorphosis is not symbolic in Goethe's sense because it is not a self-evident event. Explanation is withheld. Nor does it symbolize a universal; hence it cannot be allegorical. It is most like a dream image, the function of which is at once to express and to veil meaning.

The function of the metamorphosis is to express total ambivalence; because the latter is an empirical impossibility, only an empirically impossible event could represent it. "It integrates disintegration, not by reversing or stopping, but by embodying it" (48).

One wonders about the philosophical propriety in Sokel of labeling an empirical event the perfect expression of an essential self. The category of "expression" introduces the disjunction between essence and sign constituting (and compromising) all relations having the character of language. There cannot be a "metaphorical extension" of an essence.

The question therefore arises of the correctness of viewing *The Metamorphosis* as Expressionistic. The metamorphosis is, as Sokel says, empirically impossible. But if its impossibility–its unintelligibility, its opacity–is to remain intact, then it cannot be held to express any other sort of "impossibility"–for example, Gregor's ambivalence. The view of Kafka as Expressionist opens the door to regressive psychologizing of his work.

It is indeed instructive to view the bug as an autononous, an "uprooted" metaphor.[53] The focus is then on the character of Gregor as unintelligible language; and indeed it is his fate to incorporate a meaning which no one in the text can decipher. In the scene of the violin playing, Gregor will find himself interpreted at last by the language of music. *The Metamorphosis* thus creates a relation between the loss of meaning in one language and the acquisition of meaning in another. But these relations have nothing to do with the psychology of communication.

105-C. Sokel, Walter H. *Franz Kafka: Tragik und Ironie, Zur Struktur seiner Kunst*. Munich and Vienna: Albert Langen, Georg Müller, 1964. Pp. 77-103 and passim.

Gregor's spiritual situation in the family is reproduced in the physical layout of his room. On the one hand, he is the prisoner of his family, closed in by them on all sides. On the other hand, he is utterly secluded, locked inside himself.

Before the metamorphosis, Gregor intended to defy his parents by sending his sister to the conservatory; in thwarting this project, the metamorphosis functions as a condemnation in advance. The metamorphosis coalesces themes of condemnation, punishment, and the struggle for authority between father and son. As a consequence of Gregor's condemnation, the father regains mastery and authority within the family, while the son degenerates.

The metamorphosis is also a pleasurable wish fulfillment for Gregor: through it he flees the work he hates. And through it Gregor also expresses "the longing for the restoration in the family of the warm and harmonious relations which have disappeared" (80).

The case of a beetle metamorphosis that fulfills the intention of shirking has a precedent in the surviving fragment of a youthful novel, "Wedding Preparations in the Country." Here, Raban the beetle is the symbol of a pure, essentially inhuman self, whose deepest desire is not to be burdened with women, society, and humanity in general. He is self-sufficient and exercises a magical authority over the external world. By the act of withdrawal, the beetle attains to a perfect unity with mankind.

Meanwhile Raban's factitious, superficial self does his chores for him in the world. "Its position in life is exactly that of Gregor Samsa, the traveling salesman, before his metamorphosis, and it is therefore imperfect, unsteady, tormented and 'null.' Its relation to the world is that of struggle and strategy" (81).

The metamorphosis of Gregor Samsa also represents a tendency to retire from the world and at the same time to dominate it through a sort of magical parasitism. Gregor Samsa claims an exceptional status which exonerates him from all effort and responsibility.

Thus the metamorphosis unifies an unconscious, aiming at once for withdrawal and aggression. But because Gregor cannot admit this wish, he is denied the self-sufficiency and contentment of Raban. Gregor persists in finding his metamorphosis awkward, a disaster.

Gregor is permanently divided: on the one hand, his metamorphosed form must menace the family, while at the same time it sinks him more and more deeply into helplessness and impotence. He cannot effectually express his benevolent intentions toward the family: they have been repressed for so long that they cannot come to light anymore. The would-be supplicant emerges as the persecutor. Consciousness and body, self and world, have been hopelessly divided. Gregor's love (as toward his sister) is so mingled with aggression that it becomes impossible as a continuous feeling. "The erotic sphere serves the strategy of the hero in his struggle for self-assertion and recognition by the authority" (90).

At a crucial juncture Gregor would play the fairy-tale dragon, keeping his sister sequestered within his cave. This act is aimed against the father's authority and as such threatens to invert the purpose which the metamorphosis incarnates—to prevent Gregor from getting his sister away from the father and sending her to the conservatory. From this point on, Gregor will be more and more deeply degraded.

The passage in Gregor's sensibility from the inward experience of music to the desire to possess his sister is a parodic representation of hopeless disjunction, of the crude will to have the best of both worlds. His sister's brusque reply to Gregor's erotic wish dream "shows him the way back to the original destination of the metamorphosis" (91). This is the awareness that Gregor's authentic self is death. Gregor's genuine and tragic choice compels him to relinquish the rights of his body and person and to assume a pure seclusion and interiority whose outcome is death. In demanding Gregor's tragic sacrifice, the metamorphosis becomes the genuine meaning of his life.

The family harmony had been shattered in the past by the father's "debt" or "guilt." At first Gregor had taken this debt upon himself, not only by becoming the sole breadwinner for the family, but also by arrogating to himself the father's authority. By acquiescing to the metamorphosis, Gregor can take the debt authentically upon himself, although this acquiescence means self-abdication, not the exploitation of the aggressive and usurpatory function of the metamorphosis.

At the close Gregor perceives this point and dies, reconciled. The family is relieved of its burden of indebtedness and able to engender new life. The genuinely tragic character of *The Metamorphosis* cannot be belied with the objection that the Samsa family is so irremediably vulgar that a sacrifice on its account can only be meaningless. They belong to that common life which Kafka considered to be infinitely superior to the individual.

The metamorphosis itself is not the only miraculous, nonrealistic event in the story. What, for example, has become of the "debt," owed the boss, with which the story began? We do not hear an empirical account of how it was discharged because in this work all facts function as the representation of intentions. The "debt" was Gregor himself. Gregor's monstrous transformation drives away the office manager, who never again returns. With Gregor's physical disappearance, the debt and even all memory of it are extirpated.

In his metamorphosed form Gregor seeks to be reconciled with his family through displays of helplessness. "It is, however, Gregor's destination to be reconciled with his family through his death and not through his life with the group" (101). His deepest intention is not flight into pure self-reflection, but an act by which the family will be rejuvenated. For an instant at death he has the nourishment which he has sought and could not find "in garbage and cheese parings, and as long, too, as he hoped to find it by means of the pure self, as hunger artist, music connoisseur, and egocentric decadent" (101).

Gregor's predicament is tragic; he must redeem life by ridding it of himself, of "guilt." "No Christ, but a tragic hero—and one of the most tragic in world literature, because he must remain deprived of human dignity, of the 'beautiful form' of the human shape" (102).

105-D. Sokel, Walter H. *Franz Kafka*. Columbia Essays on Modern Writers. New York and London: Columbia University Press, 1966.

The first phase of Kafka's mature work (1912-1914) is the phase of the punitive fantasy; it is to this period, of course, that *The Metamorphosis* belongs.

The particular character of Kafka's art during this period emerges from the contrast between the wished-for beetle metamorphosis in "Wedding Preparations in the Country" and Gregor Samsa's metamorphosis. "In both stories the transformed self is the true self. However, Samsa's transformation, unlike Raban's, emerges from his night dreams and becomes reality. The text clearly refers to the subconscious origin of the metamorphosis" (16). Thus in *The Metamorphosis* what the self wants is not true, and what is true is not what the self wants. Samsa's uneasy conscience, not his beetle exterior, is his façade. His truth is the metamorphosis, no mere temporary inconvenience, as conscience would have it. The metamorphosis obliquely fulfills Gregor's repressed desires; and none of his appeasing and rationalizing reflections can mask this fact.

As a result of the metamorphosis, Gregor no longer has to labor at his job; he can enjoy a state of seclusion and irresponsibility. The price he must pay, however, is the consciousness of abandoning his family. The manifest content of the story, we see, consists of the repeated asseverations of Gregor's false consciousness that he does not wish to let the family down.

Gregor's punishment in *The Metamorphosis* comes ultimately from his desire to supplant his father; his punishment is hideous: he is transformed into a creature of another species. "The father is allied with the submerged pole of his son's divided self. He enforces those tendencies in his son that crave for regression to a child-like existence which finds its radical objectification in Gregor's vermin condition" (19). An alliance exists between the repressive force of the father and the son's subconscious desires. Three times Gregor attempts to emerge from his room to assert himself as a responsible human being. Twice his father violently drives him back and in this way "enforces Gregor's own tendency toward withdrawal and seclusion that he expressed by locking himself in his room and emerging from his dreams as a creature unable to communicate" (19). Had Gregor been faithful to his true self, he would not have attempted to emerge from his prison to impose himself on the human community. "He would have gone into ultimate loneliness, and death would have been self-fulfillment" (22). Through his sister's final judgment, spoken with the authority of the new generation, life itself speaks and condemns him.

Gregor's calm assent to her judgment is made with the voice of his inner truth; he becomes a true son, truly himself, by dying. His voluntary death leads to the sexual and procreative liberation of the family.

106. Sonnenfeld, Marion. "Paralleles in *Novelle* und *Verwandlung*." *Symposium*, XIV (Fall 1960), 221-25.

Though these works arose from different minds, under radically different historical and social circumstances, an analysis of their structure and content discloses stylistic and even conceptual parallels between them. It is not true, as **Von Wiese** maintains, that in Kafka one seeks more or less in vain for the typical narrative devices of the novella; *The Metamorphosis* conforms to Goethe's recipe for the novella, for it contains an "unprecedented event," two critical turning points, and even a so-called "falcon" [in the words of **E. K. Bennett** (15) the element which "has an inner significance and symbolizes the action"].

In *The Metamorphosis* there is an inner and an outer story. The inner story recounts Gregor's efforts to endure his metamorphosis as a man and to act for the good of his family. This story dominates the outer action, which, as in Goethe, describes the effect of love on society. In *The Metamorphosis* the outer story describes the resentment of the beloved toward the lover.

The "unprecedented event" in *The Metamorphosis* is Gregor's metamorphosis; as in Goethe's *Novelle,* the inner story arises in answer to the question of how the hero means to and can adjust to new circumstances. The unprecedented event creates a danger to the family which has been dependent on Gregor until now and which must now become independent to survive.

As in *Novelle, The Metamorphosis* has two turning points: the first is Gregor's resolution not to give in to his animal nature–he decides to keep his furniture in anticipation of his return to the human condition; the second, the decisive juncture, is Gregor's decision, after his sister's violin playing, to die. Gregor's resolve to maintain inwardly the human attitude makes the family refuse to consider him a human being: at the sight of him, his mother faints, and his father bombards him with apples. The second turning point, on the other hand, arises from the family's decision that he must go, that this being cannot indeed be Gregor, since the real Gregor would have gone by himself a long time ago.

The high points of both novellas are comparable: both treat

the soothing effect of music on a beast. And after this second turning point in both novellas there is a reconciliation; Gregor dies but thinks of his family with "deep emotion and love"; once dead, he is briefly acknowledged by the others as a member of the family, which now harbors hope for a better future.

The character of the "falcon" in these novellas is radically different, for in Goethe's story it is nature in man and in the world, a condition of harmony and perfection; the falcon in *The Metamorphosis* is the door which separates Gregor and the family, and it is for the most part locked. "In the human condition *he* had locked it; now, however, the key is inserted from the other side. Nature is banished; it is outside; but we are inside" (223).

Unlike Goethe's *Novelle, The Metamorphosis* contains no trace of allegory. Through his disfigurement or metamorphosis, the world of the bug has become real. Because *The Metamorphosis* concludes on an optimistic note, the reader is tempted to justify the outer story in terms of the inner one; he seeks Kafka's unconventional moral, which can only be negative. Here, as in Goethe, (Gregor's) love is linked to the ability to renounce, but not so as to become productive. The conclusion, practically Schopenhauerian, exacts for the sake of others the voluntary shattering of the will to live. Gregor cannot fit into the human world, and he must die. More than this, in having caused the family to grow dependent on him, he has had to be metamorphosed so as to awaken their aggressiveness. Then he has to die to liberate the family completely.

In Kafka's pessimism, inwardness has wholly lost the harmony of the natural world; Kafka's tragedy is that of the human spirit in an inhuman shape–or in an inhuman world.

1. **Foulkes** suggests on good evidence that Gregor has lost the will to live before the family explicitly demands his death. His wish to die is thus not voluntary, not ethical, but an urge.

2. The argument that Gregor has *had* to be metamorphosed, has *had* to die to liberate the family, is based on a presumption which the story does not support–namely, that the world is governed by an effectual and necessary justice which is more offended by Gregor's tyranny over the family than by the family's tyranny over Gregor.

3. **Ulshöfer** confirms the link between Goethe and Kafka. He writes: "*The Metamorphosis* is constructed on the basis of Goethe's theory of form and Goethe's aesthetics. *The Metamorphosis* shows that at the bottom of Kafka's work there is no new aesthetic but a new feeling about life and a new image of the world" (35).

107. Sparks, Kimberly. "Drei Schwarze Kaninchen: Zu einer Deutung der Zimmerherren in Kafkas 'Die Verwandlung.' " *Zeitschrift für deutsche Philologie*, 84, special issue (1965), 73-82.

The three roomers in *The Metamorphosis* are not, as **Von Wiese** (340) maintains, stereotypes and hence without significance for the progress of the story. They are supernumeraries who, after an initially senseless appearance, are ritualized—that is, absorbed into the ceremony of the story. In this work full of symmetries, they are a sort of keystone: their appearance is well prepared for, and they are essentially linked to the images, gestures, and motifs of the novella. They constitute a sort of absurd recapitulation of Gregor's metamorphosis and, in the end, a further metamorphosis of Gregor himself. Gregor is audience to their marionette's play, "which summarizes the entire course of the action up to this point: namely, the haunting of the Samsa family by a strange, uncanny being. Even the brown bug Gregor is hardly less burdensome and importunate, hardly less estranging, than these three black Hasidim" (74). It is an additional excruciation for Gregor that he must now watch the roomers (quite as Gregor himself in former days) usurp the father's chair, the father's table, and so on. He does not get to see the final act of this little drama—how the roomers are chased out of the apartment by the father after he has regained his strength—because he is already dead.

At the beginning of Section III there is an uncanny silence while the living room is literally converted into a stage in anticipation of the arrival of the roomers. Gregor watches the proceedings from his room, now an invisible loge. There follows a complicated movement consisting of variations on the first part of the story. Now it is the father who must get to work by six in the morning and who at night for fifteen minutes at a time resists leaving the chair in which he sleeps. The role of the sister as Gregor's nurse and prison warder is taken over by the cleaning woman.

The performance of the roomers is an objectification of the life of Gregor Samsa, of his condition and his effect on the family—though watching them, he cannot recognize himself. Yet this will not surprise us: Gregor is doomed never to know himself. The grotesque comedy of the roomers is linked to their puppetlike synchronization; in effect, to the condition of the loss of self. Poor Gregor is not helped by the objectification of his own predicament.

The roomers' black beards suggest the fur stole of the lady in the picture in Gregor's room; their passion for order, "especially in the kitchen," takes up Gregor's obsession with food and inverts the image of the present filthy chaos of his room.

The three roomers take over the main dining table, which had served as a sort of cult center for the life of the family. This bizarre trinity contrasts with the former trinity of father, mother, and Gregor. Many passages from the text up to this point confirm the general proposition: "whomever things are going well for, or whoever has the upper hand, sits at the head of the table and lets himself be served. It is quite characteristic now that the three roomers take over the patriarchal place and exile the family into the kitchen" (77).

It becomes clear that the behavior of the boarders is a wicked caricature of Gregor. Each of their gestures comes out of Gregor's past: for example, reading the newspaper. "Whoever sits at the head of the table has the right to read the newspaper, and the newspaper itself has become part of the ceremony" (78).

Grete begins her violin playing. There does not appear to be any external, logical reason for her to do so; a reason is supplied, however, by the hypothesis that this entire scene functions as an objectification of Gregor's self, of Gregor's past. The roomers' negative reaction to the music and Gregor's positive reaction dramatize his ambivalence toward music.

Gregor creeps out of his room into the living room; "and this is not the first time that he leaves his room in order to advance toward his polar, antagonistic self; during his first sortie into the living room he immediately glimpses a once authoritarian Gregor" (79)–Gregor in the uniform of a lieutenant. Now Gregor catches sight of the three importunate intruders. Interestingly, the boarders are not terrified of Gregor but amused by his appearance. What follows is another scene of expulsion, but now it is the roomers whom the father chases away. They do not flee; and the middle roomer gives notice in a speech that actually does perfect justice to Gregor's deeply felt resentment. The conscious Gregor could never have spoken of "disgusting conditions prevailing in this apartment and family." The fact that the middle roomer, who usually speaks through the pronoun "we," now says "I" suggests the presence and intensity of a self that in turn can only suggest Gregor's self. Now the middle roomer (and not, as at the close of Section I, the father) slams the door shut.

The remainder of the action consists of a reduction of the family number to the magic three by the clearing away of Gregor; his anti-self, the three roomers; and Grete's distorted double, the cleaning woman. After the Samsas have registered Gregor's death, the three roomers appear wanting breakfast (quite as Gregor in Section I wanted "the main thing, to have breakfast"). Their trinity is opposed by the hostile trinity of the Samsas; "but the roomers, as their role dictates, can now offer an only slight resistance: their *raison d'être* already lies dead at their six feet" (81). The insectlike character of the triad of roomers is intensified now: the two lesser members of their group, in grotesque synchronization, rub their hands together and jump away like grasshoppers. Relieved, the family watches the departure of these beings without name or profession, Gregor's "*tripelgänger*." "Their function has been to illustrate anew the burdening of the Samsa family and Gregor's burdensomeness to himself" (82).

108. Spector, Robert Donald. "Kafka's Epiphanies." *Kentucky Foreign Language Quarterly*, X (1963), 47-54.

There are three "epiphanies" or fundamental revelations in *The Metamorphosis*. The first is Gregor's metamorphosis: it is revealed from his point of view. Gregor accepts it and ascribes it to the habits and exigencies of his ordinary life. The second epiphany is told from an omniscient point of view and reveals the behavior of his family after his death. The third epiphany is generated by the contrast of the preceding two, the reciprocal betrayal of responsibility and trust by Gregor and his family. The content of this revelation is the "isolation of the individual in contemporary society." The ultimate revelation is of a son who becomes in reality what he has always been symbolically for a family whose dependence on him he has willed. The effect of the tale is to declare the impossibility of a man's "comprehending the terms of his own existence."

The episode of violin music cannot be omitted in any account of the "epiphanies" of *The Metamorphosis*. It situates the solitude *and* the bad faith of the hero at a deeper level than that of his relation to "contemporary society."

109. Spender, Stephen. "Franz Kafka's *The Metamorphosis*" (a review). *The New Republic*, XCII (Oct. 27, 1937), 347.

The Metamorphosis is a nightmare; "it contains no metaphysical purpose." Kafka describes, on his own terms, a contemporary situation: an employee, on whom his family is dependent, wakes up one morning to find that he is incurably ill.

110-A. Spilka, Mark. "Kafka's Sources for *The Metamorphosis*." *Comparative Literature,* XI (Fall 1959), 289-307.

The opening of *The Metamorphosis* seems spectacular; it enhances Kafka's reputation for originality and uniqueness as a writer. "There is growing evidence, however, that Kafka was a synthetic writer, that his greatest works were built on frames supplied by other authors, and that he was original in the best sense, in his development of the latent tendencies in older forms" (289). The content and the form of Kafka's genius belongs to the tradition of the urban grotesque, whose sources lie in late German Romanticism and the nineteenth-century realistic novel.

Kafka's creative breakthrough in the fall of 1912 was actually "a burst of 'imitative' writing" (290). His method is prefigured by the psychological fantasy of Hoffmann. Fantasy and urban realism interpenetrate in the fiction of Gogol and Dostoevsky. The central situation of *The Metamorphosis*—a son locked up in his room and despised by his family—is inspired by *David Copperfield. The Metamorphosis* creates its precursors, defines this tradition. The immediate sources of *The Metamorphosis* are supplied by Dickens and Dostoevsky.

At the beginning of this tradition stands E. T. A. Hoffmann, who explored the theme of the double, foreshadowing the split between conscious and unconscious. The self and its double are at odds. The double inhabits a fantastic world remote from its psychological and social origins.

Gogol explores the comic possibilities of Hoffmann's doubles theme by situating the fantastic in urban settings. "The Nose" is such a story. [See **Erlich** and **Parry**.] Dostoevsky grasped that "Hoffmann's doubles *belonged* in the urban world" (291), in the apartments and offices of bureaucratic drudges: and it is Dostoevsky's story, deriving from works of Gogol and Hoffmann, which is the effective origin of *The Metamorphosis*. Dostoevsky's *The Double* begins with the hero's awakening, describes in precise detail the narrowness and squalor of his room, confronts the hero with his double, and concludes: "No it was not a dream, and that was all about it."[54] Dostoevsky "was also aware of inner pressures which recur in dreams, and which continue even in the waking state. . . . For him the double . . . confirmed the *earthbound* reality of dreams, and of powers within them which oppose the conscious personality" (293). *The Double* is flawed, however, by Dostoevsky's laborious attempt to establish in the hero Golyadkin an hallucinatory madness. Kafka's technical insight allows him to be less wasteful. He replaces the hallucination with a realistically elaborated miraculous event.[55] Yet the particular character of this miracle—the transformation of a man into a bug—derives from Dostoevsky. The disgruntled clerk of *Notes from Underground* remarks that he has "tried many times to become an insect." The link between man and insect in *The Brothers Karamazov* is pronounced. There are similar images in Dickens and other writers, "but Dostoevsky alone had linked the insect state with sensual lust and inward degradation, with oppressive office life, and with the conflict between father and son over the same woman" (294). The insect metamorphosis in Kafka's story communicates the reality of the unconscious and links it to consciousness—to the sum of urban pressures. The bug is a version of the double. In introducing this more striking metaphor at the outset, Kafka imitates and intensifies the opening of *The Double.*

The opening of *The Metamorphosis* contains many details which are direct imitations of the opening of *The Double* and many "ingenious adaptations." The essential parallels are all present: "the awakening from troubled dreams; the incarnation of illness, and the discovery that the change is real; the small, familiar bedroom, in partial disorder; the tedious occupation; the attractive lady, with her proferred symbol of successful love; the bad weather, which renews the desire for sleep; and the combined effect of paralysis, weakness and pain" (295-96). All these details are organized by the dominant insect metaphor, correlative of a definite state of mind.

The drama of clerk and employer is also present in *The Double*: the hero, afraid of losing his job, manages to startle and frighten off his superior. Both Golyadkin and Gregor Samsa are tormented by social exclusion, but they are sexually repressed as well. After long torment and humiliation Golyadkin moves toward madness; Gregor Samsa, toward death.

The opening of *The Metamorphosis* constitutes a striking technical advance over *The Double*: "through this Kafka is able to move more deeply into the unconscious than Dostoevsky had penetrated. . . . For Kafka was a Freudian artist: he knew that Gregor's troubles were familial, that he was firmly fixed in the parental nest, and had never escaped from childhood pressures" (298).

This brings us to a dimension of *The Metamorphosis* not present in *The Double*. In Kafka's work the boss is a kind of office father, a figure of paternal dominance. The feelings of the work have the "*static* force of childhood feeling" (289). This aspect of *The Metamorphosis*, absent from Dostoevsky, is profoundly influenced by Dickens. "In Dickens the parental theme predominates; the father is often engaged in commerce; and the world is viewed from an infantile perspective, with all the concentrated power of a child's responses" (298). The central situation of *The Metamorphosis*—a son excluded from his family, brutally punished by the father, incarcerated in a small room, looked after by a mother-surrogate, and the like: all this was furnished Kafka by Chapter IV of *David Copperfield*. "From the end of Part I, where Gregor is thrust back into his room, until his death in Part III, the chief inspiration comes from *Copperfield*" (302).

There is another key element of *The Metamorphosis* missing from *David Copperfield*: the idea of familial support. "Gregor not only supports his parents, but is bound to his job by their debt to his office father. Their dominance thus extends to the system which deprives him of creative life and married love, and exposes him to his own suppressed desires" (302). Kafka himself did not support his family; but Dickens did. Dickens told his biographer, John Forster, of a crushing episode from his youth, when he was obliged to work in a blacking warehouse; Kafka very probably read this work. This episode yields materials that enter *The Metamorphosis*: "a whole family enveloped by the disgrace of debt and imprisonment; a young boy forced to help them through degrading labor, and made sick by his ordeal; a favored sister at the music academy; and the boy grown older, who returns in dreams to his childhood state" (304).

Gregor Samsa represents the synthesis, not only of the person Kafka, but also of David Copperfield, Dickens, and even Golyadkin. Each of these writers describes the outcast from within; thus it is through an ironic contrast that we feel the humanity of the protagonist.

110-B. Spilka, Mark. *Dickens and Kafka: A Mutual Interpretation.* Bloomington: Indiana University Press, 1963. Pp. 77-79, 252-54.

Kafka's vermin image is the product of disgust for the spirit's bodily predicament. The body is guilty, its sex is shameful, its pain marks the decline of the spirit. The bug is also a visible image of the unconscious, its vileness made objective, as in dreams. "Kafka was the first to explore the unconscious with the help of Freudian theory, and to deepen and enrich the form with conscious knowledge and control" (77). Gregor's "crust" is the image of his regression, the crystallization of his unconscious vileness. His conscious self, meanwhile, remains trapped within this insect carapace. This is the "principle at stake."

Kafka wants to show Gregor's humanity, which is larger than his insect shape. His humanity is unadaptable; there is no place for him in human society; he must die. The revulsion of his family measures the extent of his deformity. In spite of their token acts of kindness, for the family members he is only monstrous.

The comparison between *David Copperfield* and *The Metamorphosis* reveals that Gregor is guilty before human rather than divine tribunals; he is more like David Copperfield than like Joseph K. Gregor's guilt is therefore less grave than has been supposed. "His sinful state, imposed from within by unconscious yearnings, has been aggravated by social and familial pressures which reduce him to bestial immaturity. He accepts his failure, moreover, and exonerates himself through death" (253). As with David Copperfield, Gregor's punishment precedes his regression, but Gregor's shows of affection, unlike Dicken's prodigies of sentiment, are openly bound to neurotic feelings.

111. Starke, Ottomar. "Kafka und die Illustration." *Neue literarische Welt*, IX (May 10, 1953), 3.

Starke addresses himself to **Beissner**'s monograph *Der Erzähler Franz Kafka*, 13-A, which argues, in Starke's words, that "Kafka's novels and stories depict only psychopathological states. Thus the hero of *The Metamorphosis* is not really transformed into a loathsome monster. This is only his delusion." **Beissner** goes on to use Starke's illustrated title page as evidence for this contention. Starke claims that this cannot be done: he never intended to depict Gregor Samsa, only a figure fleeing with terror from an extraordinary disaster.

112. Starobinski, Jean. "La rêve architecte (A propos des intérieurs de Franz Kafka)." *Cahiers de la compagnie Madeleine Renaud-Jean Louis Barrault*, no. 50 (Feb. 1965), 21-29.

A consciousness reveals itself by the furniture with which it surrounds itself. This revelation may be of a desire to flee; but the desire may be frustrated, and (as in Kafka's case) the imagination paralyzed or frozen finds itself chained to the objects which it detests.

Architectural elements in Kafka's fiction form the threshold of a world in which absent powers–or powerful absences–hold court. Doors, windows, compartments create a separation, a near side and a far side. Whatever occurs behind the wall is out of range, beyond the imagination, but what happens there concerns us.

Yet we cannot cross this threshold. From the first moment of his metamorphosis, Gregor Samsa will not have the right to leave his room; and once outside the room, he will not dare to go back in. "The walls always tend to close up again, so that consciousness finds itself sometimes cast out into the condition of the exile, sometimes captive in the situation of the walled-up prisoner. In one position or the other, the individual always suffers the torment of not being where he should be, of not being at the right place; even inside, one is foreclosed; even outside, one is enclosed. We are always *on this side*. The animal condition is the correlative expression of this, on the level not of spatial limits, but of internal, organic limits: to be enclosed in a body and not to be able to go beyond the possibilities of this body" (28-29).

What is anomalous in Kafka's world is not the structure of things, but the relation of people to things. Natural and architectural elements remain as we know them. "If there are sudden exceptions, they take place in a universe in which everything else remains self-identical. The metamorphosis does not generalize itself." Still, incommodiousness is a characteristic of Kafka's interiors. No one in Kafka truly has his own place to live. Things and persons in Kafka have not yet entered into their own being, they remain outside themselves but captives of each other. The imagination which would perhaps flee the real world only succeeds in sharpening its outlines. A sort of invisible torpor captivates the victim, an enormous sleep envelops—or, one should say, *petrifies*—him. In Kafka the dream is an architect.

113-A. Stekel, Wilhelm. "Die Verwandlung." In *Psychosexueller Infantilismus.* Berlin, 1923. P. 263.

The Metamorphosis portrays the grotesque zooanthropic fantasy of being a louse. The afflicted creature draws all sorts of inferences from his experience as to the egoistical attitude of his family. "In most cases zooanthropism serves to symbolize the sadistic components. . . . The louse is also a bloodsucking creature."

"Schizophrenia too sometimes exhibits in the early stages transparent zooanthropic images. The psychoses also deal with regressions to an infantile period, to an archaism."

113-B. Stekel, Wilhelm. "Analyse eines Homosexuellen." In *Onanie und Homosexualität. Krankhafte Störungen des Trieb- und Affektlebens,* Vol. II. Berlin, 1923. P. 477.

While freely associating, the patient Sigma alludes to the feeling of being a louse. (The meaning of the metamorphosis dream in Kafka's story, in which a man is transformed into a louse, is very probably sadistic.) "For a time Sigma, like all homosexuals, was . . . particularly afraid of tuberculosis. . . . We are already familiar with tuberculosis' representing evil, filthiness, incest, and homosexuality."

In a letter to Felix Weltsch on September 22, 1917, Kafka asked to read these comments by Stekel. If these lines did come into his hands, he cannot have been very much instructed.

114. Tauber, Herbert. *Franz Kafka: Eine Deutung seiner Werke*. Zürich and New York: Oprecht, 1941. *Franz Kafka: An Interpretation of his Writings*, trans. by G. Humphrey Roberts and Roger Senhouse. New Haven: Yale University Press, 1948.

The Metamorphosis is more credible than "The Judgment" because it focuses on the interior of a consciousness. It has a close structural parallel with "The Judgment," with the exception of the figure of the friend, who is absent; but his distance, solitude, and inner division reappear in the nightmarish figure of Gregor. The story begins with Gregor's waking—to an awareness of his alienation from the world around him. The inaccessible dimension of his authentic self, its inner solitude, emerges in his new shape. His self has never been adequate to the claims of everyday life. The metamorphosis is an unconscious rejection of his world and of his role as provider; but the loss of this foundation discloses an inner abyss of anxiety and bad conscience. Being that has lost its foundation seems "buglike" to itself.

Gregor's terrifying appearance is the result of an unconscious self-punishment. To a self without world or structure, the sensuous givens of its existence are suspicious; the insect form expresses disgust for itself, for the bodily forces which automatically prolong a life grown dubious to itself. The metamorphosis reveals Gregor's inner being as apathetic animal hebetude—but through it is awakened Gregor's longing for higher meaning: this is the sense of his love for his sister's violin playing. The metamorphosis is thus two-sided, for it is also a liberation; it releases him from the compelling necessity of business life and leads him to an awareness of his deeper needs. The metamorphosis is a wish image, since it actualizes Gregor's inner resistance to the emptiness of everyday life. But Gregor's separation from everyday life remains unredeemed by contact with a new order of existence; his separation signifies only an irremediable backsliding into stunted animal existence, which is finally only an interpretation of the senselessness and repulsiveness of everyday life. Only the unslaked longing for a new connection remains.

Tauber stresses the farcical side of this nightmare. The

comedy arises from the contrast between the monster and the spiritual poverty of the family. The story not only shows an unhappy imprisonment in an incongruous world, but also reveals a secret ironical superiority on the part of the narrator in its atmosphere of cold-blooded description.

The family cannot see Gregor as only a monster, and so it cannot destroy him; yet neither can it see the lost soul behind the monstrous surface. It neither loves nor helps him. Gregor remains in a state of indecision.

The father detects Gregor in the bug—but with hate for the rotten trick that has been played on him. He holds Gregor responsible for the metamorphosis, and the first time he drives him back is a kind of punishment. The bug, for him, is an expression of Gregor's malice. Because Gregor can now no longer fit into the organization of family life, he becomes completely egocentric and thus falls into opposition to the father, who still considers himself the center of the family.

Gregor changes; in part he sinks more and more deeply into animal existence, although animal and human exist side by side in him. The animal would give up all mementos of the human world; the human clings to these things. The more that being an animal agrees with him, the more dispirited he becomes as a man. The animal dies, not because it does not obtain nourishment, but because the man dies of neglect. When at the close Gregor is rejected by his family, his alienation is complete; his existence has no basis whatsoever; he dies—without hatred for his family, for their cruelty is human.

The Metamorphosis belongs in part to those medieval legends in which love is put to the test through a disgusting object, as in the legend of St. Julian the Hospitaler. However, in Kafka's story the evil miracle of the metamorphosis is not withstood by a human response of comparable force. Only in a world preoccupied with superficiality could external appearance have a weight so decisive that essences are destroyed by it.

Gregor's situation is not unlike Kafka's in his family: Kafka's concerns seemed as futile to his father as those of Gregor to Mr. Samsa. Kafka maintained toward his father both a feeling of culpabilty and a claim for love, elements present in Gregor's predicament.

Internal division leads inexorably to doom: there is no retreat to a domain separate from the body. The insect cannot be an animal ironically and a man inwardly; it perishes of its unrepresentable inwardness. In Kafka, inwardness never attains the character of self-sufficient substance.

115. **Taylor, Alexander**. "The Waking: The Theme of Kafka's *Metamorphosis*." *Studies in Short Fiction*, II (Summer 1965), 337-42.

Psychoanalytic approaches to *The Metamorphosis* assume Gregor to be sick; in fact, it is his environment, "a dehumanizing world of order," which is sick (337). The story details the reaction of a perceptive being to an enslaving world.

Though Gregor understands the others, he is not understood—more, he is denied the ability to understand. In a grim sense this is true because he does not understand himself.

Gregor's reflections on his job "emphasize the distrust and suspicion surrounding Gregor and his disgust at this state of affairs. . . . This disgust stems from Gregor's desire to establish I-thou relationships in a world of I-it or I-she or I-he relationships" (338). The metamorphosis is a representation of Gregor's unconscious desire to become his true self. Ironically, this desire ruins his relation to his mother and sister—those with whom he had previously most nearly been able to achieve an intimacy.

The metamorphosis cannot have been willed consciously by Gregor; his first act is to deny it. The metamorphosis remains a continual puzzle for him. He constantly questions himself about it—for example, "Have I become less sensitive?"

Before the metamorphosis Gregor had shown almost perverse consideration to job and family, at the expense of his own desires. Afterward he gradually asserts himself at the expense of the others' feelings.

The riddle of the metamorphosis is Gregor's own. The horns of his dilemma are a desire for freedom and self-fulfillment and his knowledge of being immitigably tied to an established order. The metamorphosis shapes this riddle and provokes a cluster of feelings and intentions, the result of which is ambivalence. Gregor does not understand his desire for freedom; he cannot trace it back to its source. Meanwhile he feels "as vile as an insect, because he does not want to belong to the established order, even though he desires I-thou relationships with individuals in that established order and feels that it is his duty to his family to work within that order.[56] The beetle also represents Gregor's revolt and the established order's revulsion at such a revolt" (340).

116. Thalmann, Jörg. *Wege zu Kafka: Eine Interpretation des Amerikaromans.* Frauenfeld and Stuttgart: Huber, 1966. Pp. 230ff.

The novel *Amerika* is informed by the sentiment of owing the world something, of guilt, stemming from the "unbridgeable distance between prescribed duty and meager ability" (230). *The Metamorphosis* constitutes a striking parallel to the development of the guilt motif in *Amerika*—but the germs of the guilt theme are already present in Kafka's earliest works. "Wedding Preparations in the Country" is such a work: the hero Raban wishes to split himself into two people precisely at the moment when he is faced with a repellent unavoidable obligation. The self remains in bed, where it assumes the form of a beautiful stag beetle, while the clothed body of the self totters out into the world.

In Kafka's world neither of these possibilities of the self ever leads to success: success, for Kafka, consists in confronting the world while remaining encapsulated in the self. Only when these two possibilities coincide (something forever denied to Kafka) could there be a happy outcome. As a consequence each of these possibilities is in itself ambivalent. In Kafka's early world "inwardness [appears] as a free space and as a prison, the outer world as a threatening burden and as the goal of longing" (232)—these conceptions run parallel and do not meet. The young Kafka avoids the explicit recognition of their irreconcilability, as if this perception would be intolerable. The transformation of Kafka's naive imagination into a genuine imagination which recognizes at its own source the "swamp of debasement" occurs when the beautiful stag beetle (its meaning externalized, trivialized, through an allusion to hibernation) is transformed into the repulsive beetle of *The Metamorphosis*. Kafka's art is informed by the effort to unite opposite elements, polar movements of the spirit, neither of which is adequate to itself. This opposition–between openness to the world and self-encapsulation–is exhibited in the opposition between *The Metamorphosis* and "The Stoker," the first chapter of *Amerika*.

117. **Tindall, William York**. *The Literary Symbol.* New York: Columbia University Press, 1955. Pp. 63-64.

The body of the monstrous bug is a symbol, implying "the attitude of Samsa's family toward Samsa, his opinion of himself, and, in addition to these, ideas and feelings about our society, our time, and the miserable condition of humanity." The disgusting insect is an exemplary twentieth-century symbol, since the hero's predicament is a Freudian nightmare.

118. **Ulshöfer, Robert**. "Entseelte Wirklichkeit in Franz Kafka's 'Verwandlung,' Die Wirklichkeitsauffassung in der modernen Prosadichtung." *Der Deutschunterricht,* no. 1 (1955), 27-36.

It has been maintained that Kafka's works cannot be understood in terms of their content but only in terms of their form. In these works, it is claimed, empirical reality is deformed; action and imagery are presented, not for their own sakes, but only as functions within self-contained but meaningless wholes.

The question of the meaning and truth of Kafka's work can be posed in terms of the relation in *The Metamorphosis* between the world of the self and the world of objects.

Throughout *The Metamorphosis* Gregor increasingly lives the life of a bug. In dreams and in fairy tales men are transformed into beasts, but *The Metamorphosis* is neither of these (we are quite specifically told that the metamorphosis "was no dream"). In fables and animal epics animals think and speak, but again *The Metamorphosis* is neither of these forms because "all these genres take place, not in the empirical world, but in an illusory or visionary realm of fantasy. But our story takes place in empirical reality" (28).

Does the writer intend us to conceive the metamorphosis in the mode of reality or as an allegory, in the mode of ideality or as wild fantasy? An answer requires us to determine what in the narrative can be sensuously experienced as palpable objects and what cannot.

The story is encoded. The language of *The Metamorphosis* sometimes means what it says and sometimes must be decoded with the key which it itself provides. Kafka projects onto the plane of concrete, empirical reality ideas about the nature of man and human society in such a fashion that empirical reality and human inwardness come to light in a quite different way. The story is an interpretable structure, to a certain extent objectively true.

Gregor Samsa awakens with the notion of having the body of a large insect. The notion is bizarre; but Gregor has not lost his mind. He is a simple man without pretensions–diligent, helpful, a workhorse in the harness of an ideal of family security. "These are very good qualities" (29)–but they are his only ones. He is uncultivated, without spiritual concerns. He wants money and an attractive woman like the one in the picture that hangs on his bedroom wall.

This picture and the picture of Gregor in lieutenant's uniform –both concrete empirical objects–give the key to the understanding of the figures in this story. Both Gregor and his family appraise others by conventional standards of wealth and social prestige. "What remains when one takes away the furs from the lady and the uniform from the lieutenant? The deportment and respect others have before them disappears; beings remain–who are naked, empty, without social value.

"What is surprising and meaningful is that Gregor . . . sees himself on the first morning in his total wretchedness and worthlessness as man without a uniform" (30). The cause of this act of self-knowledge is physical sickness–a bad cold, hoarseness, and itching. Gregor's "cold shivers" are a physical symptom; they also suggest the image of the bug and induce his insight into the poverty and sickness of his soul. He suffers bodily and spiritual cold. His life is without human warmth. His recognition that he is a monstrous bug, a worthless creature, arises from the awareness that his life is without inwardness, freedom, joy, love. He is the creature of a brutal, calculating boss and of his functionaries. His family, too, is without affection—his father is a servile marionette (witness his obsequiousness in front of the manager and his behavior as bank porter).

Gregor recognizes himself on the morning of his metamorphosis as a creature without connection to any other human being or any transcendental principle. "Disgust in itself, disgust for existence, are expressed in this idea" (33).

If for Gregor the word *bug* has figurative meaning (he maintains his human shape), how can it be that those around him regard him as a real bug? The others judge all other human beings by external standards, not by their inner worth. The moment Gregor ceases to be a provider, he loses all value for them. The father drives Gregor back into his room because "he has appeared before his parents and the manager in a (socially speaking) completely impossible state—sick, unshaven, unkempt, not dressed, fearful, convinced of his unworthiness" (34).

The debacle of the first morning arises from the failure of the others. Gregor was only sick and in a bad way—they treated him like a bug. Gregor is more and more confirmed in the rightness of his despicable opinion of himself. He will no longer "open the door" to the outer world. But it is impossible for a man to live in a state of complete isolation. Kafka's theme in *The Metamorphosis* is sickness, the recognition of spiritual poverty, one's abandonment at the hands of the world, increasing torment, solitude, and death.

Kafka's technique for representing the soullessness and inhumanity of the man of our times is to flash the world as it is experienced onto the world as it is thought and reciprocally to illuminate them. In fact, the object of *The Metamorphosis* is a sick and inhumane world, a world of people who lack all love, faith, hope. *The Metamorphosis* is anticlassic (though it has the symbolic character which is characteristic of Goethe's writing) in the sense that it declines to show meaningful human connections between the psychic and the material world. It is this absence which enables Kafka's technique of flashing onto one another images from the world of thought and the world of sensation, but it also gives his work a contrived character.

119-A. Urzidil, Johannes. "Meetings with Franz Kafka." *Menorah Journal*, XL (Spring 1952), 112-16.

Among those writing in German in Prague between 1912 and 1924 was a young poet named Karl Brand who died young. "Kafka's story, 'The Metamorphosis,' describes a man, a family, and conditions of life very similar to Brand's. Brand lived with his parents and sister in a gloomy, old baroque house, where the family's attitude to his slow physical disintegration was like that of the Samsa family to the dying Gregor in 'The Metamorphosis' " (113). Urzidil and Werfel used to tell Kafka of their visits to Brand; to Kafka the case of Brand seemed a reenactment of his own story. In 1921 a little book of Brand's literary remains was published. Kafka read this book and wrote: "The book reminded me very much in essence, but also in structure, of 'Ivan Ilyich.' " Urzidil notes: "The hint at Tolstoy's 'The Death of Ivan Ilyich' "—with its initial profession of illusion, the death, the consoling epilogue—"closes the ring between the life and death of Karl Brand and the life and death of Gregor Samsa in 'The Metamorphosis' " (115).

119-B. Urzidil, Johannes. "Im Prag des Expressionismus," "Brand." In *Da Geht Kafka*. Zurich and Stuttgart: Artemis, 1965. Pp. 11-12, 60-70. Reprinted in *Da Geht Kafka*. Munich: Deutscher Taschenbuch Verlag, 1966. Pp. 11, 45-52. "In the Prague of Expressionism," "Brand." In *There Goes Kafka*, trans. by Harold A. Basilius. Detroit: Wayne State University Press, 1968. Pp. 18-19, 82-96.

Prague is in all of Kafka's work, not concretely visible perhaps, but present all the same, like salt in water. "The Prague quality in each of Kafka's figures, situations, background descriptions, could be demonstrated. Only one example: after 'The Metamorphosis' had come out, Kafka remarked to my father-in-law, Professor Karl Thieberger, whom he met on the street: 'What do you think about the terrible things going on in our house?' Whoever considers that just a joke knows absolutely nothing about Kafka. Like almost everything else about him, it was irony, of course, but not just irony; at the same time it was serious realism" (11-12).

"Brand" adds further details to **Urzidil**, 119-A. Karl Brand's real name was Karl Müller; he was Christian and of proletarian (not petty bourgeois) origins. He died of tuberculosis. Of Brand's desperate situation recounted in his book *The Bequest*, Kafka wrote: "It is no different with 'Ivan Ilyich'; only here in *The Bequest* it is more distinct, because each stage is specifically personified."

Kafka must have read "The Death of Ivan Ilyich" before 1912 because *The Metamorphosis* bears the imprint of Tolstoy's account of the gradual, inevitable, and uncomprehended death of a human being. In Brand, whom Kafka met in 1913, the figure of Gregor Samsa was palpable; Kafka might have seen in Brand, as in Samsa, his own gradual, inevitable, and uncomprehended death before it had ever been diagnosed by a doctor. The life and death of Brand, of Ivan Ilyich, and of Kafka himself are inextricably linked.

Urzidil's articles have the merit of justifying the fruitful parallel, frequently noted but never explored in depth, between Tolstoy's "The Death of Ivan Ilyich" and *The Metamorphosis.*

120-A. Vivas, Eliseo. *Creation and Discovery: Essays in Criticism and Aesthetics*. New York: Noonday Press, 1955. P.126.

The claim that literature must be plausible requires literature to refer to the world. Such an exaction, however, denies the autonomy of the artist and the self-sufficiency of the artifact. It is not plausible that overnight a man should be metamorphosed into a monstrous bug. "But the writer of *Metamorphosis* transports us . . . into a world of his own creation, by devices which the acuity of a good critic can disclose, although seldom exhaustively, and the purpose of which is to exclude from our conscious response our non-aesthetic demands in such a way that they do not become the basis of a criticism of his symbolic construction."

120-B. Vivas, Eliseo. "Imitation and Expression." *Journal of Aesthetics and Art Criticism* (Summer 1961), 428.

Aristotle claims that in a work of art a likely impossibility is preferable to an unconvincing possibility. The "admissibility" of a story such as *The Metamorphosis* disproves the claim that questions of possibility and impossibility are relevant to aesthetics. "And they are [irrelevant] because the story is self-sufficient, autonomous, and its autonomy or self-sufficiency forces us, the readers, to stay within its universe, to read it transitively." The work of art isolates the spectator, suspends for him the experience of the ordinary laws of reality, and makes comparisons impossible between these laws and the laws of the work.

Aristotelians might still argue that *The Metamorphosis* is an imitation, because the change into a beetle imitates the relations between Gregor and his family. This interpretation changes *The Metamorphosis* into an allegory—"which is all this particular story is." But it is palpably impossible to interpret *The Castle* and *The Trial* as allegories.

121. Volkening, Ernesto. "La Metamorfosis de Kafka, Preludio de una Tragedia Espiritual." *Revista de las Indas* (March-May 1948), 465-75.

Kafka's "point of departure is not constituted by form, and even less by an abstract concept, but by a nucleus of intimate experiences of a religious kind" (466). From the religious standpoint, things and relations become problematic, fragmentary, symbolic. Kafka's events do not coincide with his descriptions but reflect something beyond them that cannot be manifested in any other way; his intent is to express the infinite by means of the finite.

Understanding Kafka's works is a matter of "co-realizing" (to use Scheler's word) the basic experience of the author in an authentic spiritual act. The reader must grasp, for example, that minutely detailed descriptions of apparently trivial events register metaphysical doubt. Whatever the events of Kafka's works, they are not fantastic negations of everyday experience in the manner of Hoffmann, Poe, and Meyrink. The fragmentary character of Kafka's novels is not due to a failure of artistic discipline or of creative effort, but to an "authentic frustration" (Jaspers)—the impossibility of assigning limits to what essentially has none.

The metamorphosis of Gregor Samsa occurs with no preliminaries. There is no attempt to lead the reader by degrees from the common to the extraordinary, to accommodate evolutionary, rational notions; at the heart of the study is a transforming mystery. "It is as though in an imaginary vision [Kafka] had anticipated the sudden irruption of a powerful irrational force into his own life" (470).

Kafka's ethic "consists in enduring, under the threat of sinking into the shadows of madness, that which transcends the limits of our biological organization, *lato sensu*" (470).

In spite of his struggles, Gregor cannot return to the human world; he is hopelessly divided into beetle and man. His voice, which is lost for not being heard, his cry in the middle of a deaf and insensible night, recalls the anxiety dreams in other works of Kafka, in which someone wears himself out in the effort to transmit a message which everyone ignores. Gregor's solitude is the solitude of being one man among the many.

Gregor's metamorphosis arises in response to his impasse, his sacrifice of self on the altars of filial duty and professional responsibility. He could only become a god or an animal; in becoming the latter, he throws off the burdens of the human condition. This violent solution, however, is not in reality acceptable, since seeking refuge in "the most complete irresponsibility implies a regression contrary to the structure of our being. . . . Though we smash ourselves in the tragic struggle with the invincible forces of destiny, it is forbidden to us to return to forms already conquered by our personality, and this is what the author says when, making himself supreme judge, he condemns his creature to die an animal's death which is not a fulfillment or a rebirth but a silent transition into the inorganic" (462).[57]

The story unmasks the humanist pretensions of the world before the First World War. Gregor's fate, the retribution for his having wanted to break the limits of the human condition with impunity, reveals the extreme fragility of the family nexus. In the Samsas, craven hypocrisy is linked with coldness of heart. "When, instead of killing the monster, the family lets it agonize in the midst of its filth, it is not compassion that inspires it but that mean knowledge of decency which, once the slow punishment has been consummated, moves it to dissimulate its satisfaction" (473). The family is sick; yet it enlists the anonymous force of the species that will not tolerate aberrations of a biological kind. "Life follows its implacable march, leaving to one side all symbols of the frustrated attempt to abandon its laws–the empty shell of the beetle" (474). In the sister's yawn is reestablished, "beyond Good and Evil, the natural order of things. At the same time the reader is gripped by the sentiment of the tragic with its paradoxical double face: since, in spite of feeling compassion for the misfortune of the hero, he must nonetheless consider it justified" (474). The conclusion is Nietzschean.

The perfectly circular character of the tale distinguishes it from the Kafkan parable form, but the irony of its conclusion reasserts the intimate connection between Kafka's experience and the fragmentary parable form. In the figure of Gregor the essential themes of Kafka's art are present: the frigid isolation of the individual in the midst of an absurd and dehumanized existence; the desperation not without serenity which results from an irremediable situation; the absence of sentimentality; the effort of Kafka to probe the limits of the human by going beyond it.

122. **Wagenbach, Klaus.** *Franz Kafka in* Selbstzeugnissen *und Bilddokumenten.* Reinbek bei Hamburg: Rowohlt, 1964. Pp. 87-88 and passim.

The Metamorphosis portrays more sharply than "The Judgment" an embattled state of mind. "The destiny of Gregor Samsa is literally and figuratively the one which Raban, the main character of 'Wedding Preparations in the Country,' dreams of; it is to satisfy the claims and obligations of the world by sending it one's 'clothed body' but staying in bed oneself in the 'form of a big beetle' " (88).[58] The work is a punishing representation of the self–of its anxiety and sensitivity–and at the same time a representation of the act of reflection on these themes.

Wagenbach, Klaus. See **Palsey**.

123. **Wais, Kurt**. "Schillers Wirkungsgeschichte im Ausland." *Deutsche Vierteljahrszeitschrift für Literaturwissenschaft und Geistesgeschichte*, XXIX, no. 4 (1955), 500.

Schiller's "pure experience of [man as] cherub and worm" is present in Dostoevsky's Dmitri Karamazov; Dmitri must wait until he has grasped his own responsibility for the murder of his father for having denied his father's right to live. Then Dmitri, who has called his father "worm," will grasp the usefulness of his own self–a "useless worm"–to the sacred order. "Until he reaches this point, Dmitri repeats in stupefied expectancy: 'I am a louse,' 'a putrid insect,' and the condition of this waiting was taken up in our century by a continuator of the thread spun from Schiller to Dostoevsky: Franz Kafka in his story of the putrid louse, *Die Verwandlung*."

124. **Walzel, Oskar**. "Logik im Wunderbaren." *Berliner Tageblatt*, July 6, 1916. Cited in **Born**, Jürgen. "Franz Kafka und seine Kritiker (1912-1914)." *Kafka-Symposion*. Berlin: Wagenbach, 1965. Pp. 140-46.

The Metamorphosis constitutes a world of the marvelous by means of a logical sequence of external and internal experiences; like causes and effects, they create the effect of the necessary and the matter of fact. Romantic fairy tales slowly accustom the reader to the marvelous; they proceed by intensification; not *The Metamorphosis*, which from the outset hurtles the reader into the marvelous. However, the miracle of the metamorphosis is the only miracle postulated. The whole story is like the concrete presentation of a logical series: *if* a man were transformed into a dung beetle, *then* this must necessarily occur, given the circumstances of his life. But if Kafka works with the technique of the naturalist to secure the effect of reality once he has assumed a miraculous event, he nevertheless moves us. The repellent and incredible side of the metamorphosis recedes in our consciousness behind the pitiable spiritual torment of the man cast out of his familiar world, who must witness the gradual massing of disgust which he excites in others and recognize how swiftly he has become insufferable even to those whom he nurtured. The story ends with bitter irony; the writer exhibits the world's pitiless profile.

125. Webster, Peter Dow. "Franz Kafka's 'Metamorphosis' as Death and Resurrection Fantasy." *American Imago,* XVI (Winter 1959), 349-65.

"Here [in *The Metamorphosis*] are the eternal ones of the dream or the arche-typal constructs of the unconscious subjected to the secondary elaboration and conscious control of the artistic mind" (349). Yet the force with which these unconscious forms emerge inspires anxiety.

Kafka's unconscious was ruled by a deep-seated desire to destroy the mother image and equally by the desire, no less strong, to possess or be possessed by this figure.

Kafka's own idea was that he feared and hated his father; this idea was in fact a displaced affect aimed at the mother–"a masochistic attachment to the denying mother, whom he strove to displace in his creative work as artist" (349). He felt his weak ego as an unclean pest. This creature is figured forth in *The Metamorphosis.*

This work, in fact, comprises many metamorphoses: the whole family constellation is transformed. The drama of the introjected beloved and hated maternal imago activates a wide range of transformations: the castration fantasy is abreacted, oral and anal cathexes are dissolved, and a total phallic libido is created in the form of the three roomers. Mother and father images are restored; the emancipated anima Grete reaches maturity.

The death of Gregor is symbolic, marking the redistribution of libido throughout the family constellation; Gregor is reborn as the family group.

A crucial shift in the fixation of libido occurs as the dominant image of the earth mother (in furs) is replaced by the restored mother-sister image.

The form of the beetle is invested with the libidinal energy of the incestuous longing for the mother. "In one sense it is a fantasy introject of the . . . castrating father, for it is the father who attacks the son with the symbolic apples; yet . . . it is the apple which is used for the symbolic castration, and it is the pre-oedipal, the terrible, mother who appears at the end of the story to sweep out the remains of the beetle" (351). Gregor's task is to undergo the symbolic death of this erotic fixation, to surrender his incestuous longing and his patricidal destrudo. Within this movement the terrifying cleaning woman forces the issue, and thus she is "negatively redemptive"; once she has been discharged, her work done, "the benevolent creative phase is activated; and the mother emerges in her duplicate Grete . . . . The castration fantasy thus resolved is a necessary, impersonal drive of the psyche toward wholeness or completion" (352-53). The various forms of the anima which figure in the story—the tenderly loved mother, the infantile fantasy introject of the woman in furs, the pre-oedipal terrible mother (the cleaning woman), and finally the changing forms of Grete—constitute the "psychic progression of the anima in man as we know it in the universal symbolism of myth and dreams" (355).

Spatial and temporal elements of the story underscore its dimensions as a tale of death and resurrection.

Details of the drama contribute to this symbolic intrapsychic action; for example, the father's castration threat serves to spur on the ego to make a mature appropriation of libido. Gregor's preference for rotten food over fresh milk is the price paid and masochistically enjoyed for oral aggression. The scene outside Gregor's window is "the wasteland . . . where rebirth alone can take place" (360). The picture of Gregor in the splendid uniform of an officer and the later apparition of his father are emblems of triumphant phallic libido.

"It seems, therefore, that though 'Metamorphosis' is paradoxical because the dynamic transformation of libido does not center in the return or resurrection of the hero as centered in a new, absolute Self, Kafka has incorporated all the essential elements of the monomyth except this return. And this return is diffused into the family constellation, with the substitution of the reanimated and completely changed Grete (as anima) for the ego of the hero. We might say that Grete as anima or beloved is the psychic alternate which is resurrected or makes the return. It may be that Kafka could not project a completely redeemed ego because of the incommensurables existing between the old or artistic ego and the Self he wanted as man to be" (365).

Webster's reconstruction of the action as interacting archetypal patterns would seem hard to justify in an absolute sense, though they obviously organize the data of the piece. But what justifies the claim that Kafka's creativity flows from his striving "to displace a masochistic attachment to the denying mother"?

126. Weinberg, Kurt. *Kafkas Dichtungen: Die Travestien des Mythos.* Bern and Munich: Francke, 1963. Pp. 235-317 and passim.

Kafka's fiction has the character of a rebus. Its rhetorical figures, jokes, etymological puns, names, sums, and so on, conceal images which must be decoded. His art addresses a reader ideally qualified to generate associations and to grasp these images as referring symbolically and allegorically to a single content at the heart of the work. This is the content of traditional religion, which, despite Kafka's unbelief, arises from the basis of his imagination as "travesties of religious archetypes" (8). Kafka exorcised into his work "the protean metamorphoses of *negative* religious ideas . . . , the innumerable distortions of fragments of the divine image, shattered but indestructible" (8). Yet the puzzling chaos of figures constituting the depth of Kafka's language can be reduced to a few archetypes–"grotesque incarnations of the sacred, of Messianic hope, of faith, love, and even indifference" (41).

Gregor Samsa is a false Messiah. The matter-of-factness with which he accepts his metamorphosis is striking; "he must have been prepared for a miracle, but, equally, for a penance to be laid on him–more, for a martyrdom" (235). The five o'clock train which Gregor misses and will never take again "very clearly refers to the Pentateuch. . . . With the [train at] *seven*, one may think of the seven last words spoken on the Cross, the seven sacraments, the seven sorrows of the Mother of God, the seven Christian virtues, and so on" (235-36). Gregor soon becomes aware that he is an outcast from society; henceforth until his "croaking" he must lead the life of a kind of thing outside the human condition. "It is significant that the metamorphosis of Gregor–of all Kafka's prospective Messiahs the one most cruelly hindered in his earthly mission–begins *shortly before Christmas*" (236). Isolated in his room, Gregor thinks back to a time when he and his sister were close. (The various roles of the members of the family will emerge: the father, a Jehovah figure; the mother, the embodiment of Jewish faith and tribal consciousness; the sister, a figurative representation of the soul.) Gregor has dreamed of announcing on Christmas Eve his intention of sending his sister to the conservatory, but now Christmas has come and gone. No wonder Gregor will become "hot with shame and grief" upon learning that his sister, only a child of seventeen, will have to earn money instead of playing the violin. On Christmas Eve, Gregor was to have become his sister's savior; now, instead, he is metamorphosed into a vermin. "Instead of the longed-for redemption of his sister, instead of the eternal preservation of the life of the soul ('in the conservatory'), instead of the heavenly violin music in the chorus of angels, instead of the exultation of the daughter of Zion (Zech., 9:9)–*violin* is derived by way of the French *viole, vielle* and Provençal-Italian *viola* from the Vulgar Latin *vitula*, which goes back to the Latin *vitulari* 'rejoice,' 'exult'!–there appears the curse of the duty of 'earning money,' 'work,' 'toil,' that 'expulsion from Paradise' which 'is in its main aspect' eternal, which consists in the eternal repetition of the event" (239).

Gregor loses his body; he retains his memory but gradually loses his sense of time. Isolated in the crimping world of his room, paradigm for his inner life, which molders along with him, he exists outside human space and time. Gregor's unholy metamorphosis illustrates the ultimate judgment by the higher powers on his redemptive aspiration. Before he can live through a redemptive Christmas Eve, experience rebirth as the Christ child, the chosen Son of God, his consecration as Messiah, he must suffer the putrefaction of a blackbeetle's body.

Gregor's punishment is a moment in "the eternal recurrence of the divine punishment, which with merciless irony pursues mankind from generation to generation, threatening to transform the best, the most zealous, of each generation from prospective Messiahs into vermin" (239). The aspirant to Messiahship is cast back into his bodily finitude, a life of misery on earth, "which at the same time constitutes the value and greatness of the creature. For even from the unholy vermin Gregor Samsa his basically unchanged *essence* cannot be taken" (240).

Thus in the first section of *The Metamorphosis*, Gregor's sorrows depict the Passion and the Crucifixion as they suffer a reversal, technically correct in the Jewish perspective. The action of the second section issues from the contradictory standpoint of Messianism and Gregor Samsa's native Judaism and depicts the events from Christ's entombment until the Resurrection. Like the first section, it comes to a head in an expulsion of the son by the father and in a symbolic crucifixion. Finally, the third section shows the blossoming of the Samsa family after the trinity of boarders has been expelled and after Gregor is symbolically resurrected in the flesh (the allusion is to the ascent of the butcher boy with his carrier on his head).

Limitations of space compel me to make this abstract illustrative only of the analysis which Weinberg pursues for another eighty-two densely argued pages. But the method will have emerged. Weinberg himself notes: "These [exemplary] exegeses unfold the essential symbols and the central themes which eternally recur in Kafka's fiction with quite fascinating monotony. They will equip the reader with a method . . . for interpreting Kafka . . . on his own" (9).

Weinberg's study has stimulated a good deal of criticism, the gist of which emerges from a review article by Richard Thieberger. "To the mind of Professor Weinberg, Kafka wrote with the *intention* of creating travesties; on p. 19 we read that Kafka's symbolism was 'entirely dominated by the will of the author.' Willfully, then, this assimilated Prague Jew composed the travesties of a religion grown inaccessible to him. More than this, the 'archetypes' . . . are taken not only from the Old Testament but from the Christian tradition as well. Now, if Kafka is not ignorant of the fundamentals of Christianity, it is extremely dubious that he had a knowledge of the New Testament as detailed as that which Professor Weinberg allows *a priori* to be the case." [59]

Ulrich Weisstein makes a similar objection. "Weinberg's neo-medievalist treatment of these writers renders them a kind of modern *Speculum Humanae Salvationis*. . . . If Kafka really wanted to say what Weinberg insinuates, he would have had to bury himself deeply not only in a Middle High German dictionary but also in the *Acta Sanctorum* and Migne's *Patrologia latina*. . . . Surely, 'Die Verwandlung' is no *Faust II*, and Kafka no Goethe who needed to refresh his knowledge from a compendium like Hederich's *Mythologisches Lexikon*."[60]

127. Wiese, Benno Von. "Franz Kafka: *Die Verwandlung*." In *Die deutsche Novelle von Goethe bis Kafka, II*. Düsseldorf: Bagel, 1962. Pp. 319-45.

The many critiques of *The Metamorphosis* hardly take account of each other, although, or perhaps just because, they contradict one another in the crassest way. "German interpreters are inclined to liberate Gregor Samsa as rapidly as possible from his repulsive image and instead lend him a mysterious metaphysical status" (319). Thus **Edel** (the metamorphosed creature signifies "the distinctiveness and isolation of an existence . . . which belongs essentially to the world of the immaterial, the spiritual"); **Emrich** (the bug's existence is that of the human "self" grown strange and null in a world of empirical purposes); **Heselhaus** (the metamorphosis is both a protest from the side of the absolute against modern life and a punishment). On the other hand, English and American critiques stress the irrational and psychotic dimensions of the metamorphosis: they tend to produce psychological or symbolic readings. Witness **Reiss** (here man ceases "to be a logical being; he dehumanizes himself: it is like the fatal agony"); **Landsberg** (the life of the bug is oriented toward death, informed by the wish to regress into the inorganic, pitted against the spurious life of the others who have excluded a consciousness of death); **Sokel** (the metamorphosis is a compromise formation –of the type of the neurotic symptom or the accident–gratifying a wish to rebel *and* a wish to suffer punishment); **Angus** (behind *The Metamorphosis* is Kafka's solitude and desire for love); **Luke** (the tragi-comic dimension of *The Metamorphosis* is constituted by the contrast between reason and pseudo-reason); finally **Madden** (the metamorphosis is a parable for man's existential guilt; the family is blind to the divine action accomplishing itself on the son).

This baffling abundance of interpretations can only be countered with strict textual interpretation.

Samsa is unmistakably a code name for Kafka; the link is confirmed by the identical father-son struggle in Kafka's case as well as by passages in the letters which allude to situations in *The Metamorphosis* and in other animal stories. (See the letters to Brod and to Oskar Baum, Br 390, 434.)

There is a radical distinction between the beetle Raban of "Wedding Preparations in the Country" and Gregor Samsa; in the first case, the metamorphosis takes place in a dreamlike state of hibernation and escapes destruction at the hands of impersonal collective forces only through a sort of playful omnipotence; on the other hand, Samsa, as a beetle, has tragic reality in a world subservient to purely social forces.

The opening of the story appears to belong to the world of the fairy tale, but this aura of the miraculous is opposed by precise realistic description. There is no nightmare to wake up from; this magic cannot be revoked. The narrator does not attempt either to interpret the metamorphosis or to render it ironic. Yet this event does not have even the intelligibility of a natural catastrophe. It is incomparable, even if, as Gregor admits, something like it might possibly happen to another person.

The metamorphosis does not occur in a fairy-tale world, and its consequences are not those found in fairy tales. It occurs in a petty-bourgeois milieu and extends scarcely beyond the family's apartment. Everything that follows the metamorphosis excludes the miraculous, excludes fantasy.

It is seductive at first to grasp the metamorphosis of a man into an animal as a loss of identity, but this is not in fact the case. Throughout the entire story, it never occurs to any member of the family—except to Grete at the very end—that this bug is not Gregor. Meanwhile Gregor's identity with himself remains intact. Of course Gregor's "vital organization" is reduced to that of an animal (he suffers a change in his mode of articulation, nourishment, locomotion); "but the consciousness of the metamorphosed being is a purely human one. . . . Certainly Gregor is transformed into a repugnant animal, but for all this he does not stop being Gregor" (323).

In the whole of German epic writing there is nothing so radical as the opening of *The Metamorphosis*. Strictly speaking it is not fantastic, because no "second world," operating either without laws or under different laws, is opposed here to empirical reality. "Something wholly improbable, but not from a purely logical standpoint impossible, occurs in reality itself, belongs, so to speak, to it; and the narrator applies everything to the goal of making us forget as fast as possible the fictive character of this incursion" (324). The reality of the metamorphosis within the story is not a function of the reality of such a metamorphosis within our world. The Samsas understandably experience it as something merely improper and shameful; its reality, though, remains inescapable. Side by side with the metamorphosis the narrator describes the familiar world of Gregor's room. "Precisely this direct, immediate, but nonconflicting juxtaposition of two irreconcilable spheres makes Gregor's metamorphosis a *grotesque* event" (324). The family must come to terms with this *one* wholly unintelligible event which cannot be isolated and which penetrates into every corner of the apartment. This story is a pure example of the grotesque—according to **Kayser**, "a failure of the categories through which we orient ourselves in the world"; the world is at once recognizably our own, yet alienated, out of joint, inspiring in us an oppressive fear.

The narrator has, so to speak, inverted the point of the novel; it is found at the beginning, not at the end. What follows is more in the nature of analysis than narrative. Subsequent chapters depict the general state of affairs before coming around to new events. The tension of the narrative is not so much directed toward its unsurprising conclusion—the death of Gregor—as produced by the "constant tragi-comic contrast of the events taking place in and about Gregor, with the constantly mistaken responses which follow in the family" (325).

In contrast to **Beissner**'s notion, "Kafka does not represent only his isolated, subjective [*innerseelisch*], delusory world" (326). Kafka keeps his distance from the narrative. This distance does not emerge through overt reflection on the action, but through narration from various standpoints and through the neutral air maintained even where passionate feelings are being concealed. The family preserves its own reality, its own center of gravity, opposite to Gregor's; and this immediately prevents us from dignifying Gregor as the exclusive vehicle of the spirit vis-à-vis the damnably materialistic family. Kafka does not take sides. His personal feelings about the hateful predominance of the family are kept out of the narrative. Kafka takes the stance of baring a terrible reality and all its consequences.

A number of interpretations conceive the opening "poetic fiction" as a metamorphosis downward, a downward sinking to the level of the animal (symbolizing man's imprisonment as a creature of this world). Here man becomes a primitive, infantile automaton. But this reading is only partially correct, because Gregor's animal existence ultimately undergoes a spiritual evolution (signs for which are the keywords "nourishment" and "music"). Gregor refuses the food that can no longer satisfy his appetite. "Gregor, starved, can no longer find any 'medicine' in the world for his isolated and painful existence and exists only in a peripheral zone within which he can still, perhaps, be aware, but within which he can no longer live" (327). Excruciatingly tormented by destiny or by his own unconscious experiences, Gregor enters a domain of spiritual experience which can be linked to his being an animal. Music here is the sign of a desire for redemption transcending the animal as well as the human condition. Gregor asserts his spirit, too, in refusing to let his room be cleared of furniture and in thus rejecting a life without memory, without history. From the point of view that desires to maintain itself as an "I" against the danger of reduction into a mere "it," creeping around the bare room is "meaningless." Gregor claims the picture that hangs on the wall as a representative of the sphere of the Thou, however much it is sexually charged. This sphere must be preserved so that existence does not sink into empty spatiality. The insect's gesture of pressing himself against the glass aims at assuring him of "the vital, living basis of his *human* existence" (329). Yet there is something suspiciously instinctive about this choice of a sexual object to symbolize attachment to a historical self-consciousness.

The argument whether Gregor is essentially a human being exiled into an abominable animal state or essentially an animal who gradually loses his human identity cannot be answered. The fiction of the abominable animal has only a parabolic existence: it is the image of a hopelessly isolated human being no longer apprehended as himself, who in his sickness takes on the primitivity and innocence of the animal but is experienced by the others through the mask of a "bug" which more and more is taken for the person himself. Kafka himself stressed that he could only think in images. The image of the bug is the sensuous visualization of an inner epoch in Gregor's psyche, which extends down into archaic "animallike" levels, into the pathological states of schizophrenia. Gregor "finds himself in a condition which can be most readily understood as an analogue to sickness" (330). This is hinted at by the hospital lying outside his window. The disease is not organic; rather, it is a psychic disease with particular social consequences. The result is that Gregor can no longer provide for his family. He is socially useless. This does not, of course, exclude the positive possibilities of an "abnormal" condition which frees him from the tyranny of family and business.

To what extent can the metamorphosis be said to have been willed? Consciously, Gregor desires passionately to preserve his normal existence. There is scant evidence for the assertion of particular feelings of guilt. The guilt can only be part of the general crisis described in the diary entries for 1915. The metamorphosis is a general existential crisis, a split between conscious and unconscious. Hence Gregor's position more and more isolates him and renders his self opaque to the others. His mute suffering is the issue of an inner and outer imprisonment.

The Metamorphosis must be read primarily as a family drama. Kafka's letter of 1921 (Br 343) furnishes a crucial commentary to *The Metamorphosis*: the "family animal" is depicted as an animal organism devouring its sons. Thus Gregor tries unconsciously to escape the tyranny of the family by means of the metamorphosis; the family is prevented from secreting him from their organism because he constitutes part of it.

The Metamorphosis is divided into three distinct sections. The first details Gregor's response to the metamorphosis and the shock which it produces on the others. Gregor's reactions are inspired by the effort to explain away the bizarre change, to maintain his ordinary self-consciousness. But the reality of the change persists. "Kafka depicts Gregor's new situation with a kind of macabre gallows humor" (333), the gist of which is the contrast between animal organization and subjective reality. None of the others reflects on the inexplicable character of the metamorphosis any more than Gregor does.

Subsequent passages are marked by the dissonance between Gregor's view of the metamorphosis as "an accidental if fatal contingency that nonetheless can pass away again" and the view of the others who see only his repellent exterior and are concerned only with protecting themselves from it. The loss of human language is only one side of Gregor's disaster. No less grave is his helplessness with his body, his "language" of gestures, which is again and again misunderstood.

Gregor's wounds, mainly inflicted by the father (and reminiscent of the strange wound of the boy in the story "A Country Doctor"), have "existential significance for man's being in general" (335). The wounded animal of *The Metamorphosis* signifies man psychically wounded, man helpless, anonymous, cast out of social life by an excruciating process. "To be sure, the impediment lies on his side, tied up with the feeling of insufficiency—the debasing, humbling 'condition,' so tormenting for Kafka that he puts the terrible image of the 'monstrous bug' vicariously in its stead. But those who should help Samsa-Kafka—perhaps could help him, too—withdraw either immediately or gradually from this uncomfortable and difficult task, magnify his sufferings, and begin almost to persecute the innocent and guilty victim" (335). Gregor's rebellion in *The Metamorphosis* is weak and temporary, but in the end he finds it right that his family should demand his total disappearance. The catastrophic disturbance he causes in the family outweighs all his early merit.

In Section II it seems for a time as if a peaceful if radically segregated coexistence between the two orders had been reached; but the meager concessions made by both parties cannot arrest the disaster. In the long run Gregor cannot and will not make himself invisible. On the other hand the sister is less and less willing to look after him. The antagonism which the father feels for Gregor is acute: he considers the metamorphosis less a misfortune than a fault, as if he had expected just this sort of thing from Gregor. The apple with which he bombards Gregor appears to have a symbolic meaning, since it afterward becomes the thorn in Gregor's flesh which continuously reminds the family that they have to do with their own son, not a mere It. One thinks of the apple in the Garden of Eden, which brought man not only knowledge but also his expulsion from paradise. But what is crucial to this image is the wounding—"meant as a painful spiritual event in the innermost self" (339).

The tragic situation of the son becomes more and more clear; he is saved from his father's rage only by the practically sexual intervention of the mother. "Kafka's *The Metamorphosis* is mainly about wholly elemental disorders within the family, reaching deep down into the sexual unconscious" (339). The result is the impotent isolation of the son. The cause of this tragic event is obscure. "It appears to be provoked by the son, not through his own doing, but through his suffering a transformation, which makes his inner image unrecognizable to those near to him but makes his visible image an occasion only for anxiety and terror" (339).

In Section III Gregor is increasingly abandoned. His resentful moods are as impotent as his earlier desires to provide for the family's welfare. The three roomers play only a peripheral role. Gregor's third, now slow and hopeless, journey back into his room is more terrible, perhaps, than his father's persecutions. "Gregor is extinguished in the consciousness of the family; he still exists, only as a bug" (342). There is nothing left for him beyond a quiet death, as much unwilled as willed.

Though Kafka himself abhorred the end of this story, the end is instructive. As in "The Hunger Artist," pure vitality is contrasted with the weakness of human existence anchored in spirituality. The temptation is great to interpret this negatively, but Kafka's own ambivalence cannot be overlooked. "Although the metamorphosis is followed by a liberation from the mechanical world of profit, business, and family tyranny, it is at the same time the path that leads irreversibly to death; the depraving and punishing aspects of the outward image are not only a sign that the authentic, primordial levels of the psyche have grown unrecognizable in a world frozen into anonymity, but that the self has itself suffered an existential catastrophe; it flees into anonymity and isolation because it can no longer cope with the interpersonal and social tasks of life" (343). The story describes a double failure—from the side of the family and from the side of the individual self. Kafka shows the hopelessness of a mode of existence in which metamorphosis no longer signifies palingenesis or rebirth but the mere dislocation of the individual from the whole, a movement toward death.

Kafka's *The Metamorphosis* is not a novella in the usual sense of the word and cannot be brought under the head of the historical type of the German novella in the second half of the nineteenth century. On the other hand, its characteristics are those of modern prose. The narrator, himself the sufferer, is woven into the mysterious dimensions of the narrative and keeps his distance only with an effort. The poet's own solitude stands behind the invention of so indecipherable and grotesquely alienated a world, one representative of indissoluble contradictions in existence. Kafka creates a subjective world that assumes a compellingly objective character. This reality has a playful character, but "contains the fatal seriousness of despair that cannot be represented either by means of poetic irony or of a novellalike coincidence" (344).

Pongs takes issue with von Wiese's discussion of the tragic dimension of *The Metamorphosis*, In an earlier work (*The History of Tragedy from Lessing to Hebbel*) von Weise describes tragedy as the "conflict between man's self-affirmation and his annihilation by a divine will." Yet in his discussion of *The Metamorphosis* he stresses the ambivalence of the conclusion. Though life affirms the family, life is depicted as an inauthentic failure. Such a conclusion is grotesque. But von Wiese also speaks of the "tragic situation of the son in the family"; he sees Gregor as the victim of fate.

Pongs (278) writes: "Such a situation is 'tragic' only in the sense that the self-destructive split of character—the 'split between conscious and unconscious'—is taken to the extreme of existence as an insect. That is, the situation must be considered the representative expression of an age for the 'ambivalence' which inevitably leads to ruin. Hence, 'tragic ambivalence,' but this no longer has anything in common with the concept of the tragic dimension of tragedy." In *The Metamorphosis* the essential characteristic of tragedy, the terror of a purifying catharsis, is shrouded in "an ambivalent twilight of values." Only through his deprivation of tragic experience in the traditional sense is Gregor one of the tragic figures in literature.

128. Wilson, Colin. *The Outsider.* London and New York: Atheneum, 1956, P. 31.

Camus' and Kafka's works are alike. Kafka conveys a sense of unreality by the use of a dream technique. In *The Metamorphosis* the hero is changed into a monstrous bug. "Destiny seems to have struck with the question: If you think life is unreal, how about *this*? Its imperative seems to be: Claim your freedom, *or else*. . . . For the men who fail to claim their freedom, there is the sudden catastrophe, the nausea, the trial and execution, the slipping to a lower form of life. Kafka's *Metamorphosis* would be a perfectly commonsense parable to a Tibetan Buddhist."

By what act of will and consciousness which we will agree to call "claiming one's freedom" could Gregor have suceeded in lending his life *reality*? Kafka's point, deeper than this facile existential ethic, is: Where consciousness is, there reality is not.

Addendum to Critical Works

The following critical works on *The Metamorphosis* came to my attention too late to be included in the descriptive bibliography.

Albrecht, Erich A. "Kafka's *Metamorphosis–Realiter*." In *Homage to Charles Blaise Qualia*. Lubbock, Texas: Texas Tech Press, 1962. Pp. 55-64.

Brito, Raúl Blengio. *Aproximación a Kafka*. Montevideo: Editorial Letras, 1969. Pp. 19-45.

Fingerhut, Karl-Heinz. *Die Funktion der Tierfiguren im Werke Franz Kafkas: Offene Erzählgerüste und Figurenspiele*. Abhandlungen zur Kunst-, Musik- und Literaturwissenschaft, LXXXIX. Bonn: Bouvier & Co., 1969. Pp. 189-200 and passim.

Gilman, Sander L. "A View of Kafka's Treatment of Actuality in *Die Verwandlung*." *Germanic Notes*, II, no. 4 (1971), 26-30.

Jorge, Ruy Alves. *Interpretação de Kafka*. São Paulo: Oren, 1968. Pp. 151-57 and passim.

Kokis, Sérgio. *Franz Kafka e a Expressão da Realidade.* Rio de Janeiro: Tempo Brasileiro, 1967. Pp. 62-70.

Konder, Leandor. *Kafka: Vida e Obra*. Rio de Janeiro: Alvaro, 1966. Pp. 9-12 and passim.

Lancelotti, Mario A. *Cómo Leer a Kafka*. Buenos Aires and Barcelona, 1969. Pp. 18-36 and passim.

Moss, Leonard. "A Key to the Door Image in 'The Metamorphosis.' " *Modern Fiction Studies*, XVII, no. 1 (Spring 1971), 37-42.

Politzer, Heinz. "*Die Verwandlung des Armen Spielmanns*." In *Jahrbuch der Grillparzer-Gesellschaft*, III, no. 4 (1965), 55-64.

Ramm, Klaus. *Reduktion als Erzählprinzip bei Kafka*. Frankfurt am Main: Athenäum, 1971. Pp. 98-102 and passim.

Richter, Fritz K. ' "Verwandlungen' bei Kafka und Stehr." *Monatshefte*, LXIII, no. 2 (Summer 1971), 141-46.

Seyppel, Joachim H. "The Animal Theme and Totemism in Franz Kafka." *Universitas* (English ed.), IV, no. 2 (1961), 163-72.

NOTES

Preface

1. *Die deutsche Novelle von Goethe bis Kafka, II* (Düsseldorf: Bagel, 1962), p. 319.
2. *Strukturontologie* (Freiburg i. Br. and Munich: Alber, 1971), p. 139.

Metamorphosis of the Metaphor

1. All German titles by Kafka cited are taken from the Lizenzausgabe of Kafka's works (Frankfurt am Main: S. Fischer; New York: Schocken). All these works, except *Briefe an Felice*, were edited by Max Brod. Kafka's comments on his own writings have been conveniently brought together in *Dichter über ihre Dichtungen: Kafka*, ed. by Erich Heller and Joachim Beug (Munich, 1969).
2. **Hasselblatt**, p. 61.
3. All translations of *The Metamorphosis* are from *The Metamorphosis*, newly trans. and ed. by Stanley Corngold (New York: Bantam, 1972).
4. Edward Said, "Beginnings," *Salmagundi*, Fall 1968, p. 49.
5. **Anders**, *Kafka, pro und contra*, pp. 40-41, 20, 41. For an English version (not a literal translation), see Günther Anders, *Franz Kafka*, trans. by A. Steer and A. K. Thorlby (London, 1960).
6. **Sokel**, 105-A, p. 203.
7. **Sokel**, 105-A, p. 205; John *(sic)* Urzidil, "Recollections," *The Kafka Problem*, ed. Angel Flores (New York, 1963), p. 22.
8. **Anders**, p. 42.
9. Jacques Derrida, "Violence et Métaphysique," *L'Écriture et la différence* (Paris, 1967), p. 137; "Den Bedeutungen wachsen Worte zu." Martin Heidegger, *Sein und Zeit* (Tübingen, 1963), p. 161; Leo Weisgerber, "Die Sprachfelder in der geistigen Erschliessung der Welt," *Trier-Festschrift* (Trier, 1954), pp. 38ff.–cited in **Hasselblatt**, pp. 48-49.

10. **Blanchot**, "The Diaries: The Exigency of the Work of Art," p. 207.
11. I. A. Richards, *The Philosophy of Rhetoric* (New York and London, 1936), p. 96.
12. **Hasselblatt**, pp. 195, 200.
13. **Adorno**, *Prisms*, p. 272.
14. Kafka studied medieval German literature at the University of Prague in 1902; Klaus Wagenbach, *Franz Kafka, Eine Biographie seiner Jugend (1883-1912)*, (Bern, 1958), p. 100. He assiduously consulted Grimm's etymological dictionary; Max Brod, *Über Franz Kafka* (Frankfurt am Main: Fischer Bücherei 735, 1966), pp. 110, 213. The citation from Grimm is discussed in depth by **Weinberg**, pp. 316-17.
15. **Weinberg**, p. 317.
16. **Sparks**, pp. 78-79.
17. **Empson**, p. 653. Empson's surmise, "Maybe [Kafka] could never bear to read over the manuscript," is incorrect. Kafka speaks of proofreading *The Metamorphosis* in *Diaries, II*, p. 13. In this matter of the scrupulousness with which Kafka edited his stories, see **Dietz**, 35-A.
18. Max Brod, *Über Franz Kafka*, p. 89.
19. **Wagenbach**, pp. 41, 56.
20. **Pongs**, p. 276.
21. **Wagenbach**, p. 56.
22. **Greenberg**, *The Terror of Art: Kafka and Modern Literature* (New York, 1968), pp. 26-27.
23. Martin Walser, *Beschreibung einer Form* (Munich, 1968), p. 11.
24. Tzvetan Todorov, *Littérature et signification* (Paris, 1967), pp. 115-17.
25. Critics practising this autobiographical approach frequently attempt to force the identification of Kafka and Gregor Samsa by citing the passage from Kafka's *Letter to His Father* (H222) in which Kafka has his father compare him to a stinging, blood-sucking vermin (DF 195). This is done despite Kafka's explicit warning that "Samsa is not altogether Kafka" (**Janouch**, *Gespräche mit Kafka*, p. 55).
26. **Richter**, pp. 112-19; **Sokel** 105-A, p. 213; **Kaiser**, 41-104; **Dalmau Castañón**, pp. 385-88.
27. **Baioni**, pp. 81-100.
28. *Amerika*, p. 88. This text mistakenly reads the word *Leid* ("sorrow") as *Lied* ("song"); I have made the correction.
29. **Janouch**, p. 28.
30. **Schubiger**, pp. 55-57.
31. Jacques Lacan, "L'instance de la lettre dans l'inconscient," *Écrits* (Paris, 1966), pp. 506-07; trans. as "The Insistence of the Letter in the Unconscious," *Yale French Studies* 36-37 (October, 1966), p. 125.
32. **Hasselblatt**, p. 203.
33. **Sokel**, 105-C, p. 81.
34. **Greenberg**, p. 48.
35. *The Metamorphosis* distorts a metaphor alluding to an earlier act of writing; as such it prefigures Kafka's next published work, *In the Penal Colony*. The main action of this story, the operation of a terrible machine that kills a criminal by inscribing his fault immediately into his flesh, follows from the distortion of a metaphor about writing or engraving, of the "experience which engraves itself on a person's memory." The vehicle here,

an act of writing, is without even a residual sense of Kafka's empirical personality. Kafka himself notes: "But for me, who believe that I shall be able to lie contentedly on my deathbed, such scenes are secretly a game" (DII 102; T 448). The more comprehensive sense of this vehicle is supplied by a remark Kafka made about his inner life: I inscribe my own gravestone.

36. My colleague Theodore Ziolkowski has drawn my attention to an episode from the life of Kierkegaard paralleling remarkably this sentiment and the incident from *The Metamorphosis*: " 'Well,' the cleaning woman answered, . . . 'you don't have to worry about getting rid of the stuff next door. It's already been taken care of' " (E 140-41). Walter Lowrie writes on p. 41 of his *Short Life of Kierkegaard* (Princeton University Press Paperback, 1971) in connection with the spinal trouble that eventually caused Kierkegaard's death, "We have several accounts of similiar attacks which were not permanent. For example, at a social gathering he once fell from the sofa and lay impotent upon the floor–beseeching his friends not to pick 'it' up but to 'leave it there till the maid comes in the morning to sweep.' " For a definitive study of the relation between Kafka and Kierkegaard, see Fritz Billeter, *Das Dichterische bei Kafka und Kierkegaard* (Winterthur, 1965).

37. Maurice Merleau-Ponty, *Phénoménologie de la perception* (Paris, 1945), p. 213.

38. "Darin also besteht das eigentliche Kunstgeheimnis des Meisters, *dass er den Stoff durch die Form vertilgt*." *Über die ästhetische Erziehung des Menschen in einer Reihe von Briefen; zweiundzwanzigster Brief. Sämtliche Werke*, V (Munich: Carl Hanser, 1967), p. 639.

39. "[Music] speaks by means of mere sensations without concepts and so does not, like poetry, leave behind it any food for reflection . . . ." Kant, *The Critique of Judgement*, trans. by James Creed Meredith (Oxford, 1928), p. 193.

40. This observation and the observations in the three sentences which follow it are suggested by Paul de Man's essay, "The Rhetoric of Temporality," in *Interpretation, Theory and Practice*, ed. by Charles S. Singleton (Baltimore: The Johns Hopkins Press, 1969), esp. pp. 177 and 190.

41. Michel Foucault, *The Order of Things: An Archaeology of the Human Sciences*, a translation of *Les Mots et les choses* (New York: Atheneum, 1971), pp. 383-84.

Symbolic and Allegorical Interpretation

1. For example, Hasselblatt, and Ulrich Gaier, "Chorus of Lies–On Interpreting Kafka," *German Life and Letters*, XXII, pp. 283-96.

2. See, for example, Gaier: "Kafka's work . . . should be taken as a challenge to find an adequate approach–not to its truth–but to its reality" (p. 283).

3. DF 37; see Peter Heller, *Dailectics and Nihilism* (Amherst, Mass., 1966), for a full discussion of this aphorism.

4. *Ursprung des deutschen Trauerspiels* (Frankfurt am Main, 1963).

A Critical Bibliography of *The Metamorphosis*

1. Thus the almost total union of Gregor's parents depicted at the close of the second section of *The Metamorphosis* is not merely an illustration of Gregor's disordered state of mind.
2. Thus Gregor Samsa's metamorphosis into a thing succeeds in eluding madness but not collectivization at an archaic level of consciousness. He escapes total delusion but pays the price of becoming a thinglike arrest of consciousness, at once defiance and exhibit of a process of universal collectivization.
3. This formulation is inspired by **Anders** and in its exact wording suggests an answer to the question raised by **Pongs**: How can a work (*The Metamorphosis*), inspired by a literal reading of a figure of speech imbedded in the common language, create *the* myth of the twentieth century.
4. Perhaps in the suggestion of men who haunt rooms, or men who *are* rooms.
5. For **Hasselblatt** (203) *The Metamorphosis* is not "the trying out of a type of dehumanization" (or "the trial run of a model of dehumanization") but the exemplary or model presentation of the relation between the inconceivable and everyday reality.
6. Though Gregor and his family are inwardly alike, his motives are totally unintelligible to them. His outward difference seems a sign of the insanity of total incommunicability between beings who are absolutely alike.
7. Gregor's ongoing metamorphosis (reification) has also been explained as the dramatization of a progressively literalized metaphor.
8. Presumably, Adorno's account of the "demolished" or demystified consciousness is synchronic. Still, to violate the order of the unfolding of elements in the fable is to open the gates to such abusive readings as the psychiatric, which views the metamorphosis as a punishment in advance for oedipal passions which do not appear until two-thirds of the way through the story. Temporal precedence in narrative fiction, especially the quality of beginning and end, must be preserved as a principle of priority among elements in the synchronic structure proposed as its equivalent.
9. This observation applies cogently to Gregor's "privileged moment" in *The Metamorphosis*—the scene of the violin playing—and also poses the interesting question of why Gregor is exceptional among Kafka's heroes in reflecting so little.
10. Witness Gregor's attempted escape from his room—three times repeated and three times punished.
11. Gregor's mysterious degradation is followed by events which suggest—though never completely—its explanation.
12. **Pongs** argues that if the source of Kafka's fictions is really the figures of speech embedded in ordinary language, then it is hard to claim, as Western critics do, that *The Metamorphosis* creates the myth of the twentieth century. For a reply to this point see **Adorno**. As Kafka takes ordinary figurative language literally, so too should Kafka's language be read literally. Thus, **Adorno** (*Prismen*, 307): "The principle of literalness . . . rules out the

attempt to unite in a conception of Kafka the pretension to profundity and equivocation."

13. As **Holland** notes (146), the former traveling salesman repeats himself as a bug, still *homo viator*, crawling senselessly to and fro.

14. Is Gregor's experience of the violin music an experience of his authentic possibilities, or is it only the epiphenomenon of chaotically rebellious and incestuous desires?

15. This culpable "adherence" would appear to be a covert denunciation of the naturalistic style.

16. See Kafka's letters to Kurt Wolff (Br 116, 134); see also **Sokel**, 105-C.

17. See letter to **Brod** (Br 107).

18. The conclusion of this commentary supports the second of these views, since the judgment appears to be a self-inculpation of the father; but Gregor never attains the wisdom of "another tribunal."

19. If Kafka's guilt, according to this interesting idea, is produced by the act of writing *The Metamorphosis* "distractedly," then this guilt did not exist before. Hence the metamorphosis cannot be the punishment for a crime traceable to Kafka's life, and explorations into Kafka's life in pursuit of this crime are pointless.

20. *Letter to His Father*, p. 163 ff.

21. Letter to Kurt Wolff, *Briefe*, p. 135.

22. The fullest discussion of the double motive for the metamorphosis is to be found in **Sokel**, 105-A-D.

23. Extracts from this letter are reprinted in the Katalog der Marbacher Ausstellung, "Expressionismus: Literatur und Kunst 1910-1923" (Marbach a. N., 1960), p. 140.

24. In 35-A, **Dietz** states categorically that the third printing was "changed by Kafka himself" (416).

25. The text supports the opposite view, maintained by **Freedman**, that at least one of the meanings of the story is the progressive dissolution of Gregor's consciousness.

26. This summary is based on a discussion of Falk's work by L. Dietz in *Germanistik*, IV (Jan. 1963), 146.

27. In a page **Fast** has transformed Gregor Samsa from a "certain type of human being" to "the German petty bourgeois" to "man."

28. This argument, rudimentary and polemical as it is, shares the bias more perceptively explored in essays by **Anders** and **Richter**.

29. Then how can Foulkes conclude, as he does, that *The Metamorphosis* "is extremely autobiographical" and reflects Kafka's own experiences "in terms drawn from the author's environment" ?

30. But see **Henel** (252): "The attempt (to employ the dream idea as the starting point for a story) almost always went amiss."

31. See **Henel** (252): "Kafka wrote up his dreams . . . to lay in a stock of images which he could use in his works for the representation of inner events. This dream material, however, does not go into his work as an immediate, direct expression of something experienced in dream fashion but as the consciously manipulated device for the symbolization of inner states which Kafka precisely and consciously observed."

32. For the contrary view, which denies that *The Metamorphosis* possesses a beginning and an end in any Aristotelian sense, see **Greenberg**, 69-70.

33. This point is overstated and misses the simultaneous intensification of Gregor's bestiality and spirituality in the third section.
34. With the important exceptions of at least the unidentified animal builder of "The Burrow," the ape in "A Report to an Academy," and so on.
35. This point is made against the view of **Adorno, Greenberg**, and **Heselhaus**.
36. **Hasselblatt** denotes the man-bug simply as "the metamorphosed," wary of introducing the extraneous connotations of any other name. For "the metamorphosed" we shall write Gregor Samsa; but it should be kept in mind that Gregor Samsa is a wholly fictive entity.
37. **Luke**'s is a contrary view. He writes: "But in Kafka's stories the defense is maintained, . . . the horror is repudiated, the extraordinary is absorbed into the ordinary" (36).
38. Gregor is actually only tall enough to reach the door handle with his jaws.
39. **Beissner** supports his view that the metamorphosis is a delusion of Gregor Samsa by asserting that the figure in the foreground of the cover of the first book edition of *The Metamorphosis* is Gregor Samsa flinching away from the blackness and nothingness of his room. Kafka's letters show unequivocally that the room depicted is the insect's room; the figure turns away from the insect, and thus cannot be Gregor Samsa.
40. André Jolles, *Einfache Formen.* Sächs. Forschungsberichte, Neugermanist. Abt., II, Halle (Saale), 1930. Pp. 218-46.
41. We can see Kafka engaging with some urgency and effort in the act of interpreting one of his stories. In a diary entry for February 11, 1913, Kafka wrote: "While correcting proofs of 'The Judgment' I shall write down all the relationships which have become clear to me in the story so far as I now have them in mind. This is necessary because the story came out of me like a regular birth, covered with filth and mucus, and only I have the hand that can reach to the body itself and the desire to do so." Kafka had written in his *Diary* on September 23, 1912, that while writing "The Judgment" he had been "thinking of Freud, of course" among other writers; but this fact did not result in 1913 in his producing a Freudian interpretation.
42. H. D. Irmscher, "Nachwort." J. G. Herder, *Abhandlung über den Ursprung der Sprache*. Stuttgart: Reclam, 1966. P. 171.
43. See **Pongs**, who judges this absence as evidence of Kafka's total estrangement from language, and **Ulshöfer**, who, on the grounds of the failure of Kafka's prose to uplift, judges it anticlassic.
44. The likeness and difference between Kant's and Kafka's ethics is subtly discussed by **Anders** (*Kafka*, 77; *Franz Kafka*, 76).
45. Yet Gregor's transformation signifies that he "has become tainted by evil" (252).
46. "At a certain point in self-knowledge, when other circumstances favoring self-scrutiny are present, it will invariably follow that you find yourself execrable" (Diary entry for Feb. 7, 1915; DII 114).
47. "Reflections on Sin, Pain, Hope, and the True Way" (GW 288).
48. This perception is richly elaborated by **Anders.**
49. See **Von Wiese** (326): "However much Kafka's poetic style . . . may be conceived as the representation of his *dreamlike* inner life, nevertheless his

works do not amount to a *monologue intérieur*. The very extensive organization of the court in *The Trial* keeps its own center of gravity . . . .

"In the case of our story the family may not be seen only from the standpoint of the metamorphosed Gregor and his subjective reality, although the narration admittedly very dominantly issues from his perspective."

50. **Sokel** (105-A through 105-D) argues that Gregor awakens, not into a state of conscience, but into one enacting the conflicts of conscience, with the result that conscience is discharged.

51. Cf. Kafka's words to **Janouch**: "Samsa is not merely Kafka and nothing else."

52. For Kafka's "impressionism," see **Emrich** and **Freedman**. The most comprehensive study of Kafka's narrative perspective is Walser, *Beschreibung einer Form* (Munich, 1961).

53. In Rousseau's play *Narcisse* there is a fertile confusion on the part of one of the characters between the words *métaphoriser* and *métamorphoser.*

54. *The Short Novels of Dostoevsky*, trans. by Constance Garnett (New York: Dial Press, 1951), p. 520.

55. It would be more accurate to say, not that Kafka has done away entirely with the attempt to establish the metamorphosis as a hallucination, but that he makes the hallucination an element of Gregor's reaction in bad faith to the real event. See **Dentan** and **Luke**.

56. See the conclusion to which **Margolis** brings this dilemma.

57. For a contrary account of Gregor's death, see **Edel**, 225-26.

58. See **Sokel**, 105-C, who maintains that precisely the difference between these destinies is crucial.

59. "Kafka, Camus et le sémantique historique: Réflexions méthodologiques sur la recherche littéraire." Comparative Literature, IV, no. 3 (1967), 139-326; this citation, 322-23.

60. *Modern Language Notes*, Dec. 1966, 641-45.

INDEXES

Index of Names

Index of Kafka's Works